· 国家社科基金项目“律师法实施问题研究”成果
· 国家“2011计划”司法文明协同创新中心研究成果
· 司法部2015年国家法治与法学理论研究项目“以律师为主体的公共法律服务体系构建模式研究”成果
· 2016年度中华全国律师协会重点研究课题“律师管理体制比较研究”成果

苏格兰诉辩律师协会诉辩律师职业行为指引和惩戒规则

王进喜 ◎ 译

中国法制出版社
CHINA LEGAL PUBLISHING HOUSE

译序

苏格兰是大不列颠及北爱尔兰联合王国的一部分。苏格兰是英国重要组成部分，但却有着自己的独特法律体系。在律师制度上，苏格兰也有自己的特色。在苏格兰，专门提供庭审职业诉辩服务的叫做诉辩律师（Advocate），而不像英格兰与威尔士的相应诉辩者那样称为出庭律师（Barrister）。诉辩律师职务是一种公职，每个诉辩律师都是独立职业人员，其职业组织叫作诉辩律师协会（Faculty of Advocates）。该协会的历史可以追溯到十六世纪。诉辩律师协会负责制定准入诉辩律师公职的标准和程序，对诉辩律师的职业行为进行规制和惩戒。这些职能是苏格兰高等民事法院根据 2010 年《法律服务（苏格兰）法》委派给诉辩律师协会的。本译文的主体是《诉辩律师协会行为指引》和 2015 年《惩戒规则》，并附有《入行者条例》。此外，《诉辩律师协会行为指引》附件还含有《佩鲁贾宣言》《欧洲律师行为守则》等重要法律文件。通过这些文件我们可以了解苏格兰诉辩律师的准入、行为规制和惩戒、欧盟律师规制等基本情况。这些资料对于完善我国律师制度，无疑具有重要的借鉴意义。

是为序。

王进喜

2017 年 3 月

Contents

目录

FACULTY OF ADVOCATES

GUIDE TO THE PROFESSIONAL CONDUCT OF ADVOCATES

Published by the Faculty of Advocates, Parliament House, Edinburgh

First Published *June 1988*

Second Edition *January 2005*

Third Edition *June 2006*

Fourth Edition *August 2007*

Fifth Edition *October 2008*

诉辩律师职业行为指引

诉辩律师协会　公布

爱丁堡　国会大厦

1988 年 6 月首次公布

2005 年 1 月第二版

2006 年 6 月第三版

2007 年 8 月第四版

2008 年 10 月第五版

INTRODUCTION

The work of an Advocate is essentially the work of an individual practitioner whose conscience, guided by the advice of his seniors, is more likely to tell him how to behave than any book of rules.

In places in this Guide, it has been found convenient to state "the rule" or "the general rule" . Although convenient, use of the word "rule" would be misleading if it were thought to imply that the rule is absolute and subject to no exceptions whatever the circumstances. The Guide must be read as a whole and interpreted according to its spirit rather than its letter. For the same reasons, it must not be assumed that it is enough for an Advocate to keep within the letter of a "rule" as stated in the Guide.

It cannot be stressed too strongly that the ultimate test of an Advocate's conduct is whether it is such as to impair the trust and the confidence which others place in him and his profession.

NOTE

In this Guide, unless a contrary intention appears, the word "Advocate" or "Counsel" is used to refer to a practising Member of the Faculty of Advocates - i.e. a Member who currently holds himself out as available to be instructed as an Advocate in Scotland. For convenience, the male gender has been used for the most part when referring to Members of the Bar, but except where the context otherwise requires such references apply equally to female Members.

导言

诉辩律师的工作实质上是各个执业者这样的工作，即与任何规则之书相比，其良知在资深者的建议的指引下，更可能告诉他如何去行为。

在本指引中，你会发现在一些地方写成“规则”或者“一般规则”很方便。尽管很方便，如果“规则”一词意味着不论什么情况规则都是绝对的、没有任何例外，则“规则”一词具有误导性。对本指引的解读，必须按照它的精神而不是表面意思进行整体解读。出于同样的原因，不得认为诉辩律师遵守了本指引中的“规则”的字面意思就足够了。

诉辩律师行为的最终检验标准就是它是否破坏了他人对他及其职业付出的信任和信赖，无论如何强调这一点都不过分。

注释

在本指引中，除非有相反意图，“诉辩律师”或者“诉讼律师”是指诉辩律师协会的执业成员，即当前宣示自己能够在苏格兰作为诉辩律师接受指示的成员。为简便起见，在提及律师协会成员时，大多数情况下使用的是男性称谓，但是除非语境另有要求，所称同样适用于女性成员。

1. THE STATUS, RIGHTS AND OBLIGATIONS OF AN ADVOCATE

1.1 The Status of an Advocate

1.1.1 In law, an Advocate owes his status to the fact that he has been admitted to the office of Advocate in the Court of Session, the supreme civil Court in Scotland. Advocates so admitted have right of audience in the Court of Session and the High Court of Justiciary (the supreme criminal Courts of Scotland) , and in the other Courts (such as the Lands Valuation Appeal Court) whose judges are Senators of the College of Justice.

1.1.2 The Faculty of Advocates is a self-governing body consisting of those admitted to the office of Advocate in the Court of Session. The formal act of admission to that office is an act of the Court and an Advocate can ultimately be deprived of his office only by the Court. But, by long tradition, the Court has left it to the Faculty of Advocates (a) to lay down the qualifications for admission, (b) to determine whether an applicant for admission satisfies those qualifications, (c) to lay down the rules of professional conduct, and (d) to exercise disciplinary authority.

1.1.3 The Dean of Faculty is the elected leader of the Faculty

1. 诉辩律师的地位、权利和义务

1.1 诉辩律师的地位

1.1.1 在法律上，诉辩律师的地位取决于这样的事实，即他已经准入于高等民事法院（苏格兰最高民事法院）的诉辩律师之职务。如此准入的诉辩律师在高等民事法院、高等刑事法院（苏格兰最高刑事法院）和其法官是司法院参议官的其他法院（例如土地估价上诉法院）有出庭权。

1.1.2 诉辩律师协会是由准入于高等民事法院诉辩律师职务的人员组成的自治组织。在该职务准入之要式行为，是法院的行为，诉辩律师之职务最终只能由法院加以剥夺。但是根据长期的传统，法院已经授权诉辩律师协会（a）规定准入的资格，（b）确定准入申请人是否具有这些资格，（c）规定职业行为规则，以及（d）行使惩戒权。

1.1.3 诉辩律师协会会长是诉辩律师协会选举产生的领导人，根

of Advocates and, again by long tradition, the Faculty entrusts him with wide powers to make rulings on matters of professional conduct and, subject to the Disciplinary Rules of Faculty, to exercise disciplinary authority. The Dean's Council is a consultative body whose function is to advise the Dean on these and other matters.

1.1.4 In practice therefore, the legal and professional rights and obligations of an Advocate depend:-

(i) upon the fact that he holds the office of Advocate in the supreme Courts of Scotland; and

(ii) upon the fact that he is a Member of the Faculty of Advocates and is subject to the disciplinary authority of the Faculty and its Dean.

1.2 The Legal rights and Obligations of an Advocate

1.2.1 The historical rights and obligations of an Advocate as the holder of an office were explained by John Inglis, Lord President of the Court of Session and a former Dean of Faculty, in *Batchelor v. Pattison & Mackersy (1876) 3 R. 914, 918.*

" An Advocate in undertaking the conduct of a cause in this Court enters into no contract with his client, but takes on himself an office in the performance of which he owes a duty, not to his client only, but also to the Court, to the Members of his own profession, and to the public. .... [T] he nature of the Advocate's office makes it clear that in the performance of his duty he must be entirely independent,

据长期的传统，协会授予他广泛的权力就职业行为事项作出裁决，并且遵照协会惩戒规则行使惩戒权。会长委员会是一个咨询机构，其职能是就这些及其他事项为会长提供建议。

1.1.4 因此，在实践中，诉辩律师的法律和职业权利和义务取决于：

（i）他在苏格兰最高法院担任诉辩律师职务之事实；以及

（ii）他是诉辩律师协会成员，并受诉辩律师协会及其会长惩戒权管辖之事实。

1.2 诉辩律师的法律权利和义务

1.2.1 高等民事法院院长、诉辩律师协会前会长John Inglis在Batchelor v. Pattison & Mackersy（1876）3 R. 914, 918案件中，就诉辩律师作为公职人员的历史性权利和义务进行了解释。

“诉辩律师在本院办理案件时，与其委托人没有达成合同，而是履行其自己的职务。在履行该职务时，他不仅仅对其委托人负有职责，也对法院、其自己所属职业的成员和公众负有职责。……诉辩律师之职务的性质，明确要求他在履行其职责时，他必须完全独立，在办理其委托人案件时，依照其自己的裁量权和判断行事。他的法律权利是办理案件，无需顾及其委托人的意愿，只要他的授权没有被撤销，

and act according to his own discretion and judgment in the conduct of the cause for his client. His legal right is to conduct the cause without any regard to the wishes of his client, so long as his mandate is unrecalled, and what he does ***bonafide*** according to his own judgement will bind his client, and will not expose him to any action for what he has done, even if the client's interests are thereby prejudiced. These legal powers of Counsel are seldom, if ever, exercised to the full extent, because Counsel is restrained by consideration of propriety and expediency from doing so. But in such a case as this it is necessary to have in view what is the full extent of their legal powers.

The position of an agent ***[i.e. law agent or solicitor]*** is somewhat different. There is a contract of employment between him and his client, by virtue of which the client, for certain settled rates of remuneration, is entitled to require from the agent the exercise of care and diligence, and professional skill and experience. The general rule may fairly be stated to be that the agent must follow the instructions of his client.

But the general rule is subject to several qualifications. The agent, of course, cannot be asked to follow the client's instructions beyond what is lawful and proper. For the agent, as well as the Counsel, owes a duty to the Court, and must conform himself to the rules and practice of the Court in the conduct of every suit. He is also bound by that unwritten law of his profession which embodies the honourable understanding of the individual Members as to their bearing

他根据其自己的判断善意之所为，将对其委托人有约束力，其所为不会使其陷入任何诉讼，即使委托人的利益因此受到损害。诉讼律师的这些法律权力很少——如果有的话——充分行使，因为诉讼律师受到适当性和权宜因素的约束而不能这么做。但是在这样的情况下，有必要牢记其法律权力的全部是什么。

代理人［即诉讼代理人或者事务律师］的岗位有些不同。他与其委托人之间有雇用合同，委托人据此，因商定的特定的薪酬，有权要求代理人运用关照和勤勉，以及职业技能和经验。完全可以说，一般规则是，代理人必须遵守其委托人的指示行事。

但是一般规则受到几个限制。当然，不能要求代理人遵守委托人的非法和不当指示。对于代理人和诉讼律师而言，负有对法院的职责，在办理每起诉讼时，自己都必须遵守法院的规则和操作惯例。他还受到其职业的不成文法的约束，这些不成文法体现了各个成员就彼此的关系和行为的高贵理解。但是就当前的问题而言，最重要的是这样的毫无疑义的特殊规则，即当案件的处理交给诉讼律师时，代理人必定要根据他的指示行事，不会因善意遵守这样的指

and conduct towards each other. But above all in importance, as affecting the present question, is the undoubted special rule that when the conduct of a cause is in the hands of Counsel, the agent is bound to act according to his directions, and will not be answerable to his client for what he does *bona -fide* in obedience to such directions."

1.2.2 That traditional view of the powers and liabilities of an Advocate has been considerably altered by practice and case law in succeeding generations. It is now not possible to rely on many parts of Lord President Ingles' *dictum* with any degree of confidence. Some parts of the dictum still offer a sound analysis of the position of an Advocate.

1.2.3 An Advocate acts as such in performance of an office and has no contractual relationship with his client. It follows that he cannot perform any act which must, in law, be performed by the client or by someone empowered to act as an agent on his behalf. The acts of an Advocate are acts done upon his own responsibility in performance of an office and he does not, and cannot, in any sense, act as agent of his client; that is the function of a solicitor or other professional. Although it is commonly said that an accused person or litigant is "represented by an Advocate" or "represented by Counsel" , the use of these expressions should not be allowed to obscure the difference in law between the status and function of the Advocate and those of the agent. Thus, it is not appropriate for an Advocate to appear without an instructing agent if the client is not present. Equally, although it is said that the client

示而对其委托人承担责任。”

1.2.2 关于诉辩律师的权力和责任的传统观点，在后来被实践和判例法大大改变。现在不可能怀着什么信心来依赖 Ingles 院长的意见的许多部分来行事。其意见的一些部分仍然可以为诉辩律师的情况提供合理分析。

1.2.3 诉辩律师这样行为是在履行职务，与其委托人没有合同关系。因此，他不能从事在法律上必须由委托人或者被授权作为委托人的代理人行事的人所从事的行为。诉辩律师的行为是在尽其自己的履行职务的责任，他不是也不能在任何意义上作为其委托人的代理人，那是事务律师或者其他职业人员的职能。尽管人们常说被告或者诉讼当人是由“诉辩律师代理的”或者“诉讼律师代理的”，使用这样的表述不应当模糊了诉辩律师与那些代理人的身份和职能在法律上的差别。这样，在委托人不到庭的情况下，诉辩律师在没有进行指示的代理人在场的情况下出庭是不适当的。同样，尽管人们说是委托人或者其代理人在“指示诉辩律师”或者“指示诉讼律师”，这并不意味着他能够作出命令。然而，诉辩律师有义务就基本事项遵从指示，例如刑事案件中的辩护思路问题。如果他不能以一种允许他履行对法院的职责的方式来这么做的话，他应当退出代理。然

or his agent "instructs an Advocate" or "instructs Counsel" , this does not mean that he can give orders. An Advocate is however obliged to follow instructions as to basic matters such as the line of defence in criminal cases. If he is unable to do so in a manner which allows him to fulfil his duties to the Court he should withdraw from acting. It should be noted however that whilst Counsel is not an agent of his client he may legally bind his client in matters falling within the Advocate's particular mandate. Only in exceptional circumstances would an Advocate seek to bind his client on any matter central to a case without instructions to do so from the instructing solicitor (or other professional enjoying direct access) or the client.

1.2.4 It also follows from the fact that an Advocate acts as such in performance of an office that he cannot act in his professional capacity as an Advocate on his own behalf. He is, of course, free to plead his own cause in civil, criminal or other proceedings in exercise of his rights as an ordinary citizen, but he has no special rights or privileges by reason of the fact that he is an Advocate, nor may he wear wig or gown when doing so.

1.2.5 In order to preserve a Bar of independent Advocates it is necessary that an Advocate cannot enter into partnership with another Advocate or with any other person, or any employment or similar relationship, in connection with his practice as an Advocate.

1.2.6 An Advocate owes a variety of legal and moral obligations to his client, the Court, his professional colleagues and the legal profession generally. He does not directly owe any duty to his client's opponents.

而，应当指出的是，尽管诉讼律师不是其委托人的代理人，在属于诉辩律师特定授权范围内的事项上，他可能在法律上对其委托人有约束力。只有在特殊情况下，诉辩律师才能在没有来自进行指示的事务律师（或者有直接近用权利的其他职业人员）或者委托人的指示的情况下，试图在对案件至关重要的事项上约束其委托人。

1.2.4 从诉辩律师在履行这样的职务这一事实，也可以得出这样的结论，即他不能以为其本人以诉辩律师的身份行事。当然，他可以在民事、刑事或者其他诉讼中自由地行使他作为普通公民的权利，来对自己的案件进行诉辩，但是并不因为他是诉辩律师而有特殊的权利或者特权，也不能在这样做时戴假发或者着袍。

1.2.5 为了维护诉辩律师的独立性，诉辩律师不能与其他诉辩律师或者任何其他人员组成合伙，或者就其作为诉辩律师的执业活动，有任何雇用或者类似关系。

1.2.6 诉辩律师对其委托人、法院、其职业同僚和整个法律职业负有各种法律和伦理义务。他对其委托人的对手不直接负有任何职责。

2. THE GENERAL PRINCIPLES OF PROFESSIONAL CONDUCT

The general principles which should guide the professional conduct of an Advocate at all times are:–

2.1 Independence

2.1.1 The many duties to which an Advocate is subject require his absolute independence, free from all other influence, especially such as may arise from his personal interests or external pressure. Such independence is as necessary to trust in the process of justice as is the impartiality of the judge. An Advocate must therefore avoid any impairment of his independence and be careful not to compromise his professional standards in order to please his client, the Court or third parties.

2.1.2 This independence is necessary in non-contentious matters as well as in litigation. Advice given by an Advocate to his client has no value if it is given only to ingratiate himself, to serve his personal interests or in response to outside pressure.

2. 职业行为的一般原则

应当在任何时候指引诉辩律师职业行为的一般原则是：

2.1 独立

2.1.1 诉辩律师所承担的许多职责，要求他绝对独立，不受任何其他影响，特别是其个人利益或者外界压力可能带来的影响。这样的独立性，就像法官的不偏不倚那样，对于司法过程中的信任而言是必需的。因此，诉辩律师必须避免对其独立性的任何损害，小心谨慎，不为了取悦于其委托人、法院或者第三方而损害其职业标准。

2.1.2 这种独立性在诉讼和非争讼性事务中一样必要。如果诉辩律师为其委托人提供建议只是为了迎合自己，服务于他的个人利益，或者是为了回应外界压力，则该建议毫无价值。

2.2 Trust and Personal Integrity

Relationships of trust can only exist if an Advocate's personal honour, honesty and integrity are beyond doubt. For the Advocate, these traditional virtues are professional obligations.

2.3 Confidentiality

2.3.1 It is of the essence of an Advocate's function that he should be told by his client things which the client would not tell to others, and that he should be the recipient of other information on a basis of confidence. Without the certainty of confidentiality there cannot be trust. Confidentiality is therefore a primary and fundamental right and duty of the Advocate.

2.3.2 An Advocate shall respect the confidentiality of all information that becomes known to him in the course of his professional activity.

2.3.3 The obligation of confidentiality is not limited in time.

2.2 信任与个人适正性

只有在诉辩律师的个人荣誉、诚实性和适正性不受怀疑的情况下，才能存在信任关系。对于诉辩律师而言，这些传统美德是职业义务。

2.3 保密

2.3.1 对于诉辩律师的职能而言必不可少的是，委托人应当向其告知不会向他人告知的事项，他应当是基于信赖而获得其他信息的人。如果没有保密的确定性，就不能存在信任。因此，保密义务被视为诉辩律师的首要和基本的权利和职责。

2.3.2 诉辩律师应当就其在职业活动中知悉的所有信息保密。

2.3.3 保密义务在时间上没有限制。

3. DUTIES IN RELATION TO THE FACULTY AND OTHER ADVOCATES

3.1 An Advocate owes a duty of loyalty to the Faculty, to his fellow Members and, in particular, to the Dean.

3.2 An Advocate owes a duty not to bring the Faculty into disrepute.

3.3 It is essential that Counsel be able to discuss, negotiate and resolve cases on the basis that confidences will be respected and that agreements and undertakings will be honoured.

3. 对诉辩律师协会和其他诉辩律师的职责

3.1 诉辩律师对于协会、其他会员和——特别是——会长负有忠诚职责。

3.2 诉辩律师负有不损害诉辩律师协会之声誉的职责。

3.3 诉讼律师能够在保密得到尊重、协议和承诺将得到履行的基础上讨论、谈判和解决案件是至关重要的。

4. DUTIES IN RELATION TO THE INSTRUCTING AGENT

4.1 A corollary of the Advocate's independence from the agent is the agent's independence from the Advocate. An Advocate must respect the agent's independence - in particular, his freedom to instruct Counsel of his choice and to change Counsel at any time without explanation or apology. (An Advocate may be asked by an agent to recommend the name of another Advocate to act as his junior, or as his senior, or to replace him if he is unable to act. There is no rule against doing so, but it is preferable that the agent should be given several names from which to make his own choice after consultation with Counsel's clerk.)

4.2 An Advocate must also respect the fact that the agent's relationship with the client is different from, and likely to be more continuing than, his own. He should do nothing, beyond what his professional duty requires, to upset the agent/client relationship or destroy the trust which the client has in the agent.

4.3 When an Advocate has reason to believe that an agent has been guilty of professional misconduct (as opposed to professional negligence, as to which see paragraph 5.1.3) , he has a duty to the client, the Court and the profession to take appropriate action. If the matter comes to his knowledge in the course of

4. 与进行指示的代理人有关的职责

4.1 诉辩律师独立于代理人的一个自然结果是代理人独立于诉辩律师。诉辩律师必须尊重代理人的独立性，特别是其对其选择的诉讼律师进行指示的自由，和在任何时候不经解释或者致歉而更换诉讼律师的自由。（代理人可能请求诉辩律师推荐其他诉辩律师担任其资浅律师或者其资深律师，或者在他不能够行事的情况下取代他。没有规则禁止这么做，但是最好是为代理人提供几个姓名，使其在与诉讼律师的办事员磋商后作出自己的选择。）

4.2 诉辩律师还必须尊重这样的事实：代理人与委托人的关系不同于他自己的与委托人的关系，并可能比与自己的关系存续时间更长。除了其职业职责的要求外，他不应当做任何事情来干扰代理人 / 委托人关系或者破坏委托人对代理人的信任。

4.3 在诉辩律师有理由认为代理人在其对委托人、法院和职业负有采取适当行动的职责方面有职业不端行为（不同于职业过失，就此请参见 5.1.3）时，如果他是在法院程序过程中知悉的该事项，则可能有必要立即采取措施，如果为该目的有必要休庭，则应当请求法院休庭。如果该事项并不要求立即采

proceedings in Court, it may be necessary to take immediate action, and if an adjournment is necessary for this purpose, it should be asked for. If the matter does not call for immediate action, Counsel should consult the Dean before making any formal complaint or report.

4.4 If an Advocate feels compelled to criticise the conduct of an agent in respect of something falling short of professional misconduct, he should avoid doing so in the presence of the client and should in any event ask the agent to explain what he has done and why before criticising his conduct.

4.5 An Advocate should carefully consider whether he should attend a consultation without his instructing solicitor or a representative of his firm being present. The presence of the solicitor or representative will protect both Counsel and the solicitor should a dispute arise later as to what advice Counsel gave or what instructions he was given by the client. In cases where difficult advice is given but not accepted, it may be wise to record the advice in writing.

4.6 If Counsel has to speak to the client without the solicitor being present, the solicitor should be told as soon as possible what transpired.

4.7 There is no rule against an Advocate going to an agent's office to collect papers or to attend a consultation. Nor is there any rule which prevents an Advocate accepting a social invitation from an agent or giving such invitation to an agent. In doing so, however, the Advocate should bear in mind the considerations mentioned in preceding paragraphs.

取行动，诉讼律师在作出任何正式投诉或者举报之前，应当与会长磋商。

4.4 如果诉辩律师就没有达到职业不端行为的事项批评代理人的行为而有被迫感，他应当避免在委托人面前这么做，并在任何情况下应当在批评代理人的行为之前，要求代理人解释他做了什么，以及这么做的原因。

4.5 诉辩律师应当仔细考虑在其进行指示的事务律师或者其律师事务所的代表不在场的情况下，是否应当参加磋商。该事务律师或者代表在场，将在诉讼律师和事务律师随后就诉讼律师给出了什么建议或者委托人向他作出了什么指示发生争议的情况下，保护诉讼律师和事务律师。在给出了难以取悦的建议而没有被接受的情况下，也许最好是将建议加以书面记录。

4.6 如果在事务律师不在场的情况下，诉讼律师必须与委托人交谈，则应当就交流的内容尽可能早地告知事务律师。

4.7 没有规则禁止诉辩律师到代理人的办公室收集文件或者参与磋商。也没有规则禁止诉辩律师接受代理人的社交邀请，或者向代理人发出该邀请。然而在这么做的时候，诉辩律师应当牢记前面各段提及的因素。

5. DUTIES IN RELATION TO THE CLIENT

5.1 General

5.1.1 Confidentiality

As described in paragraph 2.3, an Advocate owes his client a duty of confidentiality.

5.1.2 The client's interest

Subject to due observance of all rules of law and professional conduct, an Advocate must always act in what he perceives in his professional judgement to be the best interests of his client and must put those interests before his own interests or those of fellow Members of the legal profession.

5.1.2.1 Conflict between client and instructing agent (e.g. where the client may have a claim for professional negligence against his agent)

Where it appears to Counsel that a conflict of interest has arisen or may arise between the client and the instructing agent, it is his duty to take steps to ensure that the client is so advised in order that he can get the advice of another agent. It will depend on the circumstances how this should be done. The great majority of solicitors and other professional

5. 对委托人的职责

5.1 总则

5.1.1 保密

就像 2.3 所规定的那样，诉辩律师对其委托人负有保密职责。

5.1.2 委托人利益

在严格遵守所有法律和职业行为规则的情况下，诉辩律师必须始终以其在职业判断中认为是出于其委托人的最大利益的方式行事，并且必须将这些利益置于他自己的利益或者法律职业其他人员的利益之上。

5.1.2.1 委托人与进行指示的代理人的利益冲突（例如，委托人可能对其代理人提出职业过失索赔的情况）

如果在诉讼律师看来，委托人与进行指示的代理人之间出现或者可能出现利益冲突，则他负有采取措施确保委托人知悉该情况的职责，以便委托人能够获得另一代理人的建议。这应当怎么做取决于有关情况。在向他们（以口头或者适当情况下采取书面形式）指出利益冲突的情况下，可以依赖绝大多数事务律师和其他职业人员代理

agents can be relied upon, when the conflict has been pointed out (orally or, if appropriate, in writing) , to take the necessary steps themselves. It will therefore normally be inappropriate to mention the matter in the presence of the client. But it may be necessary to record Counsel's advice as to the existence of a conflict in a formal note and to ask the agent to send it to the client, or to deal with the matter at consultation with the client. In extreme cases, it may be the duty of Counsel to refuse to act further on the instructions of the agent concerned.

5.1.3 Withdrawing from acting

Generally, it is desirable for Counsel to continue to act in criminal cases to assist the Court, but there are cases where it may be appropriate to withdraw from acting. In any case (criminal or civil) where Counsel feels obliged to withdraw from acting, he must do so without delay and take such steps as are necessary to ensure that the instructing solicitor and the client know why he has withdrawn. Where he feels obliged to withdraw in the course of a trial or other hearing, he must formally move the judge (or chairman) for leave to withdraw from acting and protect the interests of the client by moving for an adjournment so that the client can get other advice. He is under no obligation to explain in detail to the Court or tribunal his reasons for withdrawing, since to do so may prejudice the client, and he should not yield to pressure to do so. If Counsel is in doubt as to whether he is entitled or bound to withdraw he should seek advice (as set out in

人自己采取必要措施。因此，通常情况下，在委托人在场的情况下提及该事项是不适当的。但是，可能有必要就利益冲突的存在以正式通知的方式将诉讼律师的建议记录下来，并要求代理人将该通知送达委托人，或者在与委托人磋商时处理该事务。在极端情况下，拒绝根据有关代理人的指示采取进一步行动，可能是诉讼律师的职责。

5.1.3 退出代理

一般情况下，诉讼律师最好是继续在刑事案件中行事以协助法院，但在某些情况下，退出代理可能是适当的。在任何（刑事或者民事）案件中，如果诉讼律师感到有义务退出代理，他必须毫不迟延地这样做，并采取必要的措施，以确保进行指示的事务律师和委托人知道他为什么退出代理。在审判或者其他听证过程中，如果他感到有义务退出代理，他必须正式申请法官（或者主席）准许退出代理，并通过申请延期以便委托人获得其他建议来保护委托人的利益。他没有义务向法院或者裁判庭详细解释退出代理的原因，因为这么做可能会损害委托人，他不应当屈服于这么做的压力。如果诉讼律师就他是否有权或者有义务退出代理存在疑问，他应当寻求建议（见第 7 条之规定），并且在必要情况下申请延期以这么做。在审判即将进行或正在进行时，退出代理的后果可能特别具有破坏性。在这种情况下，在决定退出代理时应当特定谨慎。资浅诉讼律师应当寻求咨询（见第 7 条）。

Section 7) , and if necessary obtain an adjournment to do so. The consequences of withdrawing from acting when a trial is imminent or in progress may be particularly disruptive. In these circumstances care must be taken regarding the decision to withdraw from acting. Junior Counsel should seek advice (as is set out in section 7) .

5.1.4 Adequate insurance

An Advocate is obliged to maintain a reasonable level of PII cover having regard to the nature of that Advocate's practice and the extent of potential liabilities to clients in the event of a negligent error.

5.2 Special Duties in Criminal Cases

5.2.1 Pleas

5.2.2 Where the Crown offers to accept a reduced or restricted plea, the defending Advocate has a duty to advise the accused of that offer and to obtain his instructions about it. Likewise, where any limited offer to plead is made by an accused, it should (if considered in law to be appropriate) be conveyed to the Crown for consideration, without delay. For the avoidance of doubt, it is prudent to obtain written instructions from the accused, through the instructing solicitor, for the tendering of any plea. In no circumstances should Counsel tender any plea on behalf of an accused unless instructions to do so have been obtained either through, or in the presence of, the instructing solicitor.

5.1.4 充足保险

诉辩律师有义务虑及诉辩律师的业务性质和在发生职业过失情况下对委托人的潜在责任的大小，保持合理的职业赔偿保险额度。

5.2 刑事案件中的特殊职责

5.2.1 辩诉交易

5.2.2 在检控方提出接受减轻或者限制性辩诉交易的情况下，进行辩护的诉辩律师负有就此告知被告并就此获得他的指示的职责。同样，在被告提出了任何限定性答辩提议的情况下，如果从法律上看是适当的，这应当毫不迟延地传达给检控方进行考虑。为了避免疑义，最好是通过进行指示的事务律师从被告那里就提出任何辩诉交易获得书面指示。在任何情况下，诉讼律师都不应当以被告的名义提出任何辩诉交易，除非已经通过进行指示的事务律师或者在进行指示的事务律师在场的情况下获得了这么做的指示。

5.2.3 In advising as to the possible consequences of a plea of guilty, Counsel should refrain from making any positive forecast of the possible sentence beyond drawing the attention of the accused to the normally anticipated range of sentences in the circumstances of that particular case, and to any current case law indicating that a discount in sentence may be expected when a plea of guilty is tendered at an appropriate stage.

5.2.4 Confessions

Where an accused person makes a confession to Counsel and Counsel is satisfied that in law such confession amounts to guilt, Counsel must explain to the accused (if he is not pleading guilty) that the conduct of his defence will be limited by that confession as set out in paragraphs 6.3.5 and 6.3.6 below. Counsel must emphasise to the accused that no substantive defence involving an assertion or a suggestion of innocence will be put forward on his behalf and that, if he is not satisfied with this, he should seek other advice. Counsel should consider whether it advisable to obtain confirmation in writing from the accused that he has been so advised and that he accepts such an approach to the conduct of his defence.

5.2.5 So long as an accused maintains his innocence, Counsel's duty lies in advising him on the law appropriate to his case and the conduct thereof. Counsel may not put pressure on him to tender a plea of guilty, whether to a restricted charge or not, so long as he maintains his innocence. Nor should Counsel accept instructions to tender a plea in mitigation on a basis inconsistent with the plea of guilty. Counsel should always

5.2.3 在就有罪答辩的可能结果进行咨询时，诉讼律师应当避免就可能的量刑作出任何肯定性预测，只能提请被告注意在该特定案件情况下通常预计的量刑幅度，以及表明在适当阶段进行有罪答辩情况下有量刑折扣的当前判例法。

5.2.4 自白

在被告向诉讼律师作出自白且诉讼律师确信在法律上该自白等同于认罪的情况下，诉讼律师必须向被告解释，如果他不是在进行有罪答辩，则为他进行的辩护将会受到该自白的限制，这可见于以下 6.3.5 和 6.3.6。诉讼律师必须向被告强调，不会为其提出宣称或者暗示其无辜的实体辩护，如果他对此不满意，他应当寻求他人的建议。诉讼律师应当考虑是否是最好从被告这里取得书面确认，表明已经如此对其进行告知，他接受了这样为其进行辩护的方法。

5.2.5 只要被告坚持他是无辜的，诉讼律师的职责就是就与他的案件相适的法律为其提供咨询，并就此进行辩护。只要他坚持其无辜，诉讼律师不得向其施加压力来作出有罪答辩，无论是否是限制性指控。诉讼律师也不应当接受指示来提出与有罪答辩不一致的减轻答辩。诉讼律师总是应当仔细考虑接受指示提出有罪答辩是否是适当的，是否符合正义的利益。他应当确保被告充分意识到所有后果，并应当坚

consider very carefully whether it is proper, in the interests of justice, to accept instructions to tender a plea of guilty. He should ensure that the accused is fully aware of all the consequences and should insist that the instructions to plead guilty are recorded in writing.

5.2.6 Acting for co-accused

Save in the most exceptional circumstances, Counsel should not accept instructions to act for more than one accused or appellant.

持以书面形式记录进行有罪答辩的指示。

5.2.6 为共同被告行事

诉讼律师不得接受指示为一个以上的被告或者上诉人行事，最为特殊的情况除外。

6. DUTY TO THE COURT AND DUTIES CONNECTED WITH COURT AND SIMILAR PROCEEDINGS

6.1 Duties in Relation to Matters of Law

6.1.1 Where an Advocate is aware of a previous decision binding on the Court, or of a statutory provision, relevant to a point of law in issue, it is his duty to draw that decision or provision to the attention of the Court whether or not it supports his argument and whether or not it has been referred to by his opponent.

6.1.2 Where there is no contradictor, an Advocate should inform the Court of authorities relevant to the material issues in the case, even where such authority may be against his interest.

6.2 Duties in Relation to Matters of Fact

In relation to matters of fact, an Advocate should have two principles in mind -

(a) it is for the Court, not for Counsel, to assess the credibility and reliability of witnesses; And

(b) Counsel must not seek to persuade a Court to proceed on a factual basis which he with reasonable certainty

6. 对法院的职责和与法院和类似程序有关的职责

6.1 与法律事项有关的职责

6.1.1 如果诉辩律师意识到先前的判例对法院有约束力，或者与法律争点有关的制定法规定，他负有提请法院注意该判例或者规定的职责，无论这是否支持他的观点，无论其对手是否已经提及。

6.1.2 在没有反驳者的情况下，诉辩律师应当就与本案重要争议点有关的典据告知法院，即使这样的典据可能有悖于他的利益。

6.2 与事实事项有关的职责

就事实事项，诉辩律师应当牢记两个原则：

（a）是法院而不是诉讼律师来评估证人的可信性和可靠性；以及

（b）诉讼律师不得试图说服法院在他合理确定为不真实的事实基础上行事。

knows to be untrue.

6.3 In Court

6.3.1 When conducting a case in Court, an Advocate should base his questions upon his instructions, the precognitions and the productions supplemented by information obtained at consultation, and on any evidence which has already been led.

6.3.2 An Advocate should not state his personal opinion on matters of fact. It is particularly important to observe this rule when addressing a jury. Counsel must not attempt to supplement the evidence by making observations on matters of fact which are not based on, or justified by, the evidence. In a criminal trial, he should not under any circumstances express either directly or indirectly a personal belief in the innocence or guilt of an accused or any of the accused.

6.3.3 An Advocate may not be a party to the giving of evidence which he knows to be perjured evidence, or to any other course that would enable a case to be put forward on behalf of a client which the client or his solicitor has informed him is unfounded in fact.

6.3.4 An Advocate may not put to a witness any question suggesting that the witness has been guilty of a crime, fraud or other illegal or improper conduct unless he has personally satisfied himself that there is evidence to support the suggestion.

6.3.5 Confessions to Counsel by accused persons.

It follows from the rules stated in paragraphs 5.2.4 and 6.2

6.3 在法院

6.3.1 在法院办理案件时，诉辩律师应当根据他的指示、经磋商时获得的信息所补充的审前笔录和证物，以及已经导出的任何证言提出问题。

6.3.2 诉辩律师不应当就事实问题陈述其个人意见。在对陪审团致辞时遵守这一规则尤其重要。诉讼律师不得试图通过就事实问题作出不是基于证据或者没有证据支持的评论来对证据进行补充。在刑事审判中，他在任何情况下都不得直接或者间接表达对被告是否有罪的个人信念。

6.3.3 诉辩律师不得在明知情况下参与伪证，或者参与任何其他使得能够代表委托人提出委托人或者其事务律师已经告诉他没有事实根据的案件的活动。

6.3.4 诉辩律师不得向证人提出任何问题，来暗示证人犯罪、欺诈或者有其他非法或不当行为，除非他本人确信认为有证据支持该暗示。

6.3.5 被告向诉讼律师作出自白

从 5.2.4 和 6.2（b）规定的规则可以得出的结论是，在被告

(b) that, where an accused person has admitted that he committed the act with which he is charged (whether or not that admission is an explicit admission of guilt in law), an Advocate may not conduct the defence on a basis inconsistent with that admission. Thus, he may not put to a witness any question suggesting, or tending to suggest, that the accused did not commit the act. *A fortiori*, he may not seek to set up a special defence of alibi or incrimination.

6.3.6 Subject to the rule stated in the previous paragraph, Counsel may:

(a) take proper objection to the jurisdiction of the Court, to the competency or relevancy of the indictment or complaint, or to the admissibility of evidence;

(b) test the evidence for the prosecution by cross-examination;

(c) cross-examine or lead evidence in support of a special defence of insanity or (depending on the tenor of the accused's admission) self defence;

(d) cross-examine or lead evidence for the purpose of explaining the actings of the accused or supporting a plea in mitigation; and

(e) make submissions as to the sufficiency in law of the evidence to support a verdict of guilty.

6.3.7 Exparte statements of fact by Counsel at the Bar

The Court frequently must rely on statements as to matters of fact made by Counsel at the Bar - for example, in the Motion Roll and certain types of Petition procedure. Such statements are made on the responsibility of Counsel as the holder of a public office and a Member of the College of Justice. Counsel

承认他实施了被指控的行为（无论该自认是否明确承认在法律上有罪）的情况下，诉辩律师不得进行与该自认不一致的辩护。这样，他不能向证人提出任何暗示或者倾向于暗示被告没有实施该行为的问题。更不用说，他不得提出不在犯罪现场或者控告他人的特别辩护。

6.3.6 在遵守前款规定的规则的情况下，诉讼律师可以：

（a） 就法院的管辖权、起诉书或者告发书的权限或者相关性、证据的可采性提出适当异议；

（b） 通过交叉询问检验支持检控的证据；

（c） 交叉询问或者导出证据以支持精神错乱或者（取决于被告自认的要旨）自卫的特别辩护；

（d） 交叉询问或者导出证据，以解释被告的行为或者支持减轻答辩；以及

（e） 就支持有罪裁决的证据在法律上的充分性提出意见。

6.3.7 诉讼律师在法庭上的单方事实陈述

法院经常就事实事项必须依赖诉讼律师在法庭所作的陈述，例如，在动议卷程序和某些类型的请愿程序中。这样的陈述是基于诉讼律师作为公职人员和司法院成员的责任提出的。因此，诉讼律师必须谨慎小心，以确保任何作为事实陈述的事情都能由他所掌握的信息所支持。如果法院提出

must therefore be scrupulously careful to ensure that anything stated as fact is justified by the information in his possession. If the Court asks a question which Counsel cannot answer on the information in his possession, he must say that he cannot answer it and, if necessary, ask leave to take instructions on the matter. This rule applies whether or not the opposing party is represented in Court.

6.3.8 Pleadings

An Advocate must have a proper basis for stating a fact in any pleadings.

6.3.9 Interviewing witnesses

6.3.9.1 There is no general rule that an advocate may not discuss the case with a potential witness, but an advocate, when instructed by a solicitor, is entitled to insist that he accepts instructions on the basis that he, the advocate, will not do so.

6.3.9.2 Once a proof or trial has begun, an advocate must not interview any potential witness in relation to what has been said in court in the absence of that witness.

6.3.9.3 Under no circumstances should Counsel do or say anything which suggests to a witness that he should give evidence other than in accordance with the honest recollection or opinion of the witness. An advocate must avoid doing or saying anything which could have the effect of, or could be construed as, inducing the client or a skilled witness to "tailor" his evidence to suit the case.

6.3.9.4 Some cases cannot be properly prepared or conducted if the rule stated in para. 6.3.9.2 is followed strictly according to

一个问题，而诉讼律师不能根据他所掌握的信息来回答，他必须说他不能对此作出回答，如有必要，请求准许就此事获得指示。无论对方当事人是否在法院获得了代理，此规则都适用。

6.3.8 书状

在任何书状中陈述的事实，诉辩律师必须有适当根据。

6.3.9 会见证人

6.3.9.1 并不存在诉辩律师不得与潜在证人讨论案件的一般规则，但是在受到事务律师的指示时，诉辩律师有权坚持他接受指示的前提是他——诉辩律师——将不去这么做。

6.3.9.2 一旦法官单独听证或者审判已经开始，诉辩律师就不得在潜在证人不在场的情况下就法院所说的事项会见任何潜在证人。

6.3.9.3 在任何情况下，诉讼律师都不应该说或者做任何事情来暗示证人不应当按照证人的诚实记忆或者意见来作证。诉辩律师必须避免做或者说任何可能会诱使或者可解释为在诱使委托人或者有技能的证人根据案件“裁剪”其证言的事情。

6.3.9.4 如果严格按照字面来遵守 6.3.9.2 规定的规则，则一些案件就不能适当准备或者办理。陪伴委托人的亲属或者朋

the letter. The client may be accompanied by a relative or friend who is also a potential witness. Where the client is a corporate persona, those who can speak for the corporation may also be potential witnesses, although in that case it is usually better to discuss the case with someone who is not personally involved and can take a more objective view of it. Some witnesses may be witnesses to fact as to part of their evidence and expert witnesses giving opinion evidence as to another part. It may be essential in a case raising technical issues to discuss points arising from the evidence with a skilled witness who has not yet given evidence. In such cases, an Advocate must use his discretion. But he should always act according to the spirit of the rule - namely, that Counsel should not under any circumstances do or say anything which might suggest to the witness that he should give evidence otherwise than in accordance with his honest recollection or opinion.

6.3.9.5 An Advocate may not, except with the consent of his opponent or of the Court, communicate with *any* witness, including his client, once that witness has begun to give evidence until that evidence is concluded.

6.3.9.6 As to interviewing the client or witnesses in the absence of the instructing agent, see paragraphs 4.5 and 4.6 above.

6.4 The Duty of Courtesy

6.4.1 Discourtesy is as offensive in Court as it is outside, and is

友，也可能是潜在的证人。在委托人是法人的情况下，那些能够为法人代言的人也可能是潜在证人，尽管在该情况下通常最好是与本人没有卷入从而能够就案件提供更客观的看法的人员来讨论案件。一些证人可能是就其证据的一部分作证的事实证人，和就另一部分提供意见证据的专家证人。在发生了技术性问题的案件中，与还没有作证的专家证人讨论证据中的问题是很重要的。在这样的情况下，诉辩律师必须运用其自由裁量权。但是他总是应当根据规则的精神行事，即诉讼律师在任何情况下都不得做或者说可能暗示证人他应当在作证时不遵从其诚实的回忆或者意见的事情。

6.3.9.5 一旦证人开始作证，在作证结束前，诉辩律师不得与该证人进行交流，包括其自己的委托人，除非得到对方或者法院的同意。

6.3.9.6 就在进行指示的代理人不在场情况下会见委托人或者证人，参见上述 4.5 和 4.6。

6.4 礼貌职责

6.4.1 在法院失礼像在法院外失礼一样具有冒犯性，同样有损于

equally detrimental to the reputation of Counsel with the bench, to the interests of the client and to public confidence in the administration of justice.

6.4.2 In the examination of witnesses, and particularly in the cross-examination of hostile witnesses, an Advocate must remember that the law places him in a privileged position which he should not abuse - for example, by bullying or insulting behaviour or by making offensive or personal remarks.

6.4.3 There is a long-standing tradition of mutual trust and Courtesy between the bench and Bar which must be respected.

6.4.4 A failure to appear in Court on time should always, as a matter of courtesy, be the subject of an apology. If the Court is still sitting, and has not yet passed on to other business, the proper time to make the apology is at once on arrival in Court. The apology should be made in open Court to the bench.

6.5 The Duty to Attend Court

6.5.1 It is the duty of an Advocate so to arrange his affairs as to avoid a foreseeable clash of commitments.

6.5.2 Having accepted instructions to appear, it is the Advocate's responsibility to ensure, unless (in a civil case only) other arrangements have been made with the instructing solicitor, that he is present in Court on the day and at the time appointed and thereafter during the period of time for which he has been properly instructed until the trial or hearing is concluded. Where unforeseen circumstances make it

诉讼律师在法院的声望、委托人利益和公众对司法的信心。

6.4.2 在询问证人时，特别是在对敌意证人进行交叉询问时，诉辩律师必须记住，法律赋予他的受特免权保护的地位不得被滥用，例如做出恃强凌弱或者侮辱性的行为，或者说出冒犯性言论或者进行人身攻击。

6.4.3 法院与诉讼律师之间有着相互信任和以礼相待的悠久传统，对此必须尊重。

6.4.4 作为礼貌问题，应当就未能按时出庭道歉。如果法院仍未退庭，并且还没有转到处理其他事务，则道歉的适当时间是到达法院立刻进行。向法官道歉应当在公开法庭上进行。

6.5 到庭职责

6.5.1 诉辩律师负有对其事务进行安排，以避免可以预见的担当冲突的职责。

6.5.2 在接受出庭指示后，诉辩律师有责任确保他在指定的日期和时间到庭，并且此后在其被适当指示的期间到庭，直至审判或者听证结束，除非（仅限于民事案件）与进行指示的事务律师已经进行了其他安排。如果发生了不可预见的情况而使他不可能出庭，他必须确保有人在指定的时间之前或者之时到场解释其不能到庭的原因，并在必要情况下申请延期。

impossible for him to be present, he must ensure that someone else is present at or before the time appointed to explain his absence and, if necessary, to move for an adjournment.

6.5.3 If an Advocate has accepted instructions to appear in the High Court or the Inner House, including instructions for the Single Bills, it is his duty to ensure that he is present there at the appointed time, even although he also has instructions to appear in the Outer House. If a clash of commitments appears likely, he should ensure that someone else is present to appear in the Outer House in his place and, if necessary, to move for an adjournment until he is free to appear there. If a conflict arises due to unforeseen circumstances and he finds himself still detained in the Outer House when he must appear in the High Court or the Inner House, he should inform the Lord Ordinary that he requires to go to the High Court or the Inner House as the case may be and ask for an adjournment so that he can do so.

6.5.4 It is acceptable but not obligatory for Counsel to accept instruction for the Motion Roll on a day when he is engaged in a proof or other substantial hearing in the Outer House. If Counsel engaged in a proof or other hearing in the Outer House expects to be in difficulty because he has accepted instructions to attend elsewhere in the Outer House to deal with an important matter on the Motion Roll on the same day, he or his clerk should inform the Clerk of Court as soon as possible so that the judge concerned may be alerted to the problem and take such action as is appropriate. It has been

6.5.3 如果诉辩律师接受了在高等刑事法院或者内院出庭的指示，包括提出简单事项动议的指示，他有确保在指定的时间到庭的职责，即使他也接受了在外院出庭的指示。如何这些担当看起来有可能冲突，他应当确保有人代替他在外院出庭，在必要情况，申请休庭，直至他可以在那里出庭。如果由于不可预见的情况发生了冲突，他发现自己必须在高等法院或者内院出庭，而自己仍然耽误在外院时，他应当告知法官他需要到高等法院或者内院（视情况而定），并请求延期以便他能这么做。

6.5.4 诉讼律师可以——但是不是有义务——接受在诉讼律师在外院参加证据或者其他重大听证的同一天，参加动议卷程序的指示。如果在内院参加证据或者其他听证的诉讼律师因为他已经接受指示在同一天到外院处理动议卷上的重要事务，而预计有困难，他或者他的办事员应当尽可能早地告知法院书记官，以便有关法官可以留意该问题并采取适当的措施。人们已经接受的是，在这样的情况下，证据听证可以合理推迟，直至诉讼律师在其他法院的业务已经完成。

accepted that in such circumstances the start of the proof might reasonably be delayed until Counsel's business in the other Court has been completed.

6.5.5 Senior Counsel appearing with junior should only be absent from the Court if he is satisfied that his junior will be present and will be able to deal properly with any matter which may arise.

6.5.6 For the reasons mentioned in paragraph 1.2.3 above, only the agent can "represent" the client in Court. Moreover, it may be necessary at any time for the Advocate to take instructions which he cannot properly do in the absence of the agent (see paragraphs 4.5 and 4.6 above). The Advocate is not responsible for ensuring the attendance of his instructing agent and is entitled, but never bound, to proceed with the case in the agent's absence if the Court permits him to do so. He must, however, be satisfied (a) that the absence of the agent does not imply that his instructions have been withdrawn, and (b) that he can, consistently with his duty to the client and the Court, conduct the case properly in the absence of the agent.

6.6 Responsibility for Pleadings in Civil Actions

An Advocate has a professional responsibility for any pleadings drafted by him. In the case of pleadings drafted by others it is his professional duty to consider whether he can support the pleadings on the basis of the available information. If he cannot, he must insist that the pleadings are revised and, if not, refuse to act further.

6.5.5 与资浅诉讼律师一起出庭的资深诉讼律师，只有在他确信资浅诉讼律师将会到庭，并且能够适当处理任何可能发生的事项的情况下，才能不到庭。

6.5.6 出于前述 1.2.3 提及的原因，只有代理人能够在法院“代理”委托人。此外，在任何时候诉辩律师都可能有必要接受在没有代理人情况下不能适当办理的指示（参见上述 4.5 和 4.6）。诉辩律师并不负责确保对其进行指示的代理人到庭，有权——但是不是义务——在没有代理人的情况下继续办理案件，如果法院允许他这么做的话。然而，他必须确信：（a）该代理人缺席并不意味着已经撤回对他的指示；以及（b）与其对委托人和法院的职责相一致，他能够在代理人不在场的情况下适当办理案件。

6.6 民事诉讼中对书状的责任

诉辩律师对其起草的任何书状负有职业责任。在书状是他人起草的情况下，其职业职责是考虑他是否能够根据可得信息来支持该书状。如果他不能，则他必须坚持修改书状，否则拒绝采取进一步行动。

6.7 Criminal appeals

6.7.1 In advising on criminal appeals, Counsel has a duty, first, to consider whether there are grounds for an appeal which he is prepared to state to the Court and, second, if in his opinion there are none, to refuse to act further in the case.

6.7.2 Particular care must be exercised in coming to a view that an appeal which has passed a judicial sift is not stateable.

6.8 Opposing a party litigant

Where an Advocate appears against a party litigant, he should as far as consistent with his duty to his client, co-operate with the Court in enabling the party litigant's case to be fairly stated and justice to be done.

6.7 刑事上诉

6.7.1 在就刑事上诉提供咨询时，诉讼律师负有下列职责：首先，考虑是否存在他准备向法院陈述的上诉理由；其次，如果他认为不存在这样的上诉理由，则应当拒绝在该案件中采取进一步行动。

6.7.2 在形成通过了司法筛选的上诉不可辩的观点时，应当特别谨慎。

6.8 反对诉讼当事人

在诉辩律师出庭反对一方诉讼当事人的情况下，他应当尽可能与其对其委托人的职责一致，与法院合作，使得对方当事人的案件得以公平陈述和正当处理。

7. THE DUTY TO SEEK ADVICE

7.1 If an Advocate is in doubt about the proper course of conduct to adopt, he should consult the Dean or Vice-Dean. If the Dean or Vice-Dean is not available, then another office-bearer should be consulted. If no office-bearer is available, then the Advocate should consult his devilmaster or another senior Member of faculty.

7.2 In explaining his position he must be absolutely frank and conceal nothing which might be relevant to the advice he seeks.

7.3 If an Advocate is told by the Dean or Vice-Dean that it is his duty to adopt a particular course of conduct, then he must act accordingly. In other cases, if he feels unable to accept the advice given, then he must make every effort to obtain the advice of the Dean or Vice-Dean.

7. 寻求建议的职责

7.1 如果诉辩律师对采取的行为的适当性有疑问，他应该咨询于会长或者副会长。如果会长或者副会长不在，则应当咨询于其他官员。如果没有官员可进行咨询，诉辩律师应咨询他的见习生导师或者律师协会其他高级人员。

7.2 在解释他的状况时，他必须绝对坦率，毫不隐瞒可能与他寻求的建议有关的事项。

7.3 如会长或副会长告知诉辩律师，他有采取某行为的职责，他必须采取相应的行动。在其他情况下，如果他觉得不能接受所给出的建议，那么他必须尽一切努力获得会长或副会长的建议。

8. INSTRUCTIONS

8.1 General

8.1.1 By accepting instructions, an Advocate undertakes a professional commitment on which the Courts and those instructing him are entitled to rely.

8.1.2 In considering the nature of that professional commitment, two basic distinctions must be borne in mind -

(a) the distinction between (i) delivery of instructions to an Advocate, and (ii) acceptance of instructions by an Advocate; and

(b) the distinction between (i) refusal to accept instructions and (ii) the return of instructions once accepted.

8.2 From whom may an Advocate accept instructions?

8.2.1 An Advocate may not accept instructions direct from a client, except in cases detailed in Appendix D. Instructions must come from another professional person who represents the client. The persons from whom instructions may be accepted are listed in the Appendix. Instructions may only be accepted

8. 指示

8.1 总则

8.1.1 通过接受指示，诉辩律师作出了法院和对他进行指示的人有权依赖的职业担当。

8.1.2 在考虑职业担当的性质时，必须牢记两个基本区别：

（a）（i）向诉辩律师作出指示与（ii）诉辩律师接受指示之间的区别；以及

（b）（i）拒绝接受指示与（ii）接受指示后退回指示的区别。

8.2 诉辩律师可以从何人接受指示？

8.2.1 诉辩律师不得从委托人那里直接接受指示，附录D具体规定的情况除外。指示必须来自代理委托人的其他职业人员。可以从那里接受指示的人员清单请见附录。仅可以从有权在相关法院或者裁判庭执业的职业人员那里接受与在法院或者裁判庭出庭有关的指示。

in relation to Court or tribunal appearances from professionals entitled to practise before the relevant Court or tribunal.

8.2.2 Where a Dean's Ruling is in force regulating the acceptance of instructions from a particular solicitor or firm of solicitors, an Advocate may only accept instructions from that solicitor or firm on the conditions laid down by the Dean's Ruling.

8.2.3 While there is no rule which prevents an Advocate giving free legal advice at a Legal Advice Centre or similar institution, he should remember the limitations on his power to act explained in paragraph 1.2.3 above.

8.2.4 While there is no rule which prevents an Advocate giving legal advice to a relative or friend, he should remember that it is not always possible to advise a relative or friend with the degree of objectivity which the case requires.

8.3 When is an Advocate bound to accept instructions?

8.3.1 It is an important principle of practice that an Advocate should not, when available to accept instructions, refuse to accept instructions to act for any litigant before Scottish Courts which are accompanied by payment of a reasonable fee or the obligation of a Scottish solicitor to pay such a fee.

8.3.2 Advocates who are holders of the office of Advocate depute for the time being are not available to be instructed for the defence in criminal cases. They are available for instruction in civil matters, although their ability to accept instructions is constrained by the requirement that in general their duties in

8.2.2 如果从特定事务律师或者事务律师事务所接受指示，有着对此加以规制的有效会长裁决，诉辩律师仅可以根据会长裁决规定的条件接受该事务律师或者事务律师事务所的指示。

8.2.3 尽管没有规则禁止诉辩律师在法律服务中心或者类似机构提供免费法律建议，他应当记住上述1.2.3所解释的对其如此行事的权力的限制。

8.2.4 尽管没有规则禁止诉辩律师向亲属或者朋友提供法律建议，但他应当记住，为亲属或者朋友提供的建议，并不总是可能会具有案件所要求的客观程度。

8.3 诉辩律师什么时候有义务接受指示？

8.3.1 一个重要的执业原则是，诉辩律师在能够接受指示，且该指示附有合理的律师费或者苏格兰事务律师支付该费用的义务时，不得拒绝接受在苏格兰法院为任何诉讼当事人行事的指示。

8.3.2 担任检察官职务的诉辩律师，在该期间不能接受指示在刑事案件中进行辩护。他们可以在民事事务中接受指示，尽管他们接受指示的能力受到这样的要求的限制，即通常情况下，他们在公诉署的职责必须优先于其他工作。临时检察官的岗位对诉讼律师在其他方面接受指示的可得性没有

the Crown Office must take precedence over other work. The position of *adhoc* Advocates depute has no implications for the availability of Counsel to be instructed otherwise.

8.3.3 The post of standing Counsel to a government department or agency may require that Counsel not be available to be instructed against that department or agency, but does not necessarily do so. The position of Standing Counsel has no implications for the availability of Counsel to be instructed otherwise, nor grants any priority of instruction for the purposes of rule 8.5 below.

8.3.4 An Advocate should not refuse to accept instructions on :-

(i) unacceptable discriminatory grounds such as race, religion, gender or sexual orientation; or

(ii) grounds of mere personal preference or personal dislike of the potential client or his views; or

(iii) grounds that do not have some other reasonable justification.

8.3.5 An Advocate would normally be expected to be available to accept instructions to appear before Scottish Courts at times when the Court of Session is not in recess or vacation. It is however accepted that there may be circumstances such as maternity, paternity, vacation, illness or other personal circumstances which mean that an Advocate may not be available to accept any or some instructions.

8.3.6 The Dean may in exceptional circumstances require an Advocate to accept instructions to appear in Scottish Courts.

8.3.7 It is permitted and indeed encouraged to agree fees in

影响。

8.3.3 在政府部门或者机关担任常年顾问，可能要求诉讼律师不得接受指示来反对该部门或者机关，但是并不必然这么做。常年顾问岗位对诉讼律师在其他方面接受指示的可得性没有影响，也不带来下述规则 8.5 目的上的指示的优先性。

8.3.4 诉辩律师不得基于下列理由拒绝接受指示：

（i） 诸如种族、宗教、性别或者性取向等不可接受的歧视性理由；或者

（ii） 对潜在委托人及其观点的纯粹个人偏好或个人厌弃之理由；或者

（iii） 没有其他合理根据的理由。

8.3.5 在高等民事法院不闭庭或者不休假期的任何时候，诉辩律师通常应当能够接受指示在苏格兰法院出庭。然而，人们接受了这样的情况，即可能存在诸如产假、陪产假、假期、疾病或者其他个人情况，这意味着诉辩律师可能不能接受任何或者某些指示。

8.3.6 在特殊情况下，会长可以要求诉辩律师接受指示在苏格兰法院出庭。

8.3.7 允许并确实鼓励预先就律师费达成协议。在必要情况下，

advance. If necessary the Dean may be asked by Counsel to rule on whether a particular fee is "reasonable" in the circumstances.

8.3.8 There are, however, circumstances in which an Advocate is entitled, and indeed bound, to refuse instructions.

8.3.9 An Advocate may not accept instructions to act on behalf of any person or body from whom or from which he receives any remuneration other than the professional fees or retainers paid to him as an Advocate. Thus, he may not act for a company of which he is a director, or for a firm of which he is a partner, and from which he derives director's fees, a salary or a share of the profits (see also paragraph 8.3.9 below) .

8.3.10 An Advocate shall not be entitled to make a '*pactum de quota litis*' – an agreement between the Advocate and his client entered into before final conclusion of a matter to which the client is a party by virtue of which the client undertakes to pay the Advocate a share of the result regardless of whether this is represented by a sum of money or by any other benefit achieved by the client upon conclusion of the matter.

8.3.11 An Advocate may not allow his personal interests to affect the performance of his professional duty. Accordingly, he should not accept instructions to act in his professional capacity in circumstances where he has a direct personal interest in the outcome. Where he has, or may have, an indirect personal interest in the outcome (e.g. where he is asked to act for a company in which he is a major shareholder or for an organisation in which he holds office although

诉讼律师可以要求会长就特定律师费在有关情况下是否“合理”进行裁决。

8.3.8 然而，存在诉辩律师有权——实际上是有义务——拒绝指示的情况。

8.3.9 诉辩律师不得接受指示代理他从中取得任何报酬的任何人员或者组织，作为职业律师取得职业律师费或者聘请定金除外。因此，他不得在他担任公司董事、事务所合伙人，并从中取得董事费、薪金或者分红的情况下，代理这些公司或者事务所（还请参见下述 8.3.9）。

8.3.10 诉辩律师无权订立“风险代理协议”，这是诉辩律师与其委托人在委托人是一方当事人的事务终结之前订立的协议，根据该协议，委托人承诺将获得结果的一部分付给诉辩律师，不论这是事务终结时的一笔款项还是委托人取得的任何其他利益。

8.3.11 诉辩律师不得允许其个人利益影响其履行职业职责。因此，在他在结果中有直接个人利益的情况下，他不得接受指示以及以职业身份行事。在他就结果有或者可能有间接个人利益的情况下（例如，他被要求代理某公司，而他是该公司的主要股东，或者他被要求代理某组织，而他在该组织中任职，尽管是没有薪酬的），他应当在接受指示之前与会长磋商。在个人利益冲突是后来发生的情况下，他应当告知进行指示的事务律师，并谢绝继续代理。无论受

unremunerated), he should consult the Dean before accepting instructions. Where a conflict of personal interest arises later, he should inform the instructing solicitor and decline to act further. Similar difficulties may arise whether Counsel is instructed to act for or against someone he knows personally or with whose personal affairs he is familiar for other reasons, or on the instructions of an agent with whom he has a close personal relationship. Thus he should exercise particular care if proposing to act on the instructions of or against a spouse, partner or other person with whom he has a close personal relationship.

8.3.12 An Advocate may not accept instructions to act in circumstances where, in his professional opinion, the case is unstateable in law or where the case is only stateable if facts known to him are misrepresented to, or concealed from, the Court. If such circumstances arise after he has accepted instructions, he must draw the matter to the client's attention as soon as possible and indicate he is unable to act further. If necessary he may require to explain to the Court that he is unable to act further. There may, however, be exceptional circumstances in which it is proper for an Advocate, in order to assist the Court, to present a case which he believes to be unstateable in law. In such circumstances, the Advocate must explain to the client that he cannot do more than explain the client's position to the Court, and that he will be bound to draw the Court's attention to such statutory provisions or binding precedents as have led him to the conclusion that the

指示的诉讼律师是要支持还是反对他本人认识的人或者他因其他原因而熟悉其个人事务的人，或者接受与其有密切个人关系的代理人的指示，都可能发生类似的困难。因此，如果是根据与其有密切个人关系的配偶、合伙人或者其他人员的指示行事，或者是反对这些人员，他应当特别注意。

8.3.12 如果在诉辩律师看来，案件在法律上是不可辩的，或者他知道只有在向法院不实陈述或者隐瞒事实的情况下案件才可辩时，不得接受指示采取行动。如果这样的情况是在他接受指示后发生的，他必须尽可能早地提请委托人注意该事项，并表明他不能够继续行事。在必要情况下，他可以要求向法院解释他不能够继续行事。然而，可能存在这样的特殊情况，即为了帮助法院，诉辩律师提出他认为在法律上不可辩的案件是适当的。在这样的情况下，诉辩律师必须向委托人解释，他只能向法院解释委托人的立场，他有义务提请法院注意使他得出案件不可辩的结论的制定法规定或者有约束力的判例。

case is unstateable.

8.3.13 An Advocate may not advise, represent or act on behalf of two or more clients in the same matter if there is a conflict, or a significant risk of conflict, between or among the interests of those clients.

8.3.14 An Advocate must cease to act for both clients when a conflict of interests arises between those clients and also when there is a risk of a breach of confidence or where his independence may be impaired.

8.3.15 An Advocate must not accept instructions in a Legal Aid case for work for which sanction for the employment of Counsel has not been given by the Scottish Legal Aid Board. Acceptance of such instructions would almost certainly involve a breach of section 32 of the Legal Aid (Scotland) Act 1986 (as amended).

8.4 What constitutes instructions and acceptance of instructions?

8.4.1 "Instructions" would normally be constituted by a letter of instruction instructing Counsel to undertake a piece of advising or drafting work or in the case of a Court or tribunal appearance instructing Counsel to appear at a set diet. In the event that Counsel does not have sufficient information properly to decide whether he should accept these instructions, he should ask for that information before accepting the instructions.

8.3.13 如果在同一事务中，两个或者两个以上委托人之间存在利益冲突，或者有产生冲突的重大风险，则诉辩律师不得为他们提供咨询、代理或者代表他们行事。

8.3.14 在委托人之间出现利益冲突时，以及在存在泄露秘密的风险或者其独立性可能受到损害时，诉辩律师必须停止为双方委托人行事。

8.3.15 在苏格兰法律援助委员会还没有批准雇用诉讼律师的工作的法律援助案件中，诉辩律师不得接受指示。接受这样的指示几乎肯定会违反《1986 年法律援助（苏格兰）法》（已修正）第 32 条。

8.4 什么构成指示和接受指示？

8.4.1 “指示”通常由指示诉讼律师承担一项咨询或者起草工作，或者在法庭或者裁判庭出庭情况下指示诉讼律师在指定的开庭期日出庭的指示信函构成。如果诉讼律师没有足够的信息来决定他是否应该接受这些指示，他应该在接受指示之前要求取得该信息。

8.4.2 An Advocate does not accept instructions merely because they have been delivered to him with or without a fee. He is entitled to a reasonable time within which to consider whether it is proper for him to accept the instructions or whether he is bound to do so. What is a reasonable time will depend on the circumstances; but Counsel will be deemed to have accepted instructions if he has failed to take any action within a reasonable time.

8.4.3 The making of entries in the diaries kept by the Advocates' clerk does not constitute the giving or acceptance of instructions.

8.4.4 An Advocate is not bound to accept instructions unless they have been delivered to him in writing. But he is entitled to accept instructions which are given to him orally by a person entitled to instruct him or which are the subject of oral arrangements between such a person and his clerk.

8.5 Priority of instructions

8.5.1 The general rule is that instructions take priority according to the date, or if on the same date the time, when they are delivered. Once accepted, instructions would generally take priority over all subsequent instructions.

8.5.2 Entries in the diaries kept by the Advocates' clerks confer no priority whatsoever.

8.5.3 Notwithstanding the general rule, the following considerations are relevant in determining which instructions should be accepted –

8.4.2 诉辩律师不仅仅因为向其作出指示时是否附有律师费而决定是否接受指示。他有权在合理的时间内考虑他接受指示是否适当，或他是否有必要这样做。什么是合理的时间，将取决于具体情况，但是如果诉讼律师没有在合理的时间内采取任何行动，他将被视为已经接受指示。

8.4.3 在由诉辩律师的办事员保存的日志中进行记录，并不构成作出或者接受指示。

8.4.4 诉辩律师没有义务接受指示，除非以书面形式向他作出。但是他有权接受有权向他作出指示的人作出的口头指示，或者属于该人与其书记人员之间达成的口头安排中的指示。

8.5 指示的优先次序

8.5.1 一般规则是，指示的优先次序根据期日确定，如果指示是在同一期日作出的，则根据时间确定。一经接受，该指示通常将优先于所有随后的指示。

8.5.2 诉辩律师的办事员保存的日志中的登记条目不代表任何优先次序。

8.5.3 尽管存在一般规则，在确定应当接受哪个指示时，下列因素具有相关性：

(a) the precedence of the Court concerned. The order of precedence for this purpose is–

Court of Justice of European Communities

European Court of Human Rights

House of Lords and Judicial Committee of the Privy Council High Court of Justiciary exercising its appellate jurisdiction High Court of Justiciary

Inner House of the Court of Session

Outer House of the Court of Session

Other Courts and tribunals

(b) in the case of an appeal, that Counsel has appeared for the client in the Court below;

(c) in the case of an adjourned diet or continued hearing, that Counsel appeared at the previous diet or hearing;

(d) in the case of a proof or trial, that Counsel has been involved to a substantial extent in drafting the pleadings, debating the pleadings at Procedure Roll, consulting with the client and/or advising on the pre-trial or pre-proof preparations;

(e) in the case of a debate on pleadings, that Counsel was responsible for drafting or revising the pleadings, particularly where a difficult or delicate point of law is involved to which Counsel has already devoted a substantial amount of time and research;

(f) that the client and/or the instructing person has come to rely to an unusual extent on Counsel's advice and guidance;

(g) that because of the nature or circumstances of the

（a） 有关法院的优先性。为此目的，优先次序是：

欧盟法院

欧洲人权法院

上议院和枢密院司法委员会

行使上诉管辖权的高等刑事法院

高等刑事法院

高等民事法院复审部

高等民事法院初审部

其他法院和裁判庭

（b） 在上诉情况下，诉讼律师已经在下级法院代表委托人出庭；

（c） 在延期审理或者继续听证情况下，诉讼律师已经在前一审判期日或者听证中出庭；

（d） 在法官单独听证或者审判中，诉讼律师已经实质参与起草书状，在法律问题听证中就书状进行了辩论，与委托人进行了磋商，和/或就审前或者法官单独听证前准备提供了咨询；

（e） 在就书状进行辩论的情况下，诉讼律师负责起草或者修改书状，特别是在涉及困难或者微妙的法律问题，且诉讼律师已经就此投入了大量时间和研究的情况下；

（f） 委托人和/或作出指示的人员已经不同寻常地依赖于诉讼律师的建议和指引；

（g） 因为案件的性质或者情况，或者因为可得的时间有

case, or because of the limited time available, it would be unusually difficult for other Counsel adequately to prepare the case;

(h) that the instructing solicitor has taken steps beforehand to check the availability of Counsel with Counsel's clerk; and

(i) that a fee has been tendered with instructions or, conversely, that the instructions are given on the basis that no fee, or only a modified fee, will be paid.

8.5.4 The extent to which any of the foregoing considerations outweigh the others or justify a departure from the general rule is a matter of judgement and conscience in the light of all circumstances. Counsel may think it right, as a matter of Courtesy, to explain the reasons for his decision to the solicitor (s) concerned. But he should not allow himself to be drawn into an argument on the subject, and if that is likely to happen, he should explain his reasons to his clerk and leave him to deal with the matter. If in doubt as to what his decision should be, Counsel should act in accordance with Section 7 (duty to seek advice).

8.6 Return of instructions

8.6.1 An Advocate is not entitled without good cause to return instructions once accepted so as to relieve himself of that professional commitment.

8.6.2 On the other hand, an Advocate cannot be in two places at the

限，其他诉讼律师充分准备案件将存在不同寻常的困难；

（h） 进行指示的事务律师已经预先采取措施向诉讼律师的办事员核实诉讼律师的可得性；以及

（i） 律师费已经与指示一起提交，或者与此相反，是在不支付诉讼律师费或者仅支付降低的律师费的基础上作出指示的。

8.5.4 任何上述因素超过其他因素的程度，或者支持背离一般规则的理由，是根据所有情况作出判断的问题和良知问题。作为礼貌问题，诉讼律师可能认为就其决定原因向有关事务律师进行解释是对的。但是他不得允许自己陷入关于这一问题的辩论，如果这有可能发生，他应当就其原因对其办事员作出解释，让他去处理该事务。如果就他应当作出什么决定存在疑义，诉讼律师应当遵照第 7 条（寻求建议的职责）行事。

8.6 退回指示

8.6.1 一旦接受指示，诉辩律师没有正当理由，不得为解除其职业担当而退回指示。

8.6.2 另一方面，诉辩律师不能同时在两个地方，因此，在某些

same time and it is unavoidable that in some circumstances instructions will have to be returned.

8.6.3 In any event, as already stated, it may be the Advocate's professional duty to return instructions.

8.6.4 In considering whether, and if so when, to return instructions, an Advocate should have in mind the following considerations –

(a) so long as instructions to do so have been accepted and not returned, an Advocate owes a duty to the client and the Court to attend in Court when the case is called;

(b) an Advocate also owes a duty to the client and the Court to ensure, as far as he can, that the case is properly prepared and properly presented;

(c) an Advocate owes a duty to the client and the Court within the period of time for which he has accepted instructions to remain in attendance until the trial or hearing has been completed;

(d) an Advocate owes a duty to his instructing solicitor not to place him unnecessarily in a position where he has to instruct alternative Counsel at short notice and explain the situation to a dissatisfied client; and

(e) an Advocate owes a duty to his fellow Advocates not to place them unnecessarily in a position where they have to take over his case at short notice and face the client and the Court without adequate time for preparation.

It may also be appropriate to take into account the considerations mentioned in paragraph 8.5.3 above.

情况下，不得不退回指示的情况不可避免。

8.6.3 无论如何，如前所述，退回指示可能是诉辩律师的职业职责。

8.6.4 在考虑是否——如果是，在何时——退回指示时，诉辩律师应当牢记下列因素：

（a）只要接受了这么做的指示并且还没有退回，诉辩律师就对委托人和法院负有在案件召集时到庭的职责；

（b）诉辩律师还对委托人和法院负有尽其所能确保案件得到适当准备和代理的职责；

（c）诉辩律师在他接受指示的时间内，对委托人和法院负有保证到庭的职责，直至审判或者听证已经结束；

（d）诉辩律师对对他进行指示的事务律师负有这样的职责，即不得将他不必要地置于他必须在短时间内指示替代性诉讼律师，并向不满意的委托人解释情况的境地；以及

（e）诉辩律师对其他诉辩律师负有这样的职责，即不得将该诉讼律师不必要地置于必须在短时间内接办其案件，并在没有足够时间进行准备的情况下面对委托人和法院的境地。

虑及上述 8.5.3 中提到的因素，也可能是适当的。

8.6.5 As soon as it is clear that a clash of commitments is inevitable, Counsel must return without delay all instructions with which he cannot comply.

8.6.6 Where a clash of commitments is likely although not yet certain, an Advocate should take steps to see to it that his clerk and the instructing solicitor are aware of the situation. If the instructing solicitor asks that the papers be returned so that other Counsel can be instructed, the papers must be returned without delay.

8.6.7 In the case of proceedings before the High Court of Justiciary on appeal, there is an obligation on Counsel who represented the appellant at the trial and has recommended an appeal to present that appeal.

8.6.8 In certain cases the operation of the Proceeds of Crime Act 2002 may require the return of instructions.

8.6.9 In all cases, except under the Proceeds of Crime Act 2002, the paramount consideration is the interests of the client. The fact that the instructing solicitor says he is "willing to take a risk" does not absolve Counsel from his duty to the client and the Court. Counsel should not under any circumstances be influenced in his decision by the consideration that, if he returns instructions, he himself may suffer financially.

8.7 Passing on instructions to another Advocate

In principle, an Advocate is not entitled, without the prior concurrence of the instructing solicitor, to pass on instructions

8.6.5 一旦职业担当的冲突显然不可避免，诉讼律师必须立即退回他不能遵守的所有指示。

8.6.6 如果职业担当的冲突有可能发生但是还不确定，诉辩律师应该采取措施，确保他的办事员和进行指示的事务律师知道这种情况。如果进行指示的事务律师要求将文件退回，以便指示其他诉讼律师，则必须立即退回该文件。

8.6.7 就高等刑事法院上诉程序中的案件，在审判中代理上诉人并建议提出上诉的诉讼律师，有义务提出该上诉。

8.6.8 在某些案件中，2012 年《犯罪所得法》的施行可能要求退回指示。

8.6.9 在任何案件中，2002 年《犯罪所得法》案件除外，首要的因素是委托人利益。进行指示的事务律师说他“愿意承担风险”这一事实，并不能免除诉讼律师对委托人和法院的职责。在任何情况下，诉讼律师的决定都不应当受到这一因素的影响，即如果退回指示，他自己可能遭受经济损失。

8.7 将指示交给其他诉辩律师

原则上，未经进行指示的事务律师预先同意，诉辩律师无权将指示交给其他诉辩律师。由代表委托人行事的事务律师来选择他希望对谁作

to another Advocate. It is for the solicitor, acting on behalf of the client, to choose whom he wishes to instruct. Counsel is not entitled to fetter that choice.

出指示。诉讼律师无权限制该选择。

9. FEES

9.1 Fees in this section mean fees for work instructed by a solicitor. This section does not cover fees chargeable to other professionals exercising their right of direct access to the Bar. Guidance is published separately in that regard.

9.2 It has traditionally been understood that, as the law stands, an Advocate's fees are *honoraria*, and he is not entitled to sue for his fees, at least unless the solicitor has claimed payment of them from the client and the client has paid them to the solicitor.

9.3 Although he may not be entitled to sue for his fees, it is recognised that an Advocate is entitled to payment of a *reasonable* fee for his services. In the absence of express prior arrangement to the contrary, the instructing solicitor impliedly undertakes a professional commitment to pay a reasonable fee. The arrangements between the Faculty of Advocates and the Law Society of Scotland for payment of fees to Counsel are published separately, as are the arrangements for payment of fees in Legal Aid cases.

9.4 What is a "reasonable fee" depends on the whole circumstances of the particular case. Unless otherwise stipulated, Counsel's fees cover all expenses incurred by Counsel in the conduct of the case, such as travelling expenses.

9. 律师费

9.1 本条所称律师费，是指就事务律师指示的工作收取的律师费。本条并不涵盖向行使其直接近用诉辩律师的权利的其他职业人员收取的律师费。就此有单独发布的指引。

9.2 在传统上，人们认为，根据法律规定，诉辩律师的律师费是谢礼，他无权为取得其律师费而起诉，至少，除非事务律师已经宣称将由委托人支付该律师费，且委托人已经将律师费支付给事务律师。

9.3 尽管诉辩律师可能无权就其律师费提起诉讼，人们认识到，诉辩律师有权就其服务取得合理的律师费。在没有相反的明确预先安排的情况下，进行指示的事务律师默示有支付合理律师费的职业承诺。诉辩律师协会与苏格兰事务律师协会之关于向诉讼律师支付律师费的办法已经单独公布，法律援助案件中支付律师费的办法也是如此。

9.4 什么是“合理的律师费”，取决于特定案件的全部情况。除非另有约定，诉讼律师的律师费涵盖诉讼律师在办理案件过程中发生的全部耗费，例如差旅费。

9.5 Fees are normally charged after the work is done. Counsel's clerk, acting on Counsel's behalf, issues a Note of Proposed Fee to the solicitor. The solicitor is entitled to challenge the amount of the fee proposed. Failing such challenge, the solicitor is presumed to agree that the fee proposed is reasonable and comes under a professional obligation to pay it.

9.6 If the solicitor challenges the fee proposed, the matter will normally be resolved by negotiation between the solicitor and Counsel's clerk. If they cannot agree, the solicitor and/or Counsel is entitled to require that the matter be determined by the Auditor of the Court of Session. The Auditor is entitled to have regard to all the circumstances and is, in particular, entitled to allow a higher fee than would be allowed on party-and-party taxation.

9.7 Except in Legal Aid cases, where scale fees are specified more or less closely by Statutory Instrument, there is no scale of fees nor does the Faculty offer any indication as to the fees which it is appropriate for Counsel to charge, although the Dean may be asked by Counsel whether any particular fee is "reasonable" . Some guidance may be obtained from consideration of previous decisions of Auditors in the Court of Session or Sheriff Courts. Counsel is entitled to charge his fee on any basis appropriate to the work involved - for example, a composite or "block" fee for all work done, a daily rate, an hourly rate, etc. The solicitor is entitled to challenge the basis of the charge as well as the amount. As a matter of prudent practice, Counsel may wish, in appropriate cases, to keep a record of time spent and work done

9.5 律师费通常在工作完成后收取。诉讼律师的办事员代表诉讼律师向事务律师发出拟收取律师费通知。事务律师有权对拟收取的律师费的数额提出异议。如果没有提出该质疑，事务律师被推定为同意拟收取的律师费是合理的，有支付该律师费的职业义务。

9.6 如果事务律师对拟收取的律师费提出异议，该事项通常由事务律师与诉讼律师的办事员谈判解决。如果他们不能达成协议，事务律师和/或者诉讼律师有权要求由高等民事法院审计官确定该事项。审计官有权虑及所有情况，特别是有权允许比在当事人和当事人诉讼成本核定中所允许的更高的律师费。

9.7 除了法律援助案件（其收费标准或多或少地明确规定在立法文件中），并不存在收费标准，诉辩律师协会也没有就诉讼律师收取的律师费的适当性进行说明，尽管诉讼律师可能询问会长特定律师费是否是“合理的”。从高等民事法院或者郡法院的审计官作出的判决的考虑因素中，可以获得一些指引。诉讼律师有权在与有关工作相适应的基础上收取律师费，例如，针对所做全部工作的综合或者“一揽子”收费，每日费率、小时费率，等等。事务律师有权对收费根据和数额提出质疑。作为审慎的做法，在适当情况下，诉讼律师可能希望在处理特定指示方面花费的时间和工作方面进行记录。

in dealing with particular instructions.

9.8 The amount of the fee and/or the basis of charging may be agreed in advance between the solicitor and Counsel's clerk. Provided that an unequivocal agreement has been reached, the solicitor is not entitled to challenge it later.

9.9 Normally Counsel's fees are negotiated between the clerk and the solicitor. All fees should be paid to Counsel's clerk. If any fee happens to be paid direct to Counsel, Counsel must account for it forthwith to his or her clerk. Counsel should not under any circumstances whatever discuss or negotiate fees with or receive fees directly from the lay client.

9.10 Speculative actions

It is permissible for Counsel to accept instructions on the footing that there will be no remuneration for his services except in the event of success.

9.11 Fees for Settled or Discharged Cases

Normally, a fee is only chargeable when instructions have been given and accepted. Where instructions have been given and accepted, an Advocate is entitled to charge an appropriate fee for the work instructed even if the case is subsequently settled or the diet is discharged. In addition, where the solicitor knows, or ought in the circumstances reasonably to be aware, that Counsel, in order to comply with his obligations, has kept himself free from other commitments, a fee appropriate to the circumstances may be charged (see Practice Note No 5 of 1996, reproduced at Parliament House Book page C2040, and City of Aberdeen Council v W A Fairhurst 2000 SCLR

9.8 律师费数额和/或收费根据可以由事务律师和诉讼律师的办事员事先商定。只要达成了明确协议，事务律师无权此后对它提出质疑。

9.9 通常情况下，律师的律师费由办事员与事务律师谈判确定。所有的律师费应当支付给诉讼律师的办事员。如果律师费恰巧直接支付给了诉讼律师，诉讼律师必须负责立即将其交给其办事员。在任何情况下，诉讼律师都不应当直接与外行委托人就律师费进行讨论或者谈判，或者收取律师费。

9.10 投机性行动

允许诉讼律师在除非成功否则就其服务没有报酬的基础上接受指示。

9.11 和解或者撤销的案件的律师费

通常情况下，只有在已经作出指示并接受指示后才能收取律师费。如果已经作出指示并被接受，诉辩律师有权就受指示的工作收取适当的律师费，即使案件随后和解或者撤销。此外，如果事务律师知道，在有关情况下理应意识到，诉讼律师为了履行其义务，已经推掉了其他担当，可以收取与该情况相适应的律师费（参见 1996 年第 5 号执业指引，《国会报告》第 C2040 页，和 *City of Aberdeen Council v W A Fairhurst* 2000 SCLR 392 案件）。相关情况包括在准备上花费的时间，以及在多大程度上诉讼律师不能接受其他指示。诉讼律师还可以就和解谈判收取律师费。

392) . Relevant circumstances will include time spent in preparation and the extent to which Counsel has been unable to accept other instructions. Counsel may also charge a fee for negotiating a settlement.

9.12 Referral Fees

Counsel may not enter into arrangements by which a commission or referral fee is paid to any third party as a consideration for referring work, or for recommending or introducing counsel to the client or an instructing agent.

9.12 介绍费

诉讼律师不得达成这样的安排，即向第三方支付佣金或者介绍费，作为接受工作或者将诉讼律师推荐或者介绍给委托人或者进行指示的代理人的对价。

10. ADVERTISING, PUBLICITY, TOUTING AND RELATIONS WITH THE MEDIA

10.1 Subject to the provisions of paragraph 10.2 an Advocate may engage in any advertising or promotion in connection with his practice which conforms to the British Codes of Advertising and Sales Promotion and such advertising or promotion may include:

(a) photographs or other illustrations of the Advocate;

(b) statements of rates and methods of charging;

(c) statements about the nature and extent of the Advocate's services;

(d) information about any case in which the Advocate has appeared (including the name of any client for whom the Advocate acted) where such information has already become publicly available or, where it has not already become publicly available, with the express prior written consent of the lay client.

10.2 Advertising or promotion must not:

(a) be inaccurate or likely to mislead;

(b) be likely to diminish public confidence in the legal profession or the administration of justice or otherwise bring the legal profession into disrepute;

10. 广告、宣传、招揽和与媒体的关系

10.1 在遵守 10.2 之规定的情况下，诉辩律师可以就其业务进行遵守《不列颠广告和销售推销守则》的广告或者推销活动，这样的广告和推销可以包括：

（a） 诉辩律师的照片或者其他图示；

（b） 关于费率和收费方法的说明；

（c） 关于诉辩律师服务的性质和范围的说明；

（d） 关于诉辩律师代理出庭的任何案件的信息（包括诉辩律师代理的任何委托人的姓名），只要该信息已经为公众所知，或者在还没有为公众所知的情况下，取得了外行委托人的事先明确书面同意。

10.2 广告或者推销不得：

（a） 不准确或者可能具有误导性；

（b） 有可能贬损公众对法律职业或者司法的信心，或者以其他方式损害法律职业的声誉；

(c) make direct comparisons in terms of quality with or criticisms of other identifiable persons (whether they be Advocates or Members of any other profession);

(d) include statements about the Advocate's success rate;

(e) indicate or imply any willingness to accept instructions or any intention to restrict the persons from whom instructions may be accepted otherwise than in accordance with this Code;

(f) be so frequent or obtrusive as to cause annoyance to those to whom it is directed.

（c） 就质量与其他可识别人员进行直接比较，或者对其提出批评，无论他们是诉辩律师还是任何其他职业成员；

（d） 包括关于诉辩律师成功率的说明；

（e） 明示或者暗示愿意接受指示，或者限制作出指示的人员的任何意图，遵照本守则者除外；

（f） 如此频繁或者强人所难，使得其针对的人感到烦恼。

11. DISCIPLINE

11.1 Matters of discipline in respect of the conduct of Advocates are governed by the Faculty of Advocates Disciplinary Rules, which are published separately. Advocates must adhere to any statutory obligations enacted in legislation in relation to regulation of the legal profession.

11.2 Any complaint in respect of the conduct of an Advocate should be addressed to the Dean.

11.3 The Dean may summon an Advocate to explain his conduct. The Advocate must obey that summons forthwith and explain his conduct as fully as the Dean may require. Where the complaint is remitted by the Dean to the Investigating Committee or the Disciplinary Tribunal in terms of the Disciplinary Rules or is such as requires to be investigated and determined by the Scottish Legal Complaints Commission, the Advocate concerned must obey any summons to appear and must co-operate with the reasonable requirements of the Committee or Tribunal or of the Scottish Legal Complaints Commission, as the case may be.

11.4 An Advocate may, if it is necessary to his defence, disclose information communicated to him in confidence by the

11. 惩戒

11.1 诉辩律师行为的惩戒事项，由另行公布的诉辩律师协会惩戒规则调整。就法律职业的规制，诉辩律师必须遵守立法规定的任何制定法义务。

11.2 就诉辩律师行为进行投诉，应当向会长提出。

11.3 会长可以传唤诉辩律师来解释其行为。诉辩律师必须立即遵守该传唤命令，遵照会长的要求全面解释其行为。在会长根据惩戒规则或者苏格兰法律投诉委员会要求进行调查和确定而将投诉移送调查委员会或者惩戒裁判庭的情况下，有关诉辩律师必须服从任何出庭传唤，并配合调查委员会、惩戒裁判庭或者苏格兰法律投诉委员会的合理要求，视情况而定。

11.4 诉辩律师如有必要，可以披露由委托人或者任何其他人秘密交流给他的信息，只要该信息与该投诉的适当调查有关。所

client or any other person, insofar as it is relevant to a proper investigation of the complaint. All those involved in the inquiry are bound by their professional duty not to disclose confidential information so disclosed.

有参与调查的人员均有不得披露如此披露的秘密信息的职业职责。

12. DRESS

12.1 An Advocate should wear Court dress when appearing before the following Courts and tribunals:

Court of Justice of the European Communities

European Court of Human Rights

House of Lords

Judicial Committee of the Privy Council

Parliamentary Committee appointed to consider a Provisional Order or Private Bill

Court of Session and other Courts of which judges are Senators of the College of Justice (other than during vacation and in the Commercial Court when paragraph 12.4 below should be followed)

High Court of Justiciary

Land Court (if Chairman robed)

Lyon Court

Sheriff Court

District Court

General Assembly of the Church of Scotland

Courts Martial

Transport Commissioners

12.2 Court dress for a male junior consists of a wig and black stuff

12. 着装

12.1 在下列法院和裁判庭出庭时，诉辩律师应当着出庭服装：

欧盟法院

欧洲人权法院

上议院

枢密院司法委员会

被任命来审议临时命令或者不公开法案的国会委员会

高等民事法院和其法官是司法院参议官的其他法院（假期或者应当适用下列 12.4 的商事法院除外）

高等刑事法院

土地法院（如果主席着袍的话）

纹章法院

郡法院

地区法院

苏格兰长老会最高会议

军事法院

运输专员

12.2 男性资浅者的法院服装包括假发和黑色长袍，有翼领白色衬

gown, white shirt with wing collar and white bow tie, black waistcoat and tailcoat (or lightweight sleeved waistcoat) and striped or dark grey morning trousers. Court dress for male Queen's Counsel consists of a wig, black "silk" gown, wing collar and white fall, Court coat and waistcoat (or lightweight sleeved waistcoat with high collar and ornamental cuffs and pockets) and striped or dark grey trousers. Shoes should be black.

12.3 Court dress for a lady Advocate consists of a wig and the gown appropriate to her status. She should wear a black or dark grey suit or dress with a white shirt or blouse. A lady junior need not wear a white bow tie, but a lady Queen's Counsel should wear a Q.C.'s fall with a suitable shirt or blouse. Hosiery should be black or a neutral colour, and shoes black.

12.4 *Dress out of Court.* Within the precincts of Parliament House during business hours for any substantial part of the day, and when carrying on his profession in any other place of business away from Parliament House, an Advocate should wear clothing appropriate for business.

衫和白色领结，黑色马甲和燕尾服（或者轻便的有袖马甲），条纹或者深灰色长裤。男性皇家大律师的法院服装包括假发，黑色“丝绸”长袍，翼领和白色绉领，法院外套和马甲（或者轻便的高领和有装饰性袖口和口袋的有袖马甲），条纹或者深灰色长裤。 鞋子应当是黑色的。

12.3 女性诉辩律师的法院服装包括假发和与其身材相适的长袍。她应当着黑色或者深灰色套装和白色衬衫。资浅女性诉辩律师不需要系白色领结，但是女性皇家大律师应当系皇家大律师的绉领，着相配的衬衫。袜子应当是黑色或者中性色的，鞋子应当是黑色的。

12.4 法院外服装。在国会大厦内任何一天的办公时间内，以及在国会大厦之外的任何其他办公地方开展其职业活动时，诉辩律师应当着与其活动相适的服装行业。

13. DUTIES OF DEVILMASTER

13.1 An Advocate may not take a "devil" (pupil) without the consent of the Dean. He should, in normal circumstances, be at least seven years called before he will be eligible to take a devil.

13.2 It is the duty of a devilmaster, so far as he is able, to ensure that, on completion of his devilling period, the devil is fit to exercise the office of Advocate.

13.3 The duties of a devilmaster include the duty of teaching the devil the rules and customs of the Bar, and ensuring that he has read and understands this Guide.

13.4 If a devilmaster is in doubt as to whether his devil is fit to exercise the office of Advocate he should consult the Dean.

13.5 A devilmaster may not accept or request a fee for acting as a devilmaster.

13. 见习生导师的职责

13.1 未经会长同意，诉辩律师不得接受见习生。在通常情况下，在有资格接受见习生之前，他应当已经被认许至少 7 年。

13.2 尽其所能确保见习生在完成见习期后，适合担任诉辩律师职务，是见习生导师的职责。

13.3 见习生导师的职责包括就诉辩律师的规则和习俗对见习生进行教育，并确保他已经阅读并理解该指导。

13.4 如果见习生导师就其见习生是否适合担任诉辩律师职务存在疑问，他应当就此与会长磋商。

13.5 见习生导师不得因担任见习生导师而接受或者要求费用。

14. CONTINUING PROFESSIONAL DEVELOPMENT

The Faculty has a programme for Continuing Professional Development. It is the duty of an Advocate to comply with the requirements of that programme as the Faculty may specify in regulations made from time to time. Failure to do so may amount to professional misconduct.

14. 继续职业发展

诉辩律师协会有继续职业发展项目。诉辩律师负有遵守诉辩律师协会届时在条例中具体规定的该项目要求的职责。未能遵守该要求相当于职业不端行为。

15. DISCRIMINATION

Advocates should have due regard to:

(a) the need to eliminate unlawful discrimination;

(b) the need to promote equality of opportunity and;

(c) the need to promote good relations between persons of different groups; And

(d) any Faculty Code on Equality and Diversity.

15. 歧视

诉辩律师应当充分重视：

（a） 消除非法歧视的需要；

（b） 促进机会平等的需要；

（c） 促进不同群体人员之间良好关系的需要；以及

（d） 诉辩律师协会关于平等和多样性的任何守则。

16. NON-PROFESSIONAL ACTIVITIES OF PRACTISING ADVOCATES

16.1 There are no fixed rules prescribing the activities in which a practising Advocate may or may not engage outside his practice as an Advocate, except that he cannot be a solicitor or be in partnership with or employed by a solicitor or other professional person entitled to instruct Counsel directly on behalf of clients in Scotland or elsewhere.

16.2 In considering whether it is proper for him to engage in any particular activity outside his practice, an Advocate should have in mind:-

(a) the cardinal principles stated in Section 2 above; And

(b) the extent to which any duties which may be inherent in, or flow from, the activity in question are compatible with the rights and duties of an Advocate.

If he is any doubt, he should follow the procedure set out in section 7.

16.3 The Dean may, at any time, require an Advocate to cease to engage in a particular activity which in his opinion is incompatible with the rights or duties of an Advocate or, alternatively, to cease to hold himself out as a practising Advocate.

16. 执业诉辩律师的非职业活动

16.1 就执业诉辩律师在其执业活动之外，可以或者不可以从事的活动，没有固定规则，但是他不能是事务律师，或者与有权在苏格兰或其他地方直接代表委托人指示他的事务律师或者其他职业人员组成合伙，或者受雇于该事务律师或者其他职业人士。

16.2 在考虑在执业活动之外参加任何特定活动是否适当时，诉辩律师应当牢记：

（a） 上述第 2 条规定的基本原则；以及
（b） 有关活动固有的或者产生的任何职责与诉辩律师的权利和职责相容的程度。

如果他有任何疑问，应当遵循第 7 条规定的程序。

16.3 会长可以在任何时候要求诉辩律师停止参加在他看来与诉辩律师的权利或者职责不相符的任何特定活动，或者停止宣示自己为执业诉辩律师。

17. ADVOCATES HOLDING A PUBLIC OFFICE AND NON-PRACTISING ADVOCATES

17.1 Every Member of Faculty, whether practising or not, must bear in mind that his conduct may reflect upon public confidence in the Faculty and the legal profession.

17.2 Crown Counsel

Although appointed to act as deputes of the Lord Advocate, Crown Counsel are, in their relations with the Courts, with Counsel for the defence, and with others, subject to the professional obligations of a practising Advocate.

17.3 Other public offices

Where an Advocate is the holder of a public office, for appointment to which he is qualified by reason of his status as Advocate, he is bound by all the professional obligations of a practising Advocate insofar as they are relevant to the performance of his duties.

17.4 Advocates in salaried employment

An Advocate in salaried employment engaged in legal work of any kind on his employer's behalf is subject to all the professional obligations of an Advocate insofar as they are relevant to the performance of that work. He may not appear in a Court or tribunal on his employer's behalf in reliance on his

17. 担任公职的诉辩律师和非执业诉辩律师

17.1 诉辩律师协会的每个会员，无论是否执业，必须牢记他的行为可能会影响公众对诉辩律师协会和法律职业的信心。

17.2 检察官

尽管被任命为担任苏格兰检察总长的代表，检察官在处理他们与法院、辩护律师和其他人的关系上，要遵守执业诉辩律师的职业义务。

17.3 其他公职

在诉辩律师担任其他公职的情况下，如果其任命资格是基于他作为诉辩律师的身份，则在与其履行其职责有关的情况下，他应当遵守执业诉辩律师的所有职业义务。

17.4 领薪受雇的诉辩律师

领薪受雇的诉辩律师，在代表其雇主从事任何法律工作时，应当遵守与从事该工作有关的所有诉辩律师的职业义务。他不得在法院或者裁判庭以其雇主的名义用其诉辩律师身份出庭，尽管他在没有该身份的情况下有权出庭。在附录所具体规定的情况和事务中，他可以指示其他诉辩律师，但是其他

status as an Advocate, although he may so appear if he would have that right without that status. He may instruct another Advocate in the circumstances and on the matters specified in the Appendix, but not otherwise.

情况下不得这样做。

18. WORK OUTSIDE SCOTLAND

18.1 An Advocate who acts in his professional capacity in another country is subject to the rules of professional conduct of the faculty as well as the rules of the host Bar. An Advocate is, therefore, under a responsibility to take reasonable steps to familiarise himself with the relevant rules of the host Bar. If he is in any doubt as to the propriety of a particular course of conduct, he should consult the Dean.

18.2 In considering a complaint against an Advocate, the Dean will have regard to the rules governing practitioners in the country concerned as well as those of the Faculty. Where there is a conflict of rules, the Dean will determine the matter, so far as the discipline of the Faculty is concerned, in the light of the circumstances and the rules of both countries.

18.3 Where an Advocate does something in another country which would be a breach of professional rules if done by a practitioner of that country but which is not a breach of professional rules of the faculty, the breach may nonetheless in an appropriate case be justiciable by the Dean.

18.4 An Advocate practising in another country is, in relation to work in or emanating from Scotland, subject to all the rules governing the professional conduct of Advocates in Scotland.

18. 在苏格兰之外的工作

18.1 在其他国家以其职业身份行事的诉辩律师，除了遵守所在国律师协会的规则外，还应当遵守诉辩律师协会职业行为规则。因此，诉辩律师有责任采取合理措施来熟悉所在国律师协会的相关规则。如果他就任何特定行为的适当性存在怀疑，他应当与会长进行磋商。

18.2 在考虑对诉辩律师的投诉时，会长应当虑及有关国家调整职业者的规则，以及诉辩律师协会的规则。在规则存在冲突的情况下，如果涉及诉辩律师协会的惩戒，会长应当根据情况和两个国家的规则，来确定该事项。

18.3 如果诉辩律师在其他国家的所为由该国家执业者所为将是违反职业规则之行为，但是并不是违反诉辩律师协会的职业规则之行为，在适当情况下，该违规行为可由会长裁决。

18.4 在其他国家执业的诉辩律师，就在苏格兰的工作或者源于苏格兰的工作，应当遵守苏格兰调整诉辩律师职业行为的所有规则。

19. EUROPEAN LAWYERS APPEARING IN SCOTLAND

19.1 These rules are consequential upon the Council Directive (No. 77/249/E.E.C.) to facilitate the effective exercise by lawyers of freedom to provide services and the European Communities (Services of Lawyers) Order 1978 (SI 1978/1910) as amended by the European Communities (Services of Lawyers) (Amendment) Order 1980 (SI 1980/1964) and the European Communities (Services of Lawyers) Amendment (Scotland) Order 2004 (SSI 2004/186) . The expression "European lawyer" has the same meaning as it has in SI 1978/1910 as so amended.

19.2 These rules only apply to a European lawyer who provides services in Scotland, or in relation to Scottish proceedings, which apart from the said Directive and Orders and those referred to in Section 20 hereof are reserved exclusively to Advocates and/or solicitor Advocates, and who does not act along with a solicitor Advocate; and references to "services" in these rules mean services so reserved.

19.3 No European lawyer may provide any services in relation to any proceedings whether civil or criminal before any Court, tribunal or public authority unless he is instructed with and

19. 在苏格兰出庭的欧洲律师

19.1 本规则是为促进律师有效地提供服务的自由的《理事会指令》（No. 77/249/E.E.C.）和1978年《欧洲共同体（律师服务）命令》（SI 1978/1910）（经1980年《欧洲共同体（律师服务）（修正）命令》（SI 1980/1964）和2004年《欧洲共同体（律师服务）修正（苏格兰）命令》（SSI 2004/186）修正）的结果。"欧洲律师"的含义见上述修正后的SI 1978/1910。

19.2 本规则仅适用于在苏格兰提供服务或者就苏格兰程序——这些程序若非上述指令、命令和以下第20条提到的规定，将完全保留给诉辩律师和/或事务律师—诉辩律师——提供服务的欧洲律师，以及并不与事务律师—诉辩律师一道行事的欧洲律师；本规则所称"服务"，是指如此保留的服务。

19.3 任何欧洲律师都不得就法院、裁判庭或者公共机关的任何程序提供任何服务，无论是民事程序还是刑事程序，除非他与诉辩律师协会执业成员一起接受指示并一起行事。

acts in conjunction with a practising Member of faculty.

19.4 A European lawyer in salaried employment who is instructed with and acts in conjunction with a Member of Faculty in any proceedings may provide services on behalf of his employer in those proceedings only insofar as a Member of faculty in such employment could properly do so - see paragraph 17.4.

19.5 Without prejudice to such other requirements for verification of his status as may arise, a European lawyer, before appearing in the Court of Session or the High Court of Justiciary, must be introduced to the Dean of Faculty or to such Faculty Officer as may be nominated by the Dean and furnish proof of his status, preferably by production of a European Professional Identity Card. If and so long as a European lawyer fails to satisfy the Dean of Faculty with regard to verification of his status, he shall be entitled to provide services to such extent only, if at all, as the Dean of Faculty may allow.

19.6 A European lawyer providing services shall be under the disciplinary authority of the Dean of Faculty. The Dean of Faculty shall determine any matters of dispute or difficulty arising between a European lawyer and the Advocate with whom he is instructed and acting.

19.7 The Advocate with whom a European lawyer is instructed will be answerable to any Court, tribunal or other body before which they appear for the conduct of the case and for compliance with professional practice and standards. He will not be answerable, in a question with the client, for the actings of the European lawyer in relation to the duties owed by that

19.4 在任何程序中与诉辩律师协会会员一起接受指示并一道行事的受雇领薪的欧洲律师，仅在如此受雇的诉辩律师协会会员可以在这些程序中适当行事的情况下，才可以代表其雇主在这些程序中提供服务。参见 17.4。

19.5 在不影响可能存在的其他关于核实身份的要求的情况下，欧洲律师在高等民事法院或者高等刑事法院出庭之前，必须引荐给诉辩律师协会会长或者会长提名的诉辩律师协会官员，并提交关于其身份的证明，最好是出示欧洲职业人员身份证。如果欧洲律师未能就其身份核实使诉辩律师协会会长确信，他应当仅在诉辩律师协会会长可能允许的范围内提供服务。

19.6 提供服务的欧洲律师受诉辩律师协会会长的惩戒管辖。诉辩律师协会会长应当判定欧洲律师与受到指示并一起行事的诉辩律师之间发生的任何纠纷或者困难。

19.7 受欧洲律师指示的诉辩律师在办理案件时要对他们所出庭的法院、裁判庭或者其他组织负责，并要遵守职业惯例和标准。他并不就欧洲律师履行其对委托人的职责的行为而对该委托人负责。

lawyer to the client.

19.8 An Advocate accepting instructions to act with a European lawyer should recognise the responsibility which he undertakes. It would be inappropriate for any Advocate to be instructed so to act unless he has the seniority necessary to enable him to carry that responsibility. An Advocate with whom a European lawyer is instructed is entitled to withdraw from the case at any stage if he considers that such a course is expedient in the interests of the preservation of proper professional standards.

19.9 The signature of the European lawyer on any documents in the process must be accompanied by the signature of the Advocate with whom he is instructed.

19.10 Where an Advocate is required to wear Court dress, a European lawyer should wear the normal Court dress of his home Bar, or, if he belongs to more than one such Bar, the normal Court dress of one of those Bars.

19.11 The seat to be occupied by a European lawyer in Court should be determined by considerations of Courtesy and circumstances with the approval of the Court. (See also Section 21 below.)

19.8 接受指示与欧洲律师一起行事的诉辩律师，应当认识到他所承担的责任。除非他有承担该责任所必需的资历，否则这样受到指示的诉辩律师采取行动都是不适当的。欧洲律师所指示的诉辩律师有权在任何阶段退出案件，如果他认为这样的行为有利于维护适当的职业标准的话。

19.9 在程序中，欧洲律师在任何文件的签字，必须附有他所指示的诉辩律师的签字。

19.10 在诉辩律师需要着法院服装的情况下，欧洲律师应当着其所在国律师的法院服装，如果他属于多个律师协会，着其中之一的通常法院服装。

19.11 欧洲律师在法院的座位应当虑及礼貌和情况，经法院批准后确定（还请参见下列第 21 条）。

20. REGISTERED EUROPEAN LAWYERS

20.1 These rules are consequential upon the Council Directive (No. 98/5/EC) to facilitate practice of the profession of lawyer on a permanent basis in a Member State other than that in which the qualification was obtained, and the European Communities (Lawyer's Practice) (Scotland) Regulations 2000 (SSI 2000/121) . The expression "European lawyer" has the same meaning as it has in those Regulations. These rules are established by the Faculty of Advocates as the competent authority for those wishing to provide the services hereinafter referred to.

20.2 These rules apply only to a European lawyer who seeks to provide services in Scotland, or in relation to Scottish proceedings, having registered in terms of these Regulations with the faculty ("a registered European lawyer") ; and references to "services" in these rules mean services so sought to be provided.

20.3 A registered European lawyer is subject to the same rules of professional conduct as a Member of faculty in relation to all activities he pursues in the United Kingdom, and is subject to the same rules of procedure, penalties and remedies as a Member of faculty in relation to failure to comply with the

20. 注册欧洲律师

20.1 本规则是为促进职业律师在其取得国家的会员国之外永久开业的《理事会指令》(No. 98/5/EC)和2000年《欧洲共同体(律师执业)(苏格兰)条例》(SSI 2000/121)的结果。"欧洲律师"的含义见这些条例。本规则是诉辩律师协会作为那些希望提供以下服务者的主管机构制定的。

20.2 本规则仅适用于在苏格兰提供服务或者就苏格兰程序提供服务，并根据这些条例在诉辩律师协会注册的欧洲律师("注册欧洲律师")；本规则所称"服务"是指这些所要提供的服务。

20.3 就其在英国从事的任何活动，注册欧洲律师应当像诉辩律师协会会员一样遵守同样的职业行为规则，就未能遵守诉辩律师协会的职业行为规则，应当像诉辩律师协会会员一样遵守同样的程序规则、处罚和救济。

faculty's rules of professional conduct.

20.4 A registered European lawyer engaged in offering to provide services must use his home professional title. His home title must be expressed in an intelligible manner in an official language of his home state in such a way as to avoid confusion with the titles of "Advocate" or "solicitor" or both.

20.5 In representing a client in any proceedings before any Court, tribunal or public authority, (including addressing the Court, tribunal or public authority), the registered European lawyer shall act in conjunction with an Advocate who is entitled to practise before the Court, tribunal or public authority concerned who could lawfully provide those services. A registered European lawyer shall not have a right of audience before the High Court of Justiciary sitting as an appeal Court or the House of Lords or Privy Council unless he has passed the faculty's examinations for devils in evidence, pleading and practice.

20.6 A registered European lawyer in salaried employment may provide services on behalf of his employer only insofar as a Member of faculty in such employment could properly do so - see paragraph 17.4.

20.7 The Advocate referred to in paragraph 20.5 shall be answerable to the Court, tribunal or public authority concerned in relation to the proceedings. He will also be answerable to the Dean for the proper conduct of the case and for his own compliance with professional practice and standards. He will not be answerable, in a question with the client, for the actings of the registered

20.4 受聘请提供服务的注册欧洲律师，必须使用他所在国的职业头衔。他所在国的职业头衔必须使用其所在国官方语言清晰表达，避免与“诉辩律师”、“事务律师”或者二者发生混淆。

20.5 在任何法院、裁判庭或者公共机关的任何程序中代理委托人时，包括向法院、裁判庭或者公共机关呈文，注册欧洲律师应当与有权在有关法院、裁判庭或者公共机关执业而合法提供这些服务的诉辩律师一道行事。注册欧洲律师无权在作为上诉法院的高等刑事法院、上议院或者枢密院出庭，除非他已经通过了诉辩律师协会在证据、书状和操作方面为见习生举办的考试。

20.6 受雇领薪的注册欧洲律师仅可以像诉辩律师协会会员在这样的受雇中可以适当行事的情况那样，代表其雇主提供服务。参见 17.4。

20.7 20.5 所称诉辩律师应当就程序对有关法院、裁判庭或者公共机构负责。他还要就适当办理案件和自己遵守职业惯例和标准对会长负责。他并不就注册欧洲律师履行其对委托人的职责的行为而对该委托人负责。

European lawyer in relation to the duties owed by that lawyer to the client.

20.8 The signature of the registered European lawyer on any document in a process must be accompanied by the signature of the Advocate with whom he is so instructed.

20.9 An Advocate accepting instructions to act with a registered European lawyer is advised to recognise the responsibility which he undertakes referred to in the advice given in paragraph 19.8 to Advocates accepting instructions to appear with a European lawyer.

20.10 Where an Advocate is required to wear Court dress, a registered European lawyer should wear the normal Court dress of his home Bar, or, if he belongs to more than one such Bar, the normal Court dress of one of those Bars.

20.11 The seat to be occupied by a registered European lawyer in Court should be determined by considerations of Courtesy and circumstances with the approval of the Court (see also Section 21 below) .

20.8 在程序中，注册欧洲律师在任何文件的签字，必须附有他所指示的诉辩律师的签字。

20.9 接受指示与注册欧洲律师一起行事的诉辩律师，应当认识到他所承担的19.8就接受指示与欧洲律师一起出庭的诉辩律师给出的建议中所称的责任。

20.10 在诉辩律师需要着法院服装的情况下，注册欧洲律师应当着其所在国律师的法院服装，如果他属于多个律师协会，着其中之一的通常法院服装。

20.11 注册欧洲律师在法院的座位应当虑及礼貌和情况，经法院批准后确定（还请参见第21条）。

21. PRECEDENCE OF COUNSEL OF OTHER BARS

21.1 As between the Scottish, English and Irish Bars, the tradition is that juniors take precedence inter se in accordance with the date of their admission or call, and silks in accordance with the date of their patents.

21.2 As between the Scottish Bar and other Bars which do not make any distinction between senior and junior Counsel, the normal rule would be that Counsel take precedence according to their respective seniority in their own Bars.

21. 其他律师协会的诉讼律师的优先次序

21.1 在苏格兰、英格兰和爱尔兰诉辩律师之间，传统是，资浅律师根据他们准入或者认许的期日确定彼此优先次序，皇家大律师根据他们取得特权的期日确定优先次序。

21.2 在苏格兰诉辩律师与在资深和资浅诉讼律师之间并不做任何区别的诉辩律师之间，通常的规则应当是，诉讼律师根据他们各自在其自己的律师协会中的资历来确定优先次序。

22. PROCEEDS OF CRIME AND MONEY LAUNDERING

Counsel are required to acquaint themselves with the legislation in force in relation to proceeds of crime and money laundering and to take appropriate steps to comply therewith. Guidance is published separately from time to time. Counsel should follow the guidance at Appendix E and should have regard to the provisions contained in Section 7 (the duty to seek advice) .

22. 犯罪所得和洗钱

诉讼律师需要熟知关于犯罪所得和洗钱的有效立法，并采取适当措施遵守这些立法。指引将届时单独公布。诉讼律师应当遵守附录 E 中的指引，并应当虑及第 7 条（获得建议的职责）中的规定。

APPENDIX A

THE DECLARATION OF PERUGIA ON THE PRINCIPLES OF PROFESSIONAL CONDUCT OF THE BARS AND LAW SOCIETIES OF THE EUROPEAN COMMUNITY. (16.IX. 1977)

Note: This Declaration has served as the basis for the preparation by the CCBE of a code of professional conduct for cross-border transactions within the E.E.C. and Advocates should have regard to the CCBE Code of Conduct as it may be revised and adopted by the Faculty from time to time.

I The Nature of Rules of Professional Conduct

Rules of professional conduct are not designed simply to define obligations, a breach of which may involve a disciplinary sanction. A disciplinary sanction is imposed only as a remedy of last resort. It can indeed be regarded as an indication that the self-discipline of the Members of the profession has been unsuccessful.

Rules of professional conduct are designs, through their willing acceptance by the lawyers concerned, to ensure the proper performance by lawyers of a function which is recognised as essential in all civilised societies.

The particular rules of each Bar or Law Society are linked to its own traditions and are adapted to the organisation and sphere of activity of

附录 A

关于欧洲共同体各律师协会职业行为原则的佩鲁贾宣言（1977 年 9 月 16 日）

注：本宣言曾作为欧洲律师协会为欧洲经济共同体内跨边界交易而制作的职业行为守则的基础。诉辩律师应当虑及届时修改并为诉辩律师协会采纳的欧洲律师协会行为守则。

一、职业行为规则的性质

职业行为规则不仅仅旨在规定义务，并可能对违反这些义务的行为予以惩戒处罚。惩戒处罚仅仅是最后的救济手段。它确实可以被视为该职业成员的自律没有取得成功的表征。

职业行为规则旨在通过有关律师的自愿接受，确保律师适当履行在所有文明社会中被视为必不可少的职能。

每个律师协会的特定规则，都与其自己的传统联系在一起，要与有关国家该职业的组织和活动范围相适应，与其司法和行政程序和国内立

the profession in the country concerned, to its judicial and administrative procedures and to its national legislation. It is neither possible nor desirable that they should be taken out of their context nor that an attempt should be made to give general application to rules which are inherently incapable of such application.

In seeking a common basis for a code of professional conduct for the Community one must start from the common principles which are the source of specific rules in each Member country.

II The Function of the Lawyer in Society

A lawyer's function in society does not begin and end with the faithful performance of what he is instructed to do so far as the law permits. A lawyer must serve the interests of justice as well as of those who seek it and it is his duty, not only to plead his client's cause, but to be his adviser. A lawyer's function therefore lays on him a variety of duties and obligations (sometimes appearing to be in conflict with each other) towards -

- the client;
- the client's family and other people towards whom the client is under a legal or moral obligation;
- the Courts and other authorities before whom the lawyer pleads his client's cause or acts on his behalf;
- the legal profession in general and each fellow Member of it in particular; and
- the public, for whom the existence of a free and independent but regulated profession is an essential guarantee that the rights of man will be respected.

法相适应。脱离其背景来理解这些规则是不可能的、不可取的，也不应当试图将根本不能普遍适用的规则加以普遍适用。

在为欧洲共同体的职业行为守则寻求共同基础时，我们必须开始于作为每个成员国具体规则之渊源的共同原则。

二、律师在社会中的职能

律师在社会中的职能，并不限于在法律允许的范围内忠实履行他受指示要做的事情。律师必须服务于正义的利益，以及那些寻求正义的人的利益，他的职责不仅是为其委托人的案件进行诉辩，也担任其咨询者。因此，律师的职能使得他对下列主体负有各种职责和义务（这些职责和义务有时似乎是相互冲突的）：

- ◆委托人；
- ◆委托人的家庭成员和委托人对之负有法律或者伦理义务的其他人员；
- ◆律师为其委托人的案件进行诉辩或者代表其行事所涉及的法院和其他当局；
- ◆整个法律职业，特别是其每个成员；以及
- ◆公众，对于公众而言，一个自由、独立但是受到规制的职业，是使人权得以尊重的必要保障。

Where there are so many duties to be reconciled, the proper performance of the lawyer's function cannot be achieved without the complete trust of everyone concerned. All professional rules are based from the outset upon the need to be worthy of that trust.

III Personal Integrity

Relationships of trust cannot exist if a lawyer's personal honour, honesty and integrity are open to doubt. For the lawyer these traditional virtues are professional obligations.

IV Confidentially

1. It is of the essence of a lawyer's function that he should be told by his client things which the client would not tell to others, and that he should be the recipient of other information on a basis of confidence. Without the certainty of confidentially there cannot be trust. The obligation of confidentiality is therefore recognised as the primary and fundamental right and duty of the profession.

2. While there can be no doubt as to the essential principle of the duty of confidentiality, the Consultative Committee has found that there are significant differences between the Member countries as to the precise extent of the lawyer's rights and duties. These differences which are sometimes very subtle in character especially concern the rights and duties of a lawyer vis-à-vis his client, the Courts in criminal cases and administrative authorities in fiscal cases.

3. Where there is any doubt the Consultative Committee is of opinion

在如此众多的职责需要加以协调的情况下，如果没有所有有关人员的完全信任，就不可能实现律师职能的适当履行。所有的职业规则从一开始，都是基于取得该信任的需要。

三、个人适正性

如果律师的个人荣誉、诚实性和适正性受到怀疑，则就不可能存在信任关系。对于律师而言，这些传统美德是职业义务。

四、保密

1. 对于律师的职能而言必不可少的是，委托人应当向其告知不会向他人告知的事项，他应当是基于信赖而获得其他信息的人。如果没有保密的确定性，就不能存在信任。因此，保密义务被视为职业的首要和基本的权利和职责。

2. 尽管就保密职责这个基本原则不容置疑，咨询委员会发现，在成员国之间就律师的权利和职责的确切范围存在重大差别。这些差别在性质上有时是很微妙的，特别是律师对其委托人、刑事案件中的法院和财政案件中的行政当局的权利和职责。

3. 咨询委员会认为，在存在任何怀疑的情况下，应当遵守最严格的

that the strictest rule should be observed - that is, the rule which offers the best protection against breach of confidence.

4. The Consultative Committee most strongly urges the Bars and Law Societies of the Community to give their help and assistance to Members of the profession from other countries in guaranteeing protection of professional confidentiality.

V Independence

1. The multiplicity of duties to which a lawyer is subject requires his absolute independence, free from all other influence, especially such as may arise from his personal interests. The disinterestedness of the lawyer is as necessary to trust in the process of justice as the impartiality of the judge. A lawyer must therefore show himself to be as independent of his client as of the Court and be careful not to curry favour with one or the other.

2. This independence is necessary in non-contentious matters as well as in litigation. Advice given by a lawyer to his client has no real value if it is given only to ingratiate himself, to serve his personal interests or in response to outside pressure.

3. The rule against representation of conflicting interests, and the rules which prohibit a lawyer carrying on certain other forms of activity are designed to guarantee the lawyer's independence in accordance with the traditions and customs of each country.

VI The Corporate Spirit of the Profession

1. The corporate spirit of the profession ensures a relationship of

规则，即能为防止泄密提供最好的保护的规则。

4. 咨询委员会最强烈地敦促欧洲共同体各律师协会向其他国家的职员成员提供帮助和协助，以切实保护职业保密。

五、独立

1. 律师所要履行的职责的多样性，要求他有绝对的独立性，免于任何其他影响，特别是其个人利益可能产生的影响。律师的公正无私就像法官的不偏不倚那样，对于司法过程中的信任而言是必需的。因此，律师必须表明他自己像独立于法院那样独立于其委托人，并注意不去逢迎任何一方。

2. 这种独立性在诉讼和非争讼性事务中一样必要。律师为其委托人提供建议只是为了迎合自己，服务于他的个人利益，或者是为了回应外界压力，则该建议毫无价值。

3. 禁止代理冲突性利益的规则，禁止律师开展某些其他形式的活动的规则，旨在遵照每个国家的传统和习俗，保障律师的独立性。

六、职业的团体精神

1. 职业的团体精神确保律师之间为其委托人的利益和为了避免诉讼

trust between lawyers for the benefit of their clients and in order to avoid litigation. It can never justify setting the interests of the profession against those of justice or of those who seek it.

2. In some Community countries, all communications between lawyers (written or by word of mouth) are regarded as being confidential. This principle is recognised in Belgium, France, Italy, Luxembourg and the Netherlands. The law of the other countries does not accept this as a general principle: even the express statement that a letter is confidential (or "without prejudice") is not always sufficient to make it so. In order to avoid any possibility of misunderstanding which might arise from the disclosure of something said in confidence, the Consultative Committee considers it prudent that a lawyer who wishes to communicate something in confidence to a colleague the rules of whose country are different from his own, should ask beforehand whether and to what extent his colleague is able to treat it as such.

3. A lawyer who seeks the assistance of a colleague in another country must be sure that he is properly qualified to deal with the problem. Nothing is more damaging to trust between colleagues than a casual undertaking to do something which the person giving it cannot do because he is not competent to do it. It is therefore the duty of a lawyer who is approached by a colleague from another country not to accept instructions in a matter which he is not competent to undertake. He should give his colleague all the information necessary to enable him to instruct a lawyer who is truly capable of providing the service asked for.

4. As regards the financial obligations of a lawyer who instructs a lawyer of another country, the Council for Advice and Arbitration of the Consultative Committee issued the following opinion on 29th January 1977:

而存在信任关系。使得职业的利益违反正义利益或者那些寻求正义之人的利益，从而不能获得正当性。

2. 在欧洲共同体某些国家，律师之间的所有交流（书面的或者口头的）都被视为是秘密的。这一原则在比利时、法国、意大利、卢森堡和荷兰均得到了认可。其他国家的法律并没有将该原则接受为一般原则：甚至明确说明信函是保密的（或者“不受侵害”）也不总是足以使其得以保密。为了避免披露秘密所述的事情所可能造成的误解，咨询委员会认为，如果律师希望与某同僚秘密交流某事，而该同僚所在国家的规则不同于其自己所在国家的规则，为慎重起见，该律师应当首先询问其同僚是否以及在多大程度上能够就此保密。

3. 寻求其他国家同僚帮助的律师，必须确定他具备处理该问题的适当资格。随意承诺做某事，而作出承诺的人因为无资格而做不到，对于同僚之间的信任的损害莫过于此。因此，与他国的同僚打交道的律师，就其无资格承办的事务不接受指示，是其职责。他应当向其同僚提供所有必要的信息，使其能够指示真正能够提供所需服务的律师。

4. 就向其他国家的律师作出指示的律师的经济责任，咨询委员会的建议和仲裁委员会在 1977 年 1 月 29 日发布了下列意见：

In professional relations between Members of Bars of different countries, where a lawyer does not confine himself to recommending another lawyer or introducing him to the client but himself entrusts a correspondent with a particular matter or seeks his advice, he is personally bound, even if the client is insolvent, to pay the fees, costs and outlays which are due to the foreign correspondent. The lawyers concerned may, however, at the outset of the relationship between them make special arrangements on this matter. Further, the instructing lawyer may at any time limit his personal responsibility to the amount of the fees, costs and outlays incurred before intimation to the foreign lawyer of his disclaimer of responsibility for the future.

VII Professional Publicity

1. In all Member countries of the Community lawyers are forbidden to seek personal publicity for themselves or to tout for business. This prohibition is designed for the protection of the public and of the high standing of the profession. The extent of the prohibition is not the same in every country. In some countries, it is laid down in national legislation which provides for a criminal penalty in case of breach. It is therefore possible that a lawyer from another country who engages in a prohibited form of publicity may mislead the public and run the risk of criminal proceedings. In general, there is nothing to prevent a lawyer using cards and writing paper in the form authorised by his own professional body. Beyond that, he would be wise to ask the professional organisation of the host country for guidance in advance.

2. In some countries, publicity which is designed to provide

在不同国家律师协会成员之间的职业关系中，如果律师并不将自己局限于推荐其他律师或者将其介绍给委托人，而是自己将某事务委托外国同行或者寻求其建议，则他自己有义务向该外国同行支付所欠律师费、成本和支出，即使委托人资不抵债。然而，有关律师可以在他们之间的关系的一开始，就此事项作出特别安排。此外，作出指示的律师可以在任何时候将其个人责任限定在他向外国律师告知就未来拒绝承担责任之前所发生的律师费、成本和支出范围内。

七、职业宣传

1. 在共同体所有成员国中，律师均被禁止为自己或者为招徕业务而寻求个人宣传。这一禁止旨在保护公众和职业的崇高地位。禁止的范围在各国各有不同。在某些国家，国内法就此作出了规定，并规定了违反该规定的刑事处罚。因此，来自其他国家的律师，如果从事了被禁止的宣传，则可能会误导公众，因而冒有受到刑事检控的风险。一般而言，并不禁止律师使用以其自己的职业组织授权的形式使用名片和撰写文章。此外，他预先询问东道国的职业组织来获得指引是明智的。

2. 在一些国家，旨在为公众或者其他国家的律师提供信息的宣传，

information for the public or for lawyers in other countries is permitted if it is approved by or under the auspices of the professional organisations. Lawyers from other countries may use such means of publicity insofar as the rules of their own Bar or Law Society permit them to do so.

VIII Respect for the Rules of other Bars and Law Societies

The Directive of 22nd March 1977 specifies the circumstances in which a lawyer from another Community country is bound to comply with the rules at the Bar or Law Society of the host country. Lawyers have a duty to inform themselves as to the rules which will affect them in the performance of any particular activity. The Bar or Law Society of the host country has a duty to reply to their questions as to the content and effect of its own rules, always having regard to their purpose which is to protect those who require the professional services of a lawyer. Lawyers should always have in mind that the manner in which they behave will reflect on the professional organisation to which they belong, on their colleagues and on all their clients.

如果得到了职业组织的批准或者是由该组织所主办的，则是允许的。来自其他国家的律师可以使用这样的宣传手段，只要他们自己所属的律师协会的规则允许他们这么做。

八、尊重其他律师协会的规则

1977 年 3 月 22 日的指令明确规定了来自共同体其他国家的律师有义务遵守东道国律师协会的规则的情况。就影响其开展的任何特定活动的规则，律师负有自己了解该规则的职责。东道国的律师协会就他们就其自己的规则的内容和效力所提出的问题，负有进行回复的职责，并总是要虑及其目的是保护那些需要获得律师职业服务的人员。律师应当总是铭记，他们的行为方式将会影响他们所属的职业组织、其同僚和其所有委托人。

APPENDIX B

CODE OF CONDUCT FOR EUROPEAN LAWYERS

This Code of Conduct for European Lawyers was originally adopted at the CCBE Plenary Session held on 28 October 1988, and subsequently amended during the CCBE Plenary Sessions on 28 November 1998, 6 December 2002 and 19 May 2006. The Code includes an Explanatory Memorandum which was updated during the CCBE Plenary Session on 19 May 2006.

Editor : CCBE

Avenue de la Joyeuse Entrée, 1-5 – B-1040 Brussels

Tél. : +32 (0) 2 234 65 10 - Fax : +32 (0) 2 234 65 11/12

E-mail : ccbe@ccbe.org - http://www.ccbe.org

CONTENTS

附录 B

欧洲律师行为守则

欧洲律师行为准则最初是在 1988 年 10 月 28 日召开的欧洲律师协会（CCBE）全体会议上通过的，此后经 1998 年 11 月 28 日、2002 年 12 月 6 日及 2006 年 5 月 19 日召开的欧洲律师协会全体会议修正。该守则含在 2006 年 5 月 19 日召开的欧洲律师协会全体会议期间更新的解释备忘录。

编者：CCBE

Avenue de la Joyeuse Entrée, 1-5 – B-1040 Brussels

电话：+32（0）2 234 6510 传真：+32（0）2 234 65 11/12

E-mail : ccbe@ccbe.org - http://www.ccbe.org

目录

1.5 对事的效力

1.6 本守则中的定义

2. 总则

2.1 独立性

2.2 信任和个人适正性

2.3 保密

2.4 尊重其他律师协会的规则

2.5 不相容的职业

2.6 个人宣传

2.7 委托人的利益

2.8 限制律师对委托人承担的责任

3. 与委托人关系

3.1 接受和终止指示

3.2 利益冲突

3.3 风险代理协议

3.4 对律师费的规制

3.5 预付款

3.6 与非律师人员分享律师费

3.7 诉讼成本与法律援助可得性

3.8 委托人资金

3.9 职业赔偿保险

4. 与法院关系

4.1 在法院的行为规则

4.2 程序公平

4.3 在法院的举止

4.4 虚假或者误导性信息

4.5 扩展及仲裁员等人员

5. 律师之间的关系

5.1 职业的团体精神

5.2 不同成员国的律师之间的合作

5.3 律师之间的通信

5.4 介绍费

5.5 与对方当事人的交流

5.6 （根据 2002 年 12 月 6 日在都柏林召开的全体会议之决定，已经删除）

5.7 支付律师费的责任

5.8 继续职业发展

5.9 不同成员国律师之间的争端

注释备忘录

1. PREAMBLE

1.1 The Function of the Lawyer in Society

In a society founded on respect for the rule of law the lawyer fulfils a special role. The lawyer's duties do not begin and end with the faithful performance of what he or she is instructed to do so far as the law permits. A lawyer must serve the interests of justice as well as those whose rights and liberties he or she is trusted to assert and defend and it is the lawyer's duty not only to plead the client's cause but to be the client's adviser. Respect for the lawyer's professional function is an essential condition for the rule of law and democracy in society.

A lawyer's function therefore lays on him or her a variety of legal and moral obligations (sometimes appearing to be in conflict with each other) towards:

—the client;

—the Courts and other authorities before whom the lawyer pleads the client's cause or acts on the client's behalf;

—the legal profession in general and each fellow Member of it in particular;

—the public for whom the existence of a free and independent profession, bound together by respect for rules made by the profession itself, is an essential means of safeguarding human rights in face of the power of

1. 前言

1.1 律师在社会中的职能

在建立在对法治的尊重基础上的社会里，律师扮演着特殊角色。律师的职责并不限于在法律允许的范围内忠实履行他受指示要做的事情。律师必须服务于正义的利益，以及那些委托他或者她来就其权利和自由加以主张和辩护的人的利益，并且律师的职责不仅是为其委托人的案件进行诉辩，也是担任其咨询者。尊重律师的职业职能，是实现社会法治与民主的重要条件。

因此，律师的职能使得他对下列主体负有各种法律和伦理义务（这些义务有时似乎是相互冲突的）：

——委托人；

——律师为其委托人的案件进行诉辩或者代表其行事所涉及的法院和其他当局；

——整个法律职业，特别是其每个成员；

——公众，对于公众而言，一个自由、独立、因尊重职业自己制定的规则而维系在一起的职业的存在是在面对国家强力和社会中的其他利益时，维护人权的必要手段。

the state and other interests in society.

1.2 The Nature of Rules of Professional Conduct

1.2.1 Rules of professional conduct are designed through their willing acceptance by those to whom they apply to ensure the proper performance by the lawyer of a function which is recognised as essential in all civilised societies. The failure of the lawyer to observe these rules may result in disciplinary sanctions.

1.2.2 The particular rules of each Bar or Law Society arise from its own traditions. They are adapted to the organisation and sphere of activity of the profession in the Member State concerned and to its judicial and administrative procedures and to its national legislation. It is neither possible nor desirable that they should be taken out of their context nor that an attempt should be made to give general application to rules which are inherently incapable of such application.

1.3 The Purpose of the Code

1.3.1 The continued integration of the European Union and European Economic Area and the increasing frequency of the cross-border activities of lawyers within the European Economic Area have made necessary in the public interest the statement of common rules which apply to all lawyers from the European Economic Area whatever Bar or Law Society

1.2 职业行为规则的性质

1.2.1 职业行为规则旨在通过适用对象的自愿接受，确保律师适当履行在所有文明社会都被认为是必不可少的职能。如果律师未能遵守这些规则，则可能导致惩戒处罚。

1.2.2 每个律师协会的特定规则均源自其自己的传统。它们与有关成员国的职业的组织和活动范围相适应，与其司法和行政程序和国内立法相适应。脱离其背景来理解这些规则是不可能的、不可取的，也不应当试图将根本不能普遍适用的规则加以普遍适用。

1.3 守则的目的

1.3.1 随着欧盟和欧洲经济区的不断整合，以及律师在欧洲经济区内进行的跨边界活动越来越多，出于公共利益，有必要对适用于欧洲经济区内所有律师的共同规则作出说明，无论就其跨边界执业活动而言，律师属于哪个律师协会。对这些规则作出说明的特定目的，是为了减少应用“双重道德标准”而造成的困难，指令 77/249/EEC 的第 4 条和 7.2，

they belong to in relation to their cross-border practice. A particular purpose of the statement of those rules is to mitigate the difficulties which result from the application of "double deontology" , notably as set out in Articles 4 and 7.2 of Directive 77/249/EEC and Articles 6 and 7 of Directive 98/5/EC.

1.3.2 The organisations representing the legal profession through the CCBE propose that the rules codified in the following articles:

—be recognised at the present time as the expression of a consensus of all the Bars and Law Societies of the European Union and European Economic Area;

—be adopted as enforceable rules as soon as possible in accordance with national or EEA procedures in relation to the crossborder activities of the lawyer in the European Union and European Economic Area;

—be taken into account in all revisions of national rules of deontology or professional practice with a view to their progressive harmonisation.

They further express the wish that the national rules of deontology or professional practice be interpreted and applied whenever possible in a way consistent with the rules in this Code.

After the rules in this Code have been adopted as enforceable rules in relation to a lawyer's cross- border activities the lawyer will remain bound to observe the rules of the Bar or Law Society to which he or she belongs to the extent that they are consistent with the rules in this Code.

以及指令 98/5/EC 的第 6 条和第 7 条已经明确指出了这种“双重道德标准”。

1.3.2 代表法律职业的组织通过 CCBE 建议，下列条款中所列的规则，应当：

——被认为是当前欧盟与欧洲经济区内所有律师协会一致接受的表述；

——遵照国内法律或者欧洲经济区程序，尽快被采纳为可执行的规则，适用于欧盟及欧洲经济区内的律师跨边界活动；

——在对国内道德规则或者职业活动规则进行修订的所有活动中，出于进行性协调之目的而予以考虑。

上述组织进而表达了这样的希望，即对国内道德规则或者职业活动规则的解释和适用，应当尽可能与本守则中的规则相一致。

在本守则中的规则被采纳为可执行的规则，适用于律师跨边界活动后，在律师所属律师协会的规则与本守则中的规则一致的情况下，律师将仍然有义务遵守其所属律师协会的规则。

1.4 Field of Application *Ratione Personae*

This Code shall apply to lawyers as they are defined by Directive 77/249/EEC and by Directive 98/5/EC and to lawyers of the Observer Members of the CCBE.

1.5 Field of Application *Ratione Materiae*

Without prejudice to the pursuit of a progressive harmonisation of rules of deontology or professional practice which apply only internally within a Member State, the following rules shall apply to the cross-border activities of the lawyer within the European Union and the European Economic Area. Cross-border activities shall mean:

(a) all professional contacts with lawyers of Member States other than the lawyer's own;

(b) the professional activities of the lawyer in a Member State other than his or her own, whether or not the lawyer is physically present in that Member State.

1.6 Definitions In this Code

"Member State" means a Member state of the European Union or any other state whose legal profession is included in Article 1.4.

"Home Member State" means the Member State where the lawyer acquired the right to bear his or her professional title.

1.4 对人的效力

本守则应当适用于指令 77/249/EEC 和指令 98/5/EC 所定义的律师，以及 CCBE 观察员成员的律师。

1.5 对事的效力

在不损及仅在成员国内部适用的道德规则或者职业惯例的进行性协调的情况下，下列规则应当适用于律师在欧盟及欧洲经济区内进行的跨边界活动。跨边界活动是指：

（a） 与律师本人所属成员国以外的成员国律师之间的所有职业联系；

（b） 律师在其本人所属成员国以外的成员国从事的职业活动，无论该律师本人是否身在该成员国。

1.6 本守则中的定义

“成员国”，是指欧盟成员国或者其法律职业包括在 1.4 内的任何其他国家。

“所属成员国”，是指律师取得使用其职业头衔之权利的成员国。

"Host Member State" means any other Member State where the lawyer carries on cross-border activities.

"Competent Authority" means the professional organisation (s) or authority (ies) of the Member State concerned responsible for the laying down of rules of professional conduct and the administration of discipline of lawyers.

"Directive 77/249/EEC" means Council Directive 77/249/ EEC of 22 March 1977 to facilitate the effective exercise by lawyers of freedom to provide services.

"Directive 98/5/EC" means Directive 98/5/EC of the European Parliament and of the Council of 16 February 1998 to facilitate practice of the profession of lawyer on a permanent basis in a Member State other than that in which the qualification was obtained.

The particular rules of each Bar and Law Society nevertheless are based on the same values and in most cases demonstrate a common foundation.

“东道成员国”，是指律师开展跨边界活动的任何其他成员国。

“主管机构”，是指有关成员国负责制定职业行为规则和对律师实施惩戒的职业组织或者当局。

“指令 77/249/EEC”，是指 1977 年 3 月 22 日发布的理事会指令 77/249/EEC，该指令旨在促进律师有效行使提供服务之自由。

“指令 98/5/EC”，是指欧洲议会和理事会 1998 年 2 月 16 发布的指令 98/5/EC，该指令旨在促进律师职业在取得资格的成员国以外的成员国永久执业。

但是，每个律师协会的特定规则都是基于同样的价值观，且在大多数情况下，体现的是共同的基础。

2. GENERAL PRINCIPLES

2.1 Independence

2.1.1 The many duties to which a lawyer is subject require the lawyer's absolute independence, free from all other influence, especially such as may arise from his or her personal interests or external pressure. Such independence is as necessary to trust in the process of justice as the impartiality of the judge. A lawyer must therefore avoid any impairment of his or her independence and be careful not to compromise his or her professional standards in order to please the client, the Court or third parties.

2.1.2 This independence is necessary in non-contentious matters as well as in litigation. Advice given by a lawyer to the client has no value if the lawyer gives it only to ingratiate him- or herself, to serve his or her personal interests or in response to outside pressure.

2.2 Trust and Personal Integrity

Relationships of trust can only exist if a lawyer's personal honour,

2. 总则

2.1 独立性

2.1.1 律师所要履行的许多职责，要求他有绝对的独立性，免于任何其他影响，特别是其个人利益或者外部压力可能产生的影响。这样的独立性就像法官的不偏不倚那样，对于司法过程中的信任而言是必需的。因此，律师必须避免对其独立性的任何损害，小心谨慎，不要为了取悦于委托人、法院或者第三方而损害其职业标准。

2.1.2 这种独立性在诉讼和非争讼性事务中一样必要。律师为其委托人提供建议只是为了迎合自己，服务于他或者她的个人利益，或者是为了回应外界压力，则该建议毫无价值。

2.2 信任和个人适正性

只有在律师的个人荣誉、诚实性和适正性不受质疑的情况下，才可

honesty and integrity are beyond doubt. For the lawyer these traditional virtues are professional obligations.

2.3 Confidentiality

2.3.1 It is of the essence of a lawyer's function that the lawyer should be told by his or her client things which the client would not tell to others, and that the lawyer should be the recipient of other information on a basis of confidence. Without the certainty of confidentiality there cannot be trust. Confidentiality is therefore a primary and fundamental right and duty of the lawyer.
The lawyer's obligation of confidentiality serves the interest of the administration of justice as well as the interest of the client. It is therefore entitled to special protection by the State.

2.3.2 A lawyer shall respect the confidentiality of all information that becomes known to the lawyer in the course of his or her professional activity.

2.3.3 The obligation of confidentiality is not limited in time.

2.3.4 A lawyer shall require his or her associates and staff and anyone engaged by him or her in the course of providing professional services to observe the same obligation of confidentiality.

2.4 Respect for the Rules of Other Bars and Law Societies

When practising cross-border, a lawyer from another Member State may be bound to comply with the professional rules of the Host Member State. Lawyers have a duty to inform

能存在信任关系。对于律师而言，这些传统美德是职业义务。

2.3 保密

2.3.1 对于律师的职能而言必不可少的是，委托人应当向其告知不会向他人告知的事项，他应当是基于信赖而获得其他信息的人。如果没有保密的确定性，就不能存在信任。因此，保密义务被视为职业的首要和基本的权利和职责。

律师的保密义务服务于司法的利益和委托人的利益。

因此，它有权得到国家的特别保护。

2.3.2 律师应当就其在职业活动中知悉的所有信息保密。

2.3.3 保密义务在时间上没有限制。

2.3.4 律师应当要求其非合伙律师、员工和在提供职业服务过程中雇用的任何人员遵守同样的保密义务。

2.4 尊重其他律师协会的规则

在跨边界执业时，来自其他成员国的律师可能有义务遵守东道成员国的职业规则。律师负有自己了解影响其开展任何特定活动的规则的职责。

themselves as to the rules which will affect them in the performance of any particular activity.

Member organisations of the CCBE are obliged to deposit their codes of conduct at the Secretariat of the CCBE so that any lawyer can get hold of the copy of the current code from the Secretariat.

2.5 Incompatible Occupations

2.5.1 In order to perform his or her functions with due independence and in a manner which is consistent with his or her duty to participate in the administration of justice a lawyer may be prohibited from undertaking certain occupations.

2.5.2 A lawyer who acts in the representation or the defence of a client in legal proceedings or before any public authorities in a Host Member State shall there observe the rules regarding incompatible occupations as they are applied to lawyers of the Host Member State.

2.5.3 A lawyer established in a Host Member State in which he or she wishes to participate directly in commercial or other activities not connected with the practice of the law shall respect the rules regarding forbidden or incompatible occupations as they are applied to lawyers of that Member State.

2.6 Personal Publicity

2.6.1 A lawyer is entitled to inform the public about his or her

CCBE 的会员组织有义务将其行为守则存于 CCBE 秘书处，以便任何律师均能够从秘书处取得最新守则的复制件。

2.5 不相容的职业

2.5.1 为了在履行其职能时具有应有的独立性，且其方式与其参与司法的职责相一致，可能要禁止律师从事特定职业。

2.5.2 律师在东道成员国法律程序中或者任何公共机构代表委托人或者为委托人辩护时，应当遵守适用于该东道成员国律师的关于不相容职业的规则。

2.5.3 在东道国开业的律师，如果希望能直接参与与法律执业活动无关的商业活动或者其他活动，则应当尊重适用于该成员国律师的受禁止的职业或者不相容职业的规则。

2.6 个人宣传

2.6.1 律师有权就其服务告知公众，但是该信息应当准确、无误

services provided that the information is accurate and not misleading, and respectful of the obligation of confidentiality and other core values of the profession.

2.6.2 Personal publicity by a lawyer in any form of media such as by press, radio, television, by electronic commercial communications or otherwise is permitted to the extent it complies with the requirements of 2.6.1.

2.7 The Client's Interest

Subject to due observance of all rules of law and professional conduct, a lawyer must always act in the best interests of the client and must put those interests before the lawyer's own interests or those of fellow Members of the legal profession.

2.8 Limitation of Lawyer's Liability Towards the Client

To the extent permitted by the law of the Home Member State and the Host Member State, the lawyer may limit his or her liabilities towards the client in accordance with the professional rules to which the lawyer is subject.

导性，并遵守保密义务和职业的其他核心价值观。

2.6.2 律师可以通过任何媒体进行个人宣传，例如新闻、广播、电视、电子商业通信或者遵守了 2.6.1 之要求而许可的其他形式。

2.7 委托人的利益

在遵守所有法律和职业行为规则的情况下，律师必须始终为委托人的最大利益行事，必须将委托人利益置于其个人利益或者法律职业其他成员的利益之上。

2.8 限制律师对委托人承担的责任

在所属成员国法律及东道成员国法律许可的范围内，律师可以遵照其应当遵守的职业规则就对委托人承担的责任进行限制。

3. RELATIONS WITH CLIENTS

3.1 Acceptance and Termination of Instructions

3.1.1 A lawyer shall not handle a case for a party except on that party's instructions. The lawyer may, however, act in a case in which he or she has been instructed by another lawyer acting for the party or where the case has been assigned to him or her by a competent body. The lawyer should make reasonable efforts to ascertain the identity, competence and authority of the person or body who instructs him or her when the specific circumstances show that the identity, competence and authority are uncertain.

3.1.2 A lawyer shall advise and represent the client promptly, conscientiously and diligently. The lawyer shall undertake personal responsibility for the discharge of the client's instructions and shall keep the client informed as to the progress of the matter with which the lawyer has been entrusted.

3.1.3 A lawyer shall not handle a matter which the lawyer knows or ought to know he or she is not competent to handle, without cooperating with a lawyer who is competent to handle it.

3. 与委托人关系

3.1 接受和终止指示

3.1.1 律师不得办理当事人的案件，除非收到当事人的指示。然而，律师可以在其收到为当事人提供代理的其他律师的指示后或者在主管机构分配的案件中行事。如果特殊情况表明某作出指示的人员或者机构的身份、资格和权限不明确，则律师应尽合理努力查明该人员或者机构的身份、资格和权限。

3.1.2 律师在为委托人提供建议或者代理时，应当迅捷、认真和勤勉。律师应当就委托人指示的履行承担个人责任，应当使委托人了解其委托事务的进展情况。

3.1.3 律师不得办理其知道或者应当知道其无能力办理的事务，除非与具备称职性的律师合作。律师不得接受指示，除非虑及其他工作的压力，能够迅速履行这些指示。

A lawyer shall not accept instructions unless he or she can discharge those instructions promptly having regard to the pressure of other work.

3.1.4 A lawyer shall not be entitled to exercise his or her right to withdraw from a case in such a way or in such circumstances that the client may be unable to find other legal assistance in time to prevent prejudice being suffered by the client. Failing such payment, a lawyer may withdraw from the case or refuse to handle it, but subject always to paragraph 3.1.4 above.

3.2 Conflict of Interest

3.2.1 A lawyer may not advise, represent or act on behalf of two or more clients in the same matter if there is a conflict, or a significant risk of a conflict, between the interests of those clients.

3.2.2 A lawyer must cease to act for both or all of the clients concerned when a conflict of interests arises between those clients and also whenever there is a risk of a breach of confidence or where the lawyer's independence may be impaired.

3.2.3 A lawyer must also refrain from acting for a new client if there is a risk of breach of a confidence entrusted to the lawyer by a former client or if the knowledge which the lawyer possesses of the affairs of the former client would give an undue advantage to the new client.

3.2.4 Where lawyers are practising in association, paragraphs

3.1.4 在委托人不能及时获得其他法律帮助而可能遭受损害的情况下，律师不得行使其退出代理的权利。未能支付律师费，律师可以退出代理或者拒绝办理案件，但是始终要服从3.1.4 的上述规定。

3.2 利益冲突

3.2.1 在同一事务中，如果两名或者两名以上的委托人之间存在利益冲突或者存在发生冲突的重大风险，则律师不得向两名或者两名以上委托人提供建议、代理，或者代表其行事。

3.2.2 如果在有关委托人之间发生利益冲突，或者存在违反保密义务风险或者有损于律师独立性的情况，该律师必须停止代理双方或者所有相关委托人。

3.2.3 如果存在可能违反对前任委托人承担的保密义务的风险，或者律师就前任委托人事务所了解的信息可能给新委托人带来不当优势，则律师不得代理新委托人。

3.2.4 律师在某组织形式中执业时，上述 3.2.1 至 3.2.3 应当适用

3.2.1 to 3.2.3 above shall apply to the association and all its Members.

3.3 *Pactum de Quota Litis*

3.3.1 A lawyer shall not be entitled to make a *pactum de quota litis.*

3.3.2 By "*pactum de quota litis*" is meant an agreement between a lawyer and the client entered into prior to final conclusion of a matter to which the client is a party, by virtue of which the client undertakes to pay the lawyer a share of the result regardless of whether this is represented by a sum of money or by any other benefit achieved by the client upon the conclusion of the matter.

3.3.3 "*Pactum de quota litis*" does not include an agreement that fees be charged in proportion to the value of a matter handled by the lawyer if this is in accordance with an officially approved fee scale or under the control of the Competent Authority having jurisdiction over the lawyer.

3.4 Regulation of Fees

A fee charged by a lawyer shall be fully disclosed to the client, shall be fair and reasonable, and shall comply with the law and professional rules to which the lawyer is subject.

于该组织形式及其所有成员。

3.3 风险代理协议

3.3.1 律师无权订立风险代理协议。

3.3.2 “风险代理协议”是指律师与委托人在事务办结前达成的委托人作为一方当事人的协议，据此委托人承诺与律师分享其取得的结果的一部分，无论该结果是事务终结时委托人取得的钱款还是任何其他利益。

3.3.3 “风险代理协议”并不包括遵照官方批准的收费标准达成的，或者受对律师有管辖权的主管机构管辖的约定律师可按办理事务的价值的一定比例收取费用的协议。

3.4 对律师费的规制

律师收取的费用应当完全告知委托人，应当公平和合理，应当遵守律师应当遵守的法律和职业规则。

3.5 Payment on Account

If a lawyer requires a payment on account of his or her fees and/or disbursements such payment should not exceed a reasonable estimate of the fees and probable disbursements involved.

3.6 Fee Sharing with Non–Lawyers

3.6.1 A lawyer may not share his or her fees with a person who is not a lawyer except where an association between the lawyer and the other person is permitted by the laws and the professional rules to which the lawyer is subject.

3.6.2 The provisions of 3.6.1 above shall not preclude a lawyer from paying a fee, commission or other compensation to a deceased lawyer's heirs or to a retired lawyer in respect of taking over the deceased or retired lawyer's practice.

3.7 Cost of Litigation and Availability of Legal Aid

3.7.1 The lawyer should at all times strive to achieve the most cost effective resolution of the client's dispute and should advise the client at appropriate stages as to the desirability of attempting a settlement and/or a reference to alternative dispute resolution.

3.7.2 A lawyer shall inform the client of the availability of legal aid where applicable.

3.5 预付款

如果律师要求预付其律师费和 / 或者支出，则该笔款项不得超出合理估算的律师费和可能的支出数额。

3.6 与非律师人员分享律师费

3.6.1 律师不得与非律师人员分享律师费，律师应当遵守的法律和职业规则允许该律师与他人合作的除外。

3.6.2 上述 3.6.1 之规定并不禁止律师在接管已故或者退休律师的业务后，向已故律师继承人或者退休律师支付律师费、佣金或者其他报偿。

3.7 诉讼成本与法律援助可得性

3.7.1 律师应当在任何时候努力寻求最具费效比的委托人争端解决方案，并在适当的阶段就试图和解的可取性和 / 或者转向替代性纠纷解决程序的可取性，向委托人提出建议。

3.7.2 在适用情况下，律师应当告知委托人法律援助的可得性。

3.8 Client Funds

3.8.1 Lawyers who come into possession of funds on behalf of their clients or third parties (hereinafter called "client funds") have to deposit such money into an account of a bank or similar institution subject to supervision by a public authority (hereinafter called a "client account") . A client account shall be separate from any other account of the lawyer. All client funds received by a lawyer should be deposited into such an account unless the owner of such funds agrees that the funds should be dealt with otherwise.

3.8.2 The lawyer shall maintain full and accurate records showing all the lawyer's dealings with client funds and distinguishing client funds from other funds held by the lawyer. Records may have to be kept for a certain period of time according to national rules.

3.8.3 A client account cannot be in debit except in exceptional circumstances as expressly permitted in national rules or due to bank charges, which cannot be influenced by the lawyer. Such an account cannot be given as a guarantee or be used as a security for any reason. There shall not be any set-off or merger between a client account and any other bank account, nor shall the client funds in a client account be available to defray money owed by the lawyer to the bank.

3.8.4 Client funds shall be transferred to the owners of such funds in the shortest period of time or under such conditions as are authorized by them.

3.8 委托人资金

3.8.1 律师以其委托人或者第三人名义持有资金时（以下简称"委托人资金"），必须将该资金存入受公共机构监管的银行或者类似机构的账户中（以下简称"委托人账户"）。委托人账户应与律师的任何其他账户分开。律师收到的所有委托人资金应当存入该账户，除非资金所有人同意另行处理该资金。

3.8.2 律师应当保留完整、准确的记录，说明对委托人资金的全部处理情况，以及将该资金与其持有的其他资金区分的情况。律师可能必须遵照国内规则在一段时间内保存该记录。

3.8.3 委托人账户不得记入借方，国内规则明示许可的例外情形或者支付银行收费的情况除外，这些情况不受律师的影响。这样的账户不得以任何理由作为担保或者保证金使用。不得将委托人账户与任何其他银行账户进行对销或者合并，也不得以委托人账户内的委托人资金支付律师对银行的债务。

3.8.4 委托人资金应在最短时间内或者在所有人授权的条件下转给所有人。

3.8.5 The lawyer cannot transfer funds from a client account into the lawyer's own account for payment of fees without informing the client in writing.

3.8.6 The Competent Authorities in Member States shall have the power to verify and examine any document regarding client funds, whilst respecting the confidentiality or legal professional privilege to which it may be subject.

3.9 Professional Indemnity Insurance

3.9.1 Lawyers shall be insured against civil legal liability arising out of their legal practice to an extent which is reasonable having regard to the nature and extent of the risks incurred by their professional activities.

3.9.2 Should this prove impossible, the lawyer must inform the client of this situation and its consequences.

3.8.5 在未书面通知委托人的情况下，律师不得将委托人账户的资金作为支付的律师费转入其个人账户。

3.8.6 成员国主管机构应当有权核实和审查与委托人资金相关的任何文件，但是应当尊重可能适用的保密要求或者法律职业特免权。

3.9 职业赔偿保险

3.9.1 律师应当就法律执业活动发生的民事法律责任购买保险，该保险范围应当合理虑及律师职业活动可能发生的风险的性质和程度。

3.9.2 如果证明不能获得上述保险，律师必须就此及其后果告知委托人。

4. RELATIONS WITH THE COURTS

4.1 Rules of Conduct in Court

A lawyer who appears, or takes part in a case, before a Court or tribunal must comply with the rules of conduct applied before that Court or tribunal.

4.2 Fair Conduct of Proceedings

A lawyer must always have due regard for the fair conduct of proceedings.

4.3 Demeanour in Court

A lawyer shall while maintaining due respect and Courtesy towards the Court defend the interests of the client honourably and fearlessly without regard to the lawyer's own interests or to any consequences to him- or herself or to any other person.

4.4 False or Misleading Information

A lawyer shall never knowingly give false or misleading information to

4. 与法院的关系

4.1 在法院的行为规则

律师在法院或者裁判出庭或者参与案件审理时，必须遵守适用于该法院或者裁判庭的行为规则。

4.2 程序公平

律师必须始终虑及程序公平。

4.3 在法院的举止

在对法院予以应有尊重和礼貌的同时，律师应得体、无畏地为委托人利益进行辩护，不考虑律师个人利益或者对其本人或者任何其他人员产生的后果。

4.4 虚假或者误导性信息

律师不得故意向法院提供虚假或者误导性信息。

the Court.

4.5 Extension to Arbitrators etc.

The rules governing a lawyer's relations with the Courts apply also to the lawyer's relations with arbitrators and any other persons exercising judicial or quasi-judicial functions, even on an occasional basis.

4.5 扩展及仲裁员等人员

调整律师与法院关系的规则，也适用于律师与仲裁员及其他行使司法或者准司法职能的人员的关系，即使这样的情况偶尔发生。

5. RELATIONS BETWEEN LAWYERS

5.1 Corporate Spirit of the Profession

5.1.1 The corporate spirit of the profession requires a relationship of trust and co-operation between lawyers for the benefit of their clients and in order to avoid unnecessary litigation and other behaviour harmful to the reputation of the profession. It can, however, never justify setting the interests of the profession against those of the client.

5.1.2 A lawyer should recognise all other lawyers of Member States as professional colleagues and act fairly and Courteously towards them.

5.2 Co–operation among Lawyers of Different Member States

5.2.1 It is the duty of a lawyer who is approached by a colleague from another Member State not to accept instructions in a matter which the lawyer is not competent to undertake. The lawyer should in such case be prepared to help that colleague to obtain the information necessary to enable him or her to

5. 律师之间的关系

5.1 职业的团体精神

5.1.1 职业的团体精神要求律师之间为其委托人的利益、为了避免不必要诉讼和其他有损于职业的声望的行为而存在信任关系。然而，使得职业的利益违反委托人的利益，从不能获得正当性。

5.1.2 律师应承认成员国所有其他律师的职业同僚地位，并公平、礼貌地对待他们。

5.2 不同成员国的律师之间的合作

5.2.1 接洽来自其他成员国的同僚的律师，就超出其称职能力范围的事务负有不接受指示的职责。在这样的情况下，律师应当乐于帮助该同僚获取必要信息，使其能够指示真正能够提供所需服务的律师。

instruct a lawyer who is capable of providing the service asked for.

5.2.2 Where a lawyer of a Member State co-operates with a lawyer from another Member State, both have a general duty to take into account the differences which may exist between their respective legal systems and the professional organisations, competences and obligations of lawyers in the Member States concerned.

5.3 Correspondence between Lawyers

5.3.1 If a lawyer intends to send communications to a lawyer in another Member State, which the sender wishes to remain confidential or without prejudice he or she should clearly express this intention prior to communicating the documents.

5.3.2 If the prospective recipient of the communications is unable to ensure their status as confidential or without prejudice he or she should inform the sender accordingly without delay.

5.4 Referral Fees

5.4.1 A lawyer may not demand or accept from another lawyer or any other person a fee, commission or any other compensation for referring or recommending the lawyer to a client.

5.4.2 A lawyer may not pay anyone a fee, commission or any other compensation as a consideration for referring a client to him- or herself.

5.2.2 当某一成员国的律师与其他成员国的律师合作时，二者均有考虑有关成员国各自的法律制度和职业组织、律师的称职性和义务之差异的一般职责。

5.3 律师之间的通信

5.3.1 如果律师欲与其他成员国的律师进行交流，且发出交流者希望予以保密或者不受侵害，则他或者她应当在交流之前清晰表达该意图。

5.3.2 如果交流的预期接收者不能保证该交流的保密性或者不受侵害，则其应当就此毫不迟延地通知发出交流者。

5.4 介绍费

5.4.1 律师不得以向委托人介绍或者推荐其他律师为由，要求其他律师或者任何其他人支付费用、佣金或者任何其他报偿，或者接受上述费用、佣金或者任何其他报偿。

5.4.2 律师不得向任何人员支付费用、佣金或者其他任何报偿，作为向其介绍委托人的对价。

5.5 Communication with Opposing Parties

A lawyer shall not communicate about a particular case or matter directly with any person whom he or she knows to be represented or advised in the case or matter by another lawyer, without the consent of that other lawyer (and shall keep the other lawyer informed of any such communications).

5.6 (Deleted by decision of the Plenary Session in Dublin on 6 December 2002)

5.7 Responsibility for Fees

In professional relations between Members of Bars of different Member States, where a lawyer does not confine him- or herself to recommending another lawyer or introducing that other lawyer to the client but instead him- or herself entrusts a correspondent with a particular matter or seeks the correspondent's advice, the instructing lawyer is personally bound, even if the client is insolvent, to pay the fees, costs and outlays which are due to the foreign correspondent. The lawyers concerned may, however, at the outset of the relationship between them make special arrangements on this matter. Further, the instructing lawyer may at any time limit his or her personal responsibility to the amount of the fees, costs and outlays incurred before intimation to the foreign lawyer of the instructing lawyer's disclaimer of responsibility for the future.

5.5 与对方当事人的交流

律师不得就特定案件或者事务直接与其已知在该案件或者事务中得到其他律师代理或者建议的任何人员进行交流，除非得到该其他律师的同意（并且应当使该其他律师了解任何这样的交流）。

5.6 （根据 2002 年 12 月 6 日在都柏林召开的全体会议之决定，已经删除）

5.7 支付律师费的责任

在不同成员国律师协会的成员之间的职业关系中，如果律师并不将自己局限于推荐其他律师或者将其介绍给委托人，而是自己将某事务委托外国同行或者寻求其建议，则作出指示的律师自己有义务向该外国同行支付所欠律师费、成本和支出，即使委托人资不抵债。然而，有关律师可以在他们之间的关系的一开始，就此事项作出特别安排。此外，作出指示的律师可以在任何时候将其个人责任限定在他向外国律师告知就未来拒绝承担责任之前所发生的律师费、成本和支出的范围内。

5.8 Continuing Professional Development

Lawyers should maintain and develop their professional knowledge and skills taking proper account of the European dimension of their profession.

5.9 Disputes amongst Lawyers in Different Member States

5.9.1 If a lawyer considers that a colleague in another Member State has acted in breach of a rule of professional conduct the lawyer shall draw the matter to the attention of that colleague.

5.9.2 If any personal dispute of a professional nature arises amongst lawyers in different Member States they should if possible first try to settle it in a friendly way.

5.9.3 A lawyer shall not commence any form of proceedings against a colleague in another Member State on matters referred to in 5.9.1 or 5.9.2 above without first informing the Bars or Law Societies to which they both belong for the purpose of allowing both Bars or Law Societies concerned an opportunity to assist in reaching a settlement.

5.8 继续职业发展

律师应当在适当考虑欧洲地区律师职业发展的情况下，维持并不断发展其职业知识和技能。

5.9 不同成员国律师之间的争端

5.9.1 如果律师认为其他成员国的同僚的行为违反了职业行为规则，该律师应当提请该同僚注意该事项。

5.9.2 如果不同成员国律师之间发生了职业性质的个人争端，在可能的情况下，他们首先应当以友好的方式解决该争端。

5.9.3 在未首先通知双方所属律师协会，以允许有关的律师协会有机会帮助达成和解的情况下，律师不得就 5.9.1 或者 5.9.2 所述事项，对其他成员国的同僚提起任何程序。

EXPLANATORY MEMORANDUM

This Explanatory Memorandum was prepared at the request of the CCBE Standing Committee by the CCBE's deontology working party, who were responsible for drafting the first version of the Code of Conduct itself. It seeks to explain the origin of the provisions of the Code, to illustrate the problems which they are designed to resolve, particularly in relation to cross-border activities, and to provide assistance to the Competent Authorities in the Member States in the application of the Code. It is not intended to have any binding force in the interpretation of the Code. The Explanatory Memorandum was updated on the occasion of the CCBE Plenary Session on 19 May 2006. The original versions of the Code are in the French and English languages. Translations into other Community languages are prepared under the authority of the national delegations.

Commentary on Article 1.1—The Function of the Lawyer in Society

The Declaration of Perugia, adopted by the CCBE in 1977, laid down the fundamental principles of professional conduct applicable to lawyers throughout the EC. The provisions of Article 1.1 reaffirm the statement in the Declaration of Perugia of the function of the lawyer in society which forms the basis for the rules governing the performance of that function.

注释备忘录

本解释备忘录由 CCBE 道德标准工作小组应 CCBE 常设委员会的要求制作，该工作小组曾负责起草行为守则第一版。本解释备忘录试图解释本守则的规定之渊源，说明旨在解决的问题，尤其是针对跨边界活动，并为成员国的主管机构就本守则的适用提供帮助。本解释备忘录并不旨在在守则注释方面具有任何约束力。本解释备忘录已在 2006 年 5 月 19 日召开的 CCBE 全体大会中进行了更新。本守则的原始版本为法语和英语版本。将守则译为其他共同体语言的工作，是在各国代表团的管理下进行的。

1.1 律师在社会中的职能

CCBE 在 1977 年通过的《佩鲁贾宣言》，规定了在整个欧洲共同体适用于律师职业行为的基本原则。1.1 之规定重申了《佩鲁贾宣言》就律师社会职能所作的陈述，该陈述是调整履行该职能的规则的基础。

Commentary on Article 1.2—The Nature of Rules of Professional Conduct

These provisions substantially restate the explanation in the Declaration of Perugia of the nature of rules of professional conduct and how particular rules depend on particular local circumstances but are nevertheless based on common values.

Commentary on Article 1.3—The Purpose of the Code

These provisions introduce the development of the principles in the Declaration of Perugia into a specific Code of Conduct for lawyers throughout the EU and the EEA, and lawyers of the Observer Members of the CCBE, with particular reference to their cross-border activities (defined in Article 1.5) . The provisions of Article 1.3.2 lay down the specific intentions of the CCBE with regard to the substantive provisions in the Code.

Commentary on Article 1.4—Field of Application Ratione Personae

The rules are stated to apply to all lawyers as defined in the Lawyers Services Directive of 1977 and the Lawyers Establishment Directive of 1998, and lawyers of the Observer Members of the CCBE. This includes lawyers of the states which subsequently acceded to the Directives, whose names have been added by amendment to the Directives. The Code accordingly applies to all the lawyers represented on the CCBE, whether as full

1.2 职业行为规则的性质

这些规定实质上重申了《佩鲁贾宣言》对律师职业行为规则性质的解释，并说明特定的规则不论如何取决于地方性情况，都是以共同的价值观为基础的。

1.3 守则的目的

这些规定介绍了《佩鲁贾宣言》所述原则发展成为整个欧盟及欧洲经济区律师以及 CCBE 观察员国的律师的具体行为守则的过程，尤其是提到了跨边界活动（定义见 1.5）的参照准则的过程。1.3.2 规定了 CCBE 制定本守则实体规定的具体意图。

1.4 对人的效力

这些规则适用于 1977 年《律师服务指令》和 1998 年《律师开业指令》定义的所有律师和 CCBE 观察员国的律师。包括之后同意加入这些指令且其国家名称已通过修正加入到指令中的国家的律师。因此，本守则适用于 CCBE 所代表的所有律师，无论是作为正式成员国律师还是观察员国律师，即：

Members or as Observer Members, namely:

Austria Rechtsanwalt;

Belgium avocat / advocaat / Rechtsanwalt;

Bulgaria advokat;

Croatia odvjetnik;

Cyprus dikegóros;

Czech Republic advokát;

Denmark advokat;

Estonia vandeadvokaat;

Finland asianajaja / advokat;

FYROMacedonia advokat;

France avocat;

Germany Rechtsanwalt;

Greece dikegóros;

Hungary ügyvéd;

Iceland lögmaður;

Ireland Barrister, solicitor;

Italy avvocato;

Latvia zvērināts advokāts;

Liechtenstein Rechtsanwalt;

Lithuania advokatas;

Luxembourg avocat / Rechtsanwalt;

Malta avukat, prokuratur legali;

Netherlands advocaat;

Norway advokat;

Poland adwokat, radca prawny;

Portugal advogado;

奥地利：Rechtsanwalt；

比利时：avocat / advocaat / Rechtsanwalt；

保加利亚：advokat；

克罗地亚：odvjetnik；

塞浦路斯：dikegóros；

捷克共和国：advokát；

丹麦：advokat；

爱沙尼亚：vandeadvokaat；

芬兰：asianajaja / advokat；

马其顿：advokat；

法国：avocat；

德国：Rechtsanwalt；

希腊：dikegóros；

匈牙利：ügyvéd；

冰岛：lögmaður；

爱尔兰：Barrister, solicitor；

意大利：avvocato；

拉脱维亚：zvērināts advokāts；

列支敦士登：Rechtsanwalt；

立陶宛：advokatas；

卢森堡：avocat / Rechtsanwalt；

马尔他：avukat, prokuratur legali；

荷兰：advocaat；

挪威：advokat；

波兰：adwokat, radca prawny；

葡萄牙：advogado；

Romania avocat;

Slovakia advokát / advokátka;

Slovenia odvetnik / odvetnica;

Spain abogado / advocat / abokatu / avogado;

Sweden advokat;

Switzerland Rechtsanwalt / Anwalt / Fürsprech / Fürsprecher / avocat / avvocato /advokat;

Turkey avukat;

Ukraine Advocate;

United Kingdom Advocate, Barrister, solicitor.

It is also hoped that the Code will be acceptable to the legal professions of other non-Member states in Europe and elsewhere so that it could also be applied by appropriate conventions between them and the Member States.

Commentary on Article 1.5—Field of Application Ratione Materiae

The rules are here given direct application only to "cross-border activities" , as defined, of lawyers within the EU and the EEA and lawyers of the Observer Members of the CCBE - see above on Article 1.4, and the definition of "Member State" in Article 1.6. (See also above as to possible extensions in the future to lawyers of other states.) The definition of crossborder activities would, for example, include contacts in state A even on a matter of law internal to state A between a lawyer of state A and a lawyer of state B; it would exclude contacts between lawyers of state A in state A of a matter arising in state B, provided that none of their professional activities takes place in state B; it would include any activities

罗马尼亚：avocat；

斯洛伐克：advokát / advokátka；

斯洛文尼亚：odvetnik / odvetnica；

西班牙：abogado / advocat / abokatu / avogado；

瑞典：advokat；

瑞士：Rechtsanwalt / Anwalt / Fürsprech / Fürsprecher / avocat / avvocato / advokat；

土耳其：avukat；

乌克兰：Advocate；

英国：Advocate, Barrister, solicitor.

也希望欧洲和其他地方的非成员国的法律职业能够接受本守则，以便可以通过它们与成员国之间订立的适当公约来适用本守则。

1.5 对事的效力

这里的规则仅直接适用于欧盟和欧洲经济区的律师以及 CCBE 观察员国（参见上述 1.4 和 1.6 中对“成员国”的定义）的律师所从事的“跨边境活动”（见上述定义）。（关于未来对其他国家律师的可能扩展，也请参见上述规定）。例如，跨边境活动的定义包括：A 国的某位律师与 B 国的某位律师在 A 国建立的联系，即使是关于 A 国内部的法律事务；但是不包括 A 国的律师们因 B 国发生的事项而在 A 国建立的联系，只要他们的职业活动都没有发生在 B 国；跨边境活动应当包括 A 国律师在 B 国进行的任何活动，即使是采用从 A 国到 B 国的通信形式。

of lawyers of state A in state B, even if only in the form of communications sent from state A to state B.

Commentary on Article 1.6—Definitions

This provision defines a number of terms used in the Code, "Member State", "Home Member State", "Host Member State", "Competent Authority", "Directive 77/249/EEC" and "Directive 98/5/EC".

The reference to "where the lawyer carries on cross-border activities" should be interpreted in the light of the definition of "cross-border activities" in Article 1.5.

Commentary on Article 2.1—Independence

This provision substantially reaffirms the general statement of principle in the Declaration of Perugia.

Commentary on Article 2.2—Trust and Personal Integrity

This provision also restates a general principle contained in the Declaration of Perugia.

Commentary on Article 2.3—Confidentiality

This provision first restates, in Article 2.3.1, general principles laid down in the Declaration of Perugia and recognised by the ECJ in the *AM&S* case (157/79). It then, in Articles 2.3.2 to 4, develops them into a specific

1.6 定义

本条规定就本守则使用的一系列术语，包括“成员国”、“所属成员国”、“东道成员国”、“主管机构”、“指令 77/249/EEC”和“指令 98/5/EC”，规定了定义。

所称“在律师从事跨边境活动的情况下”，应当根据 1.5 中“跨边境活动”的定义进行解释。

2.1 独立性

本条规定实质上重申了《佩鲁贾宣言》所述一般原则声明。

2.2 信任和个人适正性

本条规定同样重述了《佩鲁贾宣言》中的一个一般原则。

2.3 保密

本条规定首先在 2.3.1 重述了《佩鲁贾宣言》规定的并被欧洲共同体法院在 AM&S 案件（157/79）中认可的一般原则。在 2.3.2 至 4 中，它们被阐述为与保护秘密相关的具体规则。2.3.2 包含要求尊重保密的

rule relating to the protection of confidentiality. Article 2.3.2 contains the basic rule requiring respect for confidentiality. Article 2.3.3 confirms that the obligation remains binding on the lawyer even if he or she ceases to act for the client in question.

Article 2.3.4 confirms that the lawyer must not only respect the obligation of confidentiality him- or herself but must require all Members and employees of his or her firm to do likewise.

Commentary on Article 2.4—Respect for the Rules of Other Bars and Law Societies

Article 4 of the Lawyers Services Directive contains the provisions with regard to the rules to be observed by a lawyer from one Member State providing services on an occasional or temporary basis in another Member State by virtue of Article 49 of the consolidated EC treaty, as follows:

(a) activities relating to the representation of a client in legal proceedings or before public authorities shall be pursued in each Host Member State under the conditions laid down for lawyers established in that state, with the exception of any conditions requiring residence, or registration with a professional organisation, in that state;

(b) a lawyer pursuing these activities shall observe the rules of professional conduct of the Host Member State, without prejudice to the lawyer's obligations in the Member State from which he or she comes;

(c) when these activities are pursued in the UK, "rules of professional conduct of the Host Member State" means the rules of

基本规则。2.3.3 确认了律师在不再代理委托人后，仍然对律师有约束力的义务。

2.3.4 确认，律师不仅自己需要遵守保密义务，还必须要求其事务所所有成员和员工同样遵守该义务。

2.4 尊重其他律师协会的规则

《律师服务指令》的第 4 条所含的是成员国律师依据合并后的欧洲共同体条约第 49 条偶尔或者临时在另一成员国提供服务时应当遵守的规则，这些规定如下：

（a） 与在法律诉讼中或者公共机构代理委托人有关的活动，应当在东道成员国进行，并应遵守该国就律师规定的条件，但是不包括要求在该国居住或者在该国的职业组织注册的条件；

（b） 律师在从事这些活动时，应当遵守东道成员国的职业行为规则，无损于律师在其所属成员国的义务；

（c） 当在英国从事这些活动时，如果这些活动没有保留给出庭律师和诉辩律师，“东道成员国职业行为规则”是指适用于事务

professional conduct applicable to solicitors, where such activities are not reserved for Barristers and Advocates. Otherwise the rules of professional conduct applicable to the latter shall apply. However, Barristers from Ireland shall always be subject to the rules of professional conduct applicable in the UK to Barristers and Advocates. When these activities are pursued in Ireland "rules of professional conduct of the Host Member State" means, in so far as they govern the oral presentation of a case in Court, the rules of professional conduct applicable to Barristers. In all other cases the rules of professional conduct applicable to solicitors shall apply. However, Barristers and Advocates from the UK shall always be subject to the rules of professional conduct applicable in Ireland to Barristers; and

(d) a lawyer pursuing activities other than those referred to in (a) above shall remain subject to the conditions and rules of professional conduct of the Member State from which he or she comes without prejudice to respect for the rules, whatever their source, which govern the profession in the Host Member State, especially those concerning the incompatibility of the exercise of the activities of a lawyer with the exercise of other activities in that state, professional secrecy, relations with other lawyers, the prohibition on the same lawyer acting for parties with mutually conflicting interests, and publicity. The latter rules are applicable only if they are capable of being observed by a lawyer who is not established in the Host Member State and to the extent to which their observance is objectively justified to ensure, in that state, the proper exercise of a lawyer's activities, the standing of the

律师的职业行为规则。否则，就是指适用于出庭律师和诉辩律师的职业行为规则。然而，来自爱尔兰的出庭律师应当始终遵守适用于英国出庭律师和诉辩律师的职业行为规则。当在爱尔兰从事这些活动时，“东道成员国职业行为规则”，在调整的是在法院口头陈述案件的情况下，是指适用于出庭律师的职业行为规则。在所有其他情况下，适用于事务律师的职业行为规则应当适用。然而，来自英国的出庭律师和诉辩律师应当始终遵守适用于爱尔兰出庭律师的职业行为规则；

（d） 在从事上述（a）所述活动以外的活动时，律师仍然应当遵守其所属成员国的条件和职业行为规则，同时不得有损于对东道成员国调整法律职业的规则的尊重，无论其来源如何，尤其是涉及这些事项的规则：律师从事的活动与其在该国从事的其他活动的不相容性，职业秘密，与其他律师的关系，禁止同一律师为存在利益冲突的多位委托人提供代理，以及律师宣传。后述这些规则仅在下列情况下才能适用：它们能够被不在东道成员国开业的律师所遵守，且对这些规则的遵守在客观上有利于保证在该国律师适当开展活动、法律职业的地位和尊重关于不相容性的规则。

profession and respect for the rules concerning incompatibility.

The Lawyers Establishment Directive contains the provisions with regard to the rules to be observed by a lawyer from one Member State practicing on a permanent basis in another Member State by virtue of Article 43 of the consolidated EC treaty, as follows:

(a) irrespective of the rules of professional conduct to which he or she is subject in his or her Home Member State, a lawyer practicing under his home-country professional title shall be subject to the relevant professional title of the Host Member State in respect of all the activities the lawyer pursues in its territory (Article 6.1);

(b) the Host Member State may require a lawyer practising under his or her home-country professional title either to take out professional indemnity insurance or to become a Member of a professional guarantee fund in accordance with the rules which that state lays down for professional activities pursued in its territory. Nevertheless, a lawyer practising under his or her home-country professional title shall be exempted from that requirement if the lawyer can prove that he or she is covered by insurance taken out or a guarantee provided in accordance with the rules of the Home Member State, insofar as such insurance or guarantee is equivalent in terms of the conditions and extent of cover. Where the equivalence is only partial, the Competent Authority in the Host Member State may require that additional insurance or an additional guarantee be contracted to cover the elements which are not already covered by the insurance or guarantee contracted in accordance with the rules of the Home Member State (Article 6.3); and

《律师开业指令》包含了来自成员国的律师依据合并后的欧洲共同体条约第 43 条在另一成员国永久开业时应当遵守的规则，这些规定如下：

（a） 无论律师在其所属成员国应当遵守的职业行为规则如何，律师以其所属国的职业头衔执业时，应当像以东道成员国相关职业头衔执业的律师一样，就其在其领土从事的所有活动，遵守同样的行为规则（6.1）。

（b） 东道成员国可能要求律师在以其所属国职业头衔执业时，办理职业责任保险，或者遵照该东道成员国就其领土内进行的职业活动制定的规则参加律师职业担保基金。但是，以其所属国职业头衔执业的律师，如果能证明其已遵照所属国规则投保或者参加担保，只要该保险或者担保在条件和范围方面与上述保险和担保相当，则该律师可免于该要求。如果仅有部分相当，东道成员国的主管机构可以要求签订额外的保险或担保，以涵盖遵照所属国规则参加的保险或担保未涵盖的要素（6.3）；以及

(c) a lawyer registered in a Host Member State under his or her home country professional title may practise as a salaried lawyer in the employ of another lawyer, an association or firm of lawyers, or a public or private enterprise to the extent that the Host Member State so permits for lawyers registered under the professional title used in that state (Article 8).

In cases not covered by either of these Directives, or over and above the requirements of these Directives, the obligations of a lawyer under Community law to observe the rules of other Bars and Law Societies are a matter of interpretation of any relevant provision, such as the Directive on Electronic Commerce (2000/31/EC). A major purpose of the Code is to minimise, and if possible eliminate altogether, the problems which may arise from "double deontology", that is the application of more than one set of potentially conflicting national rules to a particular situation (see Article 1.3.1).

Commentary on Article 2.5—Incompatible Occupations

There are differences both between and within Member States on the extent to which lawyers are permitted to engage in other occupations, for example in commercial activities. The general purpose of rules excluding a lawyer from other occupations is to protect the lawyer from influences which might impair the lawyer's independence or his or her role in the administration of justice. The variations in these rules reflect different local conditions, different perceptions of the proper function of lawyers and different techniques of rule-making. For instance in some cases there is a complete prohibition of engagement in certain named occupations, whereas

（c） 以其所属国的职业头衔在东道成员国注册的律师，可受雇于另一位律师、律师合作形式或者律师事务所、国有或者私营企业，担任领薪律师，但是不得超过东道成员国对使用所属国职业头衔注册的律师所许可的范围（第8条）。

对于不属于这些指令范围内的情况，或超出这些指令要求的情况，律师所负有的根据欧洲共同体法律遵守其他律师协会的规则的义务，是一个对任何相关规定加以解释的问题，例如《电子商务指令》（2000/31/EC）。本准则的主要目的，是减少及在可行的情况下全面消除因“双重道德标准”可能产生的问题，即避免就特定情形适用一套以上存在潜在冲突的国家的规则（参见1.3.1）。

2.5 不相容的职业

各成员国间和成员国内对允许律师从事其他职业——例如商业活动——的程度，是存在差异的。禁止律师从事其他职业的规则的一般目的，是保护律师不受可能损害其独立性或者在司法中的角色的影响。这些规则的不同，反映了不同的地方情况，对律师职能的不同认识，以及制定规则的不同技术。例如，在某些情况下，完全禁止从事某些特定列名的职业，而在另一些情况下，通常允许从事其他职业，但是要遵守为保护律师独立性所采取的具体措施。2.5.2和3针对来自某成员国的律师在未成为东道成员国法律职业成员时在东道国从事跨边境活动（定义见1.5）的不同情况作了相关规定。2.5.2要求律师在东道成员国法律程

in other cases engagement in other occupations is generally permitted, subject to observance of specific safeguards for the lawyer's independence. Articles 2.5.2 and 3 make provision for different circumstances in which a lawyer of one Member State is engaging in cross-border activities (as defined in Article 1.5) in a Host Member State when he or she is not a Member of the Host State legal profession. Article 2.5.2 imposes full observation of Host State rules regarding incompatible occupations on the lawyer acting in national legal proceedings or before national public authorities in the Host State. This applies whether the lawyer is established in the Host State or not.

Article 2.5.3, on the other hand, imposes "respect" for the rules of the Host State regarding forbidden or incompatible occupations in other cases, but only where the lawyer who is established in the Host Member State wishes to participate directly in commercial or other activities not connected with the practice of the law.

Commentary on Article 2.6—Personal Publicity

The term "personal publicity" covers publicity by firms of lawyers, as well as individual lawyers, as opposed to corporate publicity organised by Bars and Law Societies for their Members as a whole. The rules governing personal publicity by lawyers vary considerably in the Member States. Article 2.6 makes it clear that there is no overriding objection to personal publicity in cross-border practice. However, lawyers are nevertheless subject to prohibitions or restrictions laid down by their home professional rules, and a lawyer will still be subject to prohibitions or restrictions laid down by Host State rules when these are binding on the lawyer by virtue of the

序中或者任何公共机构中行事时，应当全面遵守该东道成员国关于律师的相容职业的规则。不论律师是否在东道成员国开业，这一规定均适用。

另一方面，2.5.3 要求律师“尊重”东道成员国有关在其他情况下被禁止或者不相容职业的规定，但是仅限于在东道国开业的律师希望直接参与与法律执业活动无关的商业活动或者其他活动的情况。

2.6 个人宣传

“个人宣传”，指的是相对于律师协会为其成员整体所做的集体宣传，由律师事务所和律师个人所做的宣传。各成员国制定的调整律师个人宣传的规则有很大不同。2.6 明确规定，在跨边界执业活动中，不存在反对个人宣传的压倒性理由。然而，律师仍然需遵守其来源国职业规则规定的禁令或者限制，同时还应当遵守根据《律师服务指令》或者《律师开业指令》对律师有约束力的东道国规则规定的禁令或限制。

Lawyers Services Directive or the Lawyers Establishment Directive.

Commentary on Article 2.7—The Client's Interest

This provision emphasises the general principle that the lawyer must always place the client's interests before the lawyer's own interests or those of fellow Members of the legal profession.

Commentary on Article 2.8—Limitation of Lawyer's Liability towards the Client

This provision makes clear that there is no overriding objection to limiting a lawyer's liability towards his or her client in cross-border practice, whether by contract or by use of a limited company, limited partnership or limited liability partnership. However it points out that this can only be contemplated where the relevant law and the relevant rules of conduct permit - and in a number of jurisdictions the law or the professional rules prohibit or restrict such limitation of liability.

Commentary on Article 3.1—Acceptance and Termination of Instructions

The provisions of Article 3.1.1 are designed to ensure that a relationship is maintained between lawyer and client and that the lawyer in fact receives instructions from the client, even though these may be transmitted through a duly authorised intermediary. It is the responsibility of the lawyer to satisfy him- or herself as to the authority of the intermediary

2.7 委托人利益

本条规定强调了这样的一般原则，即律师必须始终将委托人利益置于律师自己的利益或者法律职业同行的利益之上。

2.8 限制律师对委托人的责任

本条规定清楚说明，对律师在跨边境执业活动中限制对委托人承担的责任的做法，不存在压倒性反对，无论是通过合同，还是通过有限公司、有限合伙还是有限责任合伙。然而，本条规定指出，仅在相关法律及相关行为规则准许的情况下，才可以考虑这么做，在许多司法管辖区，法律或者职业规则禁止或者限制这种对责任的限制。

3.1 接受和终止指示

3.1.1 款之规定，旨在确保维持律师与委托人之间的关系，律师事实上从委托人那里接受指示，即使这些指示是通过妥为授权的中介转发的。律师有责任确信该中介的权限和委托人的意愿。

and the wishes of the client.

Article 3.1.2 deals with the manner in which the lawyer should carry out his or her duties. The provision that the lawyer shall undertake personal responsibility for the discharge of the instructions given to him or her means that the lawyer cannot avoid responsibility by delegation to others. It does not prevent the lawyer from seeking to limit his or her legal liability to the extent that this is permitted by the relevant law or professional rules - see Article 2.8.

Article 3.1.3 states a principle which is of particular relevance in cross-border activities, for example when a lawyer is asked to handle a matter on behalf of a lawyer or client from another state who may be unfamiliar with the relevant law and practice, or when a lawyer is asked to handle a matter relating to the law of another state with which he or she is unfamiliar. A lawyer generally has the right to refuse to accept instructions in the first place, but Article 3.1.4 states that, having once accepted them, the lawyer has an obligation not to withdraw without ensuring that the client's interests are safeguarded.

Commentary on Article 3.2—Conflict of Interest

The provisions of Article 3.2.1 do not prevent a lawyer acting for two or more clients in the same matter provided that their interests are not in fact in conflict and that there is no significant risk of such a conflict arising. Where a lawyer is already acting for two or more clients in this way and subsequently there arises a conflict of interests between those clients or a risk of a breach of confidence or other circumstances where the lawyer's independence may be impaired, then the lawyer must cease to act for both

3.1.2 规定了律师在履行其职责时应当采用的方式。关于律师应当就执行其所受指示承担个人责任的规定，意思是律师不能通过委派他人来逃避责任。本规定并不禁止律师将其承担的法律责任限制在相关法律或者职业规则允许的范围内。参见 2.8。

3.1.3 规定的是与跨边境活动特别相关的原则，例如律师接受请求代表其他国家不熟悉相关法律和惯例的律师或者委托人办理某事务的情况，或律师接受请求办理涉及其所不熟悉的其他国家法律的事务的情况。通常情况下，律师有权利在一开始就拒绝接受指示，但是 3.1.4 规定，一旦接受指示，律师即负有这样的义务，即不得在无法保证委托人利益不受损的情况下退出代理。

3.2 利益冲突

3.2.1 之规定并不禁止律师在同一事务中代理两名或者两名以上的委托人，只要他们的利益不存在实际利益冲突，或者不存在发生这种冲突的重大风险。如果律师已经这样担任两名或者两名以上委托人的代理人，在随后这些委托人之间出现利益冲突或者出现违反保密义务的风险的情况下，或者在可能影响律师独立性的其他情况下，律师必须停止代理双方或者所有相关委托人。

or all of them.

There may, however, be circumstances in which differences arise between two or more clients for whom the same lawyer is acting where it may be appropriate for the lawyer to attempt to act as a mediator. It is for the lawyer in such cases to use his or her own judgement on whether or not there is such a conflict of interest between them as to require the lawyer to cease to act. If not, the lawyer may consider whether it would be appropriate to explain the position to the clients, obtain their agreement and attempt to act as mediator to resolve the difference between them, and only if this attempt to mediate should fail, to cease to act for them.

Article 3.2.4 applies the foregoing provisions of Article 3 to lawyers practicing in association. For example a firm of lawyers should cease to act when there is a conflict of interest between two clients of the firm, even if different lawyers in the firm are acting for each client. On the other hand, exceptionally, in the "chambers" form of association used by English Barristers, where each lawyer acts for clients individually, it is possible for different lawyers in the association to act for clients with opposing interests.

Commentary on Article 3.3—Pactum de Quota Litis

These provisions reflect the common position in all Member States that an unregulated agreement for contingency fees (*pactum de quota litis*) is contrary to the proper administration of justice because it encourages speculative litigation and is liable to be abused. The provisions are not, however, intended to prevent the maintenance or introduction of arrangements under which lawyers are paid according to results or only if the action or matter is successful, provided that these arrangements are

然而，可能存在这样的情况，即受同一位律师代理的两名或者两名以上的委托人之间发生了分歧，而该律师作为调停人可能是适当的。在这种情况下，该律师应当自行判断他们之间是否存在需要律师停止代理的利益冲突。如果没有这种冲突，该律师应当考虑是否可向委托人阐明其立场，获得他们的同意，并作为调停人解决他们之间的分歧。只有在调停失败后，才能停止对他们的代理。

3.2.4 将第 3 条的前述规定适用于一起执业的律师。例如，律师事务所应停止为存在利益冲突的两位委托人代理，即使律师事务所不同的律师在代理各个委托人。但是，存在一个例外情况，即：在英国出庭律师以“工作室”形式建立的合作中，每个律师可各自为利益相对的委托人代理，因为每个律师都是为其委托人单独代理的。

3.3　风险代理协议

这些规定反映了所有成员国的共同立场，即订立不受规制的风险代理协议（讨债分成协议）是有悖于适当司法的，因为它将鼓励投机性诉讼行为，并且容易被滥用。然而，这些规定并不是要禁止保持或者引入这样的安排：律师就其结果或者仅在案件或者事务成功后取得律师费，但是这种安排要有充分的规制和控制，以保护委托人和适当司法。

under sufficient regulation and control for the protection of the client and the proper administration of justice.

Commentary on Article 3.4—Regulation of Fees

Article 3.4 lays down three requirements: a general standard of disclosure of a lawyer's fees to the client, a requirement that they should be fair and reasonable in amount, and a requirement to comply with the applicable law and professional rules. In many Member States machinery exists for regulating lawyers' fees under national law or rules of conduct, whether by reference to a power of adjudication by the Bar authorities or otherwise. In situations governed by the Lawyers Establishment Directive, where the lawyer is subject to Host State rules as well as the rules of the Home State, the basis of charging may have to comply with both sets of rules.

Commentary on Article 3.5—Payment on Account

Article 3.5 assumes that a lawyer may require a payment on account of the lawyer's fees and/or disbursements, but sets a limit by reference to a reasonable estimate of them. See also on Article 3.1.4 regarding the right to withdraw.

Commentary on Article 3.6—Fee Sharing with Non-Lawyers

In some Member States lawyers are permitted to practise in

3.4 对律师费的规制

3.4 规定了三项要求：向委托人披露律师费的一般标准，律师费数额应当公平、合理，以及遵守现行法律和职业规则。在许多成员国，都存在根据国家法律或者行为规则规制律师费的机制，或是通过律师协会的裁判权，或是通过其他形式。对于受到《律师开业指令》调整的情况，律师需遵守东道成员国规则和所在国规则，其收费根据可能要遵守两套规则的规定。

3.5 预付款

3.5 认为，律师可以要求预付其律师费和 / 或者支出，但是限制在了合理估算的数额内。还请参见关于退出代理的权利的 3.1.4。

3.6 与非律师人员分享律师费

一些成员国允许律师与经核准的其他职业的成员一起合作执业，无

association with Members of certain other approved professions, whether legal professions or not. The provisions of Article 3.6.1 are not designed to prevent fee sharing within such an approved form of association. Nor are the provisions designed to prevent fee sharing by the lawyers to whom the Code applies (see on Article 1.4 above) with other "lawyers" , for example lawyers from non-Member States or Members of other legal professions in the Member States such as notaries.

Commentary on Article 3.7—Cost of Litigation and Availability of Legal Aid

Article 3.7.1 stresses the importance of attempting to resolve disputes in a way which is cost- effective for the client, including advising on whether to attempt to negotiate a settlement, and whether to propose referring the dispute to some form of alternative dispute resolution.

Article 3.7.2 requires a lawyer to inform the client of the availability of legal aid where applicable. There are widely differing provisions in the Member States on the availability of legal aid. In cross- border activities a lawyer should have in mind the possibility that the legal aid provisions of a national law with which the lawyer is unfamiliar may be applicable.

Commentary on Article 3.8—Client Funds

The provisions of Article 3.8 reflect the recommendation adopted by the CCBE in Brussels in November 1985 on the need for minimum regulations to be made and enforced governing the proper control and disposal of clients' funds held by lawyers within the Community. Article 3.8

论该等职业是否属于法律职业。3.6.1 所述规定，并非旨在禁止律师在这种经核准的合作形式内共享律师费。这些规定也不是要禁止本守则所适用的律师（参见上述 1.4）与其他“律师”共享律师费，例如，来自非成员国的律师或者成员国的其他法律职业的成员（例如公证人）。

3.7 诉讼成本和法律援助的可得性

3.7.1 强调了以经济高效的方式为委托人解决争端的重要性，包括建议委托人是否通过谈判达成和解，以及是否建议适用某些替代性争端解决方法来解决争端。

3.7.2 要求律师在可行情况下，应当告知委托人法律援助的可得性。成员国之间在法律援助可得性的规定上差别很大。在跨边境活动中，律师应当牢记其不熟悉的国家法律所可能提供的法律援助。

3.8 委托人资金

3.8 之规定反映了 CCBE 于 1985 年 11 月在布鲁塞尔通过的建议，目的是在欧洲共同体内解决适当控制和处置律师持有的委托人资金的最低规制要求的制定和执行问题。3.8 规定了应当遵守的最低标准，但同时不影响各国委托人资金保护制度中更为全面、严格的详细规定。如果

lays down minimum standards to be observed, while not interfering with the details of national systems which provide fuller or more stringent protection for clients' funds. The lawyer who holds clients' funds, even in the course of a cross-border activity, has to observe the rules of his or her home Bar. The lawyer needs to be aware of questions which arise where the rules of more than one Member State may be applicable, especially where the lawyer is established in a Host State under the Lawyers Establishment Directive.

Commentary on Article 3.9—Professional Indemnity Insurance

Article 3.9.1 reflects a recommendation, also adopted by the CCBE in Brussels in November 1985, on the need for all lawyers in the Community to be insured against the risks arising from professional negligence claims against them.

Article 3.9.2 deals with the situation where insurance cannot be obtained on the basis set out in Article 3.9.1.

Commentary on Article 4.1—Rules of Conduct in Court

This provision applies the principle that a lawyer is bound to comply with the rules of the Court or tribunal before which the lawyer practises or appears.

Commentary on Article 4.2—Fair Conduct of Proceedings

This provision applies the general principle that in adversarial

律师持有委托人资金，即使是跨边境活动过程中，也必须遵守其所在国律师协会制定的规则。律师需要意识到多个成员国的规则同时适用可能会引发的问题，特别是在该律师根据《律师开业指令》在东道成员国开业的情况下。

3.9 职业赔偿保险

3.9.1 反映的是 CCBE 于 1985 年 11 月在布鲁塞尔通过的建议，即欧洲共同体所有律师都需要购买保险，以防范职业过失索赔带来的风险。

3.9.2 针对的是无法根据 3.9.1 获得保险的情况。

4.1 在法院的行为规则

本条规定适用了这样的原则，即律师在法院或者裁判庭执业或者出庭时，有义务遵守法院或者裁判庭的规则。

4.2 程序公平

本条规定适用了这样的一般原则，即在对抗式程序中，律师不得试

proceedings a lawyer must not attempt to take unfair advantage of his or her opponent. The lawyer must not, for example, make contact with the judge without first informing the lawyer acting for the opposing party or submit exhibits, notes or documents to the judge without communicating them in good time to the lawyer on the other side unless such steps are permitted under the relevant rules of procedure. To the extent not prohibited by law a lawyer must not divulge or submit to the Court any proposals for settlement of the case made by the other party or its lawyer without the express consent of the other party's lawyer. See also on Article 4.5 below.

Commentary on Article 4.3—Demeanour in Court

This provision reflects the necessary balance between respect for the Court and for the law on the one hand and the pursuit of the client's best interest on the other.

Commentary on Article 4.4—False or Misleading Information

This provision applies the principle that the lawyer must never knowingly mislead the Court. This is necessary if there is to be trust between the Courts and the legal profession.

Commentary on Article 4.5—Extension to Arbitrators etc.

This provision extends the preceding provisions relating to Courts and other bodies exercising judicial or quasi-judicial functions.

图取得不利于对手的不公平优势。例如，该律师不得在未首先通知对方当事人代理律师的情况下接触法官，或者在未与对方律师及时沟通的情况下向法官提交展示件、票据或者文件，除非相关程序规则允许这样的做法。在法律未禁止的范围内，在未取得对方律师的明示同意时，律师不得向法院透露或者提交对方当事人或者其律师提出的任何案件和解建议。还请参见下文 4.5。

4.3 在法院的举止

本规定反映了在尊重法院、尊重法律与维护委托人最大利益之间应达到的必要平衡。

4.4 虚假或者误导性信息

本条规定适用了这一原则，即律师不得有意误导法院。如果要在法院与法律职业之间存在信赖，这将是必需的。

4.5 扩展及仲裁员等人员

本条规定就前述关于履行司法职能或者准司法职能的法院和其他组织的规定，进行了扩展适用。

Commentary on Article 5.1—Corporate Spirit of the Profession

These provisions, which are based on statements in the Declaration of Perugia, emphasise that it is in the public interest for the legal profession to maintain a relationship of trust and cooperation between its Members. However, this cannot be used to justify setting the interests of the profession against those of justice or of clients (see also on Article 2.7) .

Commentary on Article 5.2—Co-operation among Lawyers of Different Member States

This provision also develops a principle stated in the Declaration of Perugia with a view to avoiding misunderstandings in dealings between lawyers of different Member States.

Commentary on Article 5.3—Correspondence between Lawyers

In certain Member States communications between lawyers (written or by word of mouth) are normally regarded as to be kept confidential as between the lawyers. This means that the content of these communications cannot be disclosed to others, cannot normally be passed to the lawyers' clients, and at any event cannot be produced in Court. In other Member States, such consequences will not follow unless the correspondence is marked as "confidential" . In yet other Member States, the lawyer has to keep the client fully informed of all relevant communications from a

5.1 职业的团体精神

这些规定是基于《佩鲁贾宣言》所述声明而制定的，强调出于法律界的公共利益，成员间应当建立一种信任和合作关系。然而，这不应当被用作支持将法律职业的利益与司法或者委托人利益相对立(参见 2.7)。

5.2 不同成员国的律师之间的合作

本规定也阐述了《佩鲁贾宣言》所述的一个原则，目的是为了避免不同成员国律师在交往中产生误解。

5.3 律师之间的通信

在某些成员国，律师之间的交流（书面或者口头的）通常被视为律师之间的秘密而加以保守。这意味着这些交流的内容不得披露给他人，通常不得传递给律师的委托人，且在任何情况下均不得在法院提出。在其他成员国则无此类结果，除非通信注明为“秘密”。然而，在其他成员国，律师必须让委托人全面了解所有来自代理对方当事人的职业同僚的所有相关交流，并且，在信件上标示“秘密”字样，仅仅意味着该信件是发送给接收信件的律师及其委托人的法律资料，第三方不得滥用。在某些国家，如果律师希望表明寄出的信件是为了就争端进行和解，且

professional colleague acting for another party, and marking a letter as "confidential" only means that it is a legal matter intended for the recipient lawyer and his or her client, and not to be misused by third parties. In some states, if a lawyer wishes to indicate that a letter is sent in an attempt to settle a dispute, and is not to be produced in a Court, the lawyer should mark the letter as "without prejudice" . These important national differences give rise to many misunderstandings. That is why lawyers must be very careful in conducting cross-border correspondence.

Whenever a lawyer wants to send a letter to a professional colleague in another Member State on the basis that it is to be kept confidential as between the lawyers, or that it is "without prejudice" , the lawyer should ask in advance whether the letter can be accepted on that basis. A lawyer wishing that a communication should be accepted on such a basis must express that clearly at the head of the communication or in a covering letter. A lawyer who is the intended recipient of such a communication, but who is not in a position to respect, or to ensure respect for, the basis on which it is to be sent, must inform the sender immediately so that the communication is not sent. If the communication has already been received, the recipient must return it to the sender without revealing its contents or referring to it in any way; if the recipient's national law or rules prevent the recipient from complying with this requirement, he or she must inform the sender immediately.

Commentary on Article 5.4—Referral Fees

This provision reflects the principle that a lawyer should not pay or receive payment purely for the reference of a client, which would risk

不得在法院出示，则该律师应当在信件上注明“不受侵害”字样。这些国家间的重大差异会引起许多误解。这就是为什么律师在进行跨边境通信时必须非常小心的原因。

如果律师想要在律师之间的秘密基础上，或者在“不受侵害”的基础上，向另一成员国的职业同僚发出信件，则该律师应当预先询问该信件能否在该基础上被接收。如果律师希望该交流在该基础上被接收，则该律师必须在信头或在附信中明确说明这一点。作为该交流指定收件人的律师，如果无法尊重或者确保该发信基础，则必须立即告知发信任，以确保不发送该交流。如果已收悉该交流，则收件人必须退回发件人，不得披露其内容或者以任何方式提及信件内容；如果收件人所属国家的法律或者规则禁止收件人遵守该要求，则必须立即告知发件人。

5.4 介绍费

这一规定反映了这样的原则，即律师不应当纯粹出于介绍委托人的目的支付或者收取费用，这会有影响委托人自由选择律师的权利的风

impairing the client's free choice of lawyer or the client's interest in being referred to the best available service. It does not prevent fee-sharing arrangements between lawyers on a proper basis (see also on Article 3.6 above) . In some Member States lawyers are permitted to accept and retain commissions in certain cases provided the client's best interests are served, there is full disclosure to the client and the client has consented to the retention of the commission. In such cases the retention of the commission by the lawyer represents part of the lawyer's remuneration for the service provided to the client and is not within the scope of the prohibition on referral fees which is designed to prevent lawyers making a secret profit.

Commentary on Article 5.5—Communication with Opposing Parties

This provision reflects a generally accepted principle, and is designed both to promote the smooth conduct of business between lawyers and to prevent any attempt to take advantage of the client of another lawyer.

Commentary on Article 5.6—Change of Lawyer

Article 5.6 dealt with change of lawyer. It was deleted from the Code on 6 December 2002.

Commentary on Article 5.7—Responsibility for Fees

These provisions substantially reaffirm provisions contained in the Declaration of Perugia. Since misunderstandings about responsibility for

险，或者对把能够得到的最佳服务介绍给委托人产生影响的风险。但是这并不禁止律师之间在适当基础上达成律师费分享协议（参见上述 3.6）。在某些成员国，允许律师在特定情况下接受和保留佣金，只要委托人的最大利益得以维护，并就保留该佣金完全告知委托人，且委托人表示同意。在这种情况下，律师保留的佣金代表的是律师为委托人提供服务的部分报酬，且不在旨在防止律师谋取秘密利润的介绍费禁令的范围内。

5.5 与对方当事人的交流

本条规定反映了一项普遍接受的原则，且旨在推动律师之间的业务顺利进行，防止任何利用对方律师的委托人的企图。

5.6 更换律师

5.6 涉及律师的更换。该条已于 2002 年 12 月 6 日从本守则中删除。

5.7 对律师费的责任

这些规定实质上重申了《佩鲁贾宣言》包含的规定。对未付律师费的责任存在误解，是导致不同成员国律师产生分歧的常见原因。因此，

unpaid fees are a common cause of difference between lawyers of different Member States, it is important that a lawyer who wishes to exclude or limit his or her personal obligation to be responsible for the fees of a foreign colleague should reach a clear agreement on this at the outset of the transaction.

Commentary on Article 5.8—Continuing Professional Development

Keeping abreast of developments in the law is a professional obligation. In particular it is essential that lawyers are aware of the growing impact of European law on their field of practice.

Commentary on Article 5.9—Disputes amongst Lawyers in Different Member States

A lawyer has the right to pursue any legal or other remedy to which he or she is entitled against a colleague in another Member State. Nevertheless it is desirable that, where a breach of a rule of professional conduct or a dispute of a professional nature is involved, the possibilities of friendly settlement should be exhausted, if necessary with the assistance of the Bars or Law Societies concerned, before such remedies are exercised.

如果律师希望排除或者限制其向国外同僚承担的付费个人义务，则该律师应当在交易开始之初就此达成明确协议，这一点很重要。

5.8 继续职业发展

与法律的发展俱进，是律师的职业义务。特别是，律师能够意识到欧洲法律对其执业领域日益增长的影响，这是至关重要的。

5.9 不同成员国律师之间的争端

律师有权针对其有权反对的另一成员国同僚提出任何法律或其他救济要求。但是，在出现任何违反职业行为规则的行为时，或者涉及具有职业性质的争端时，在寻求这些救济之前，应当尽可能穷尽以友好方式解决争端的可能性，如有必要，可以向相关律师协会寻求协助。

APPENDIX C

THE CONTINUING PROFESSIONAL DEVELOPMENT REGULATIONS

(Approved by Faculty Council on 3 November 2003)

Application

1. These Regulations apply:

    (a) to all practising Members of Faculty from 1st January 2004;

    (b) to a non-practising Member of Faculty who returns to practice on or after 1st January 2004.

The Mandatory Continuing Professional Development Requirements

2. (1) For the purpose of these Regulations the "mandatory requirements" are those set out in sub-paragraph (2).

    (2) Subject to sub-paragraph (3), any Member of Faculty to whom these Regulations apply must complete a minimum of 10 hours of continuing professional development during each

附录 C

继续职业发展条例

（诉辩律师协会委员会 2003 年 11 月 3 日批准）

适用

1. 本条例：

（a） 从 2004 年 1 月 1 日起适用于诉辩律师协会所有执业会员；

（b） 适用于在 2004 年 1 月及以后重新执业的诉辩律师协会非执业会员。

强制性继续职业发展要求

2. （1）为本条例之目的，“强制性要求”是指（2）所列要求。

（2） 在遵守（3）的情况下，本条例所适用的诉辩律师协会任何会员必须在每个日历年度完成最低 10 小时的继续职业发展。

calendar year.

(3) A Member of Faculty who commences or returns to practice after 30th June in any year must complete a minimum of 5 hours continuing professional development during each calendar year.

3. Members of Faculty to whom these regulations apply shall complete the mandatory requirements by attendance at courses, conferences, symposia and similar events organised by training providers accredited for the purpose by the Director of Training & Education, and "continuing professional development" shall be construed accordingly.

4. The Faculty Council, on the advice of the Training & Admission Committee, may if it thinks fit specify the nature, content and format of particular courses and other activities which may be undertaken by Members of Faculty in order to satisfy the mandatory requirements.

5. (1) Every Member of Faculty to whom these regulations apply shall keep a record of his or her performance of the mandatory requirements on a form provided for that purpose by the Director of Training & Education.

(2) Every Member of Faculty to whom these regulations apply shall forward that record of performance to the Director of Training & Education no later than 1st March of the year following that to which it relates.

6. The Faculty Council, on the advice of the Training & Admission Committee, may increase the minimum number of hours of continuing professional development which must be completed in

（3） 在每年 6 月 30 日后开始或者重新执业的诉辩律师协会会员，必须在每个日历年度完成最低 5 小时的继续职业发展。

3. 本条例所适用的诉辩律师协会每个会员，应当通过参加培训和教育主管为本目的认可的培训提供者组织的课程、会议、研讨班和类似活动，来完成强制性要求，对“继续职业发展”应当作相应解释。

4. 诉辩律师协会委员会，根据培训和准入委员会的建议，可以在其认为适当的情况下具体规定诉辩律师协会会员为达到强制要求而参加的特定课程和其他活动的性质、内容和模式。

5. （1）本条例所适用的诉辩律师协会每个会员，应当就其对强制性要求的履行，在培训和教育主管为本目的提供的表单上进行记录。

（2） 本条例所适用的诉辩律师协会每个会员，应当在第二年的 3 月 1 日之前，将该履行情况记录提交培训和教育主管。

6. 诉辩律师协会委员会，根据培训和准入委员会建议，可以提高为达到任何强制性要求必须完成的继续职业发展最低小时数。

order to satisfy any of the mandatory requirements.

Waivers

7. The Faculty Council, on the advice of the Professional Standards Committee shall have the power in relation to any Member of Faculty to waive any or all of the mandatory requirements in whole or in part, on such conditions as it may think fit.

Failure to comply with the mandatory requirements

1. (1) Where a Member of Faculty to whom these regulations apply fails to satisfy the mandatory requirements, the Director of Training & Education shall notify the Professional Standards Committee of the Faculty.

(2) The Professional Standards Committee shall consider the matter and after making such enquiry as they consider appropriate, they may:

(a) dismiss the complaint; or

(b) report the matter to the Dean.

(3) When the Dean receives a notification under sub-paragraph (2), he shall treat it as a complaint made under rule 1 (1) (a) of the Faculty of Advocates Disciplinary Rules 2001.

Citation and commencement

2. (1) These regulations may be cited as the Faculty of Advocates

弃权

7. 诉辩律师协会委员会，根据职业标准委员会建议，应当有权就诉辩律师协会任何会员根据其认为适当的条件，全部或者部分放弃任何或者全部强制性要求。

未能遵守强制性要求

1. （1） 在本条例适用的诉辩律师协会会员未能达到强制性要求的情况下，培训和教育主管应当通知诉辩律师协会职业标准委员会。

（2） 职业标准委员会应当审议该事项，在进行他们认为适当的调查后，他们可以：

（a） 驳回投诉；或者

（b） 就该事项向会长报告。

（3） 在会长收到根据（2）发出的通知时，他应当将其视为根据诉辩律师协会《2001 年惩戒规则》1（1）（a）提出的投诉。

引用和施行

2. （1） 本条例可以被引为诉辩律师协会《2003 年继续职业发展

Continuing Professional Development Regulations 2003.

(2) These regulations shall come into force on 1st January 2004.

条例》。

（2）本条例在 2004 年 1 月 1 日起生效。

APPENDIX D

FROM WHOM MAY AN ADVOCATE ACCEPT INSTRUCTIONS?

An Advocate may accept instructions from any person or body detailed in the appendix hereto and in terms of the Direct Access Rules and Standard Terms of Instruction as they may be updated by the faculty from time to time.

DIRECT ACCESS RULES (October 2006)

1. An Advocate may accept instructions from any person or body detailed in the Appendix hereto, whether on their own behalf or on behalf of a client. Instructions under these rules will be referred to as "Direct Access Instructions" .
2. Advocates may not, however, accept instructions to act from, or on behalf of, any person or body from which they receive any remuneration other than the professional fees or retainers paid to them as Advocate. Thus they may not act for, or accept instructions from, a company of which they are a director, or any person or body by which they are employed, or a firm of which

附录 D

诉辩律师可以从何人那里接受指示?

诉辩律师可以从附录中所列的任何人员或者组织那里依照诉辩律师协会届时可能更新的《直接近用规则》和《指示标准条款》接受指示。

直接近用规则（2006 年 10 月）

1. 诉辩律师可以从附录中所列的任何人员或者组织那里接受指示，无论是以其自己的名义还是以委托人的名义。根据这些规则作出的指示，称为“直接近用指示”。

2. 然而，诉辩律师不得从他们接受任何薪酬的任何人员或者组织那里接受指示或者代表他们行事，作为诉辩律师取得职业律师费或者聘请费除外。这样，他们不得接受他们实名或者实际上取得董事费、薪酬或者分红的担任董事、受雇、担任合伙人的公司、任何人员或者组织、事务所的指示来行事。

they are a partner, and from which they derive director's fees, a salary, or a share of the profits either in name or in reality.

3. Advocates may not accept instructions to receive or handle clients' money; nor to do administrative work which would normally be carried out by an instructing solicitor; nor to carry out investigative work which would normally be carried out by an instructing solicitor, any more than they might do so when instructed by a solicitor. An Advocate acting under these rules may, however, meet and discuss matters with a client or a potential witness without a representative of the instructing body or person being present, so long as both the Advocate and the instructing person or body consider this appropriate in terms of the code of conduct.
4. An Advocate who is instructed by any person or body detailed in the Appendix other than a Scottish solicitor must satisfy himself or herself so far as appears necessary of:
   (i) their competence to give the instructions in question;
   (ii) if those instructions are given on behalf of a client, their authority to do so; and
   (iii) their understanding of the terms of engagement and their effect, and in particular the limitations on the work which an Advocate may do and also any disadvantage which may, as a real possibility, be suffered by the client if the client does not act through a Scottish solicitor. If an Advocate cannot be satisfied of these matters, they may not accept those instructions. If an Advocate at any time concludes that they are no longer satisfied of any of these matters, or

3. 诉辩律师不得接受指示来接受或者处理委托人的资金，不得担任通常由进行指示的事务律师开展的行政性工作，不得承担通常由进行指示的事务律师开展的调查性工作，除非是受到事务律师的指示。然而，根据本规则行事的诉辩律师可以与委托人或者潜在证人会面和讨论问题，而不需要进行指示的组织或者人员的代表在场，只要诉辩律师和进行指示的人员或者组织都认为从行为守则的角度看这是适当的。

4. 如果诉辩律师受到附录详细所列的苏格兰事务律师之外的任何人员和组织的指示，则在看来必要情况下，必须确信：

（i） 他们有作出有关指示的能力；

（ii） 如果这些指示是代表委托人作出的，他们有权这么做；以及

（iii） 他们理解委托条款及其效力，特别是对诉辩律师可以从事的工作的限制，以及他们不通过苏格兰事务律师来行事可能遭受的不利的现实可能性。如果诉辩律师不能确信这些事项，他们不得接受这些指示。如果诉辩律师在任何时候得出结论认为，他们不再确信任何这些事项，或者因为这样的指示不是通过苏格兰事务律师这一中介作出的而不符合委托人的利益或者正义的利益，他们必须就此告知进行指示的人员，可以拒绝进一步采取行

that it is not in the interest of the client or the interests of justice that such instructions be given other than through the medium of a Scottish solicitor, they must so inform the person instructing and may refuse to act further except through that medium.

5. For the avoidance of doubt, the "cab rank" rule does not apply to instructions provided under these rules.
6. It is expected that an Advocate who accepts instructions under Direct Access Rules shall follow any guidance issued by the Direct Access Guidance Committee from time to time.

APPENDIX TO DIRECT ACCESS RULES

1. Legal professionals:
   (i) Members of the Law Societies of England and Wales, and Northern Ireland;
   (ii) Non-practising Members of Faculty;
   (iii) European lawyers registered under the European Communities (Lawyers Practice) (Scotland) Regulations;
   (iv) Persons on the register of foreign lawyers held by the Law Society of Scotland;
   (v) Qualified conveyancing and executry practitioners in Scotland;
   (vi) Persons or bodies qualified to practise law in a jurisdiction other than Scotland who actually do so practise law.
2. Other professionals:
   (i) Members of any professional body recognised for this purpose by the Faculty, and any such body itself;

动，除非通过该中介。

5. 为避免疑义，“出租车待雇”规则并不适用于本规则规定的指示。
6. 根据《直接近用规则》接受指示的诉辩律师，应当遵守直接近用指导委员会届时发布的指引。

《直接近用规则》附录

1. 法律职业人员：
   (i) 英格兰和威尔士、北爱尔兰事务律师协会成员；
   (ii) 诉辩律师协会非执业成员；
   (iii) 根据《欧洲共同体（律师执业）（苏格兰）条例》注册的欧洲律师；
   (iv) 苏格兰事务律师协会持有的外国律师登记簿上的人员；
   (v) 苏格兰有资格的产权转让和遗嘱执行执业者；
   (vi) 有资格在苏格兰之外的司法辖区从事法律执业活动并实际从事该法律执业活动的人员或者组织。
2. 其他职业人员：
   (i) 诉辩律师协会为本目的承认的任何职业组织的成员，以及任何该组织本身；

(ii) Parliamentary agents;

(iii) Any person or body on the register maintained by the Office of the Immigration Services Commissioner.

3. Public authorities:

(i) Any person or body subject to complaint to the Scottish Public Services Ombudsman;

(ii) Any public authority in terms of the Freedom of Information (Scotland) Act 2002 or the Freedom of Information Act 2000;

(iii) Any person or body subject to complaint to the European Ombudsman;

(iv) Any public authority under the law of the European Union;

(v) Any person or body acting under law in a governmental, judicial or legislative capacity;

(vi) Members of the British and Irish Ombudsman Association or the International Ombudsman Institute.

4. Other persons and bodies:

(i) Any person or body on the Financial Services Authority Register;

(ii) Any voluntary organisation in Membership of the Scottish Council for Voluntary Organisations, the National Council for Voluntary Organisations, the Northern Ireland Council for Voluntary Action, or the Wales Council for Voluntary Action;

(iii) Any body on the register maintained by the office of the Scottish Charity Regulator or the Central Register of Charities maintained by the Charity Commission for

（ii） 议会代理人；

（ii） 移民服务委员会办公室设立的登记簿上的任何人员或者组织。

3. 公共机关：

（i） 任何可被投诉到苏格兰公共服务监察专员的人员或者组织；

（ii）《2012 年信息自由（苏格兰）法》或者《2000 年信息自由法》规定的任何公共机关；

（iii） 任何可被投诉到欧洲监察专员的人员或者组织；

（iv） 欧盟法规定的任何公共机关；

（v） 任何依法以政府、司法或者立法身份行事的人员或者组织；

（vi） 不列颠和爱尔兰监察专员协会会员或者国际监察专员协会会员。

4. 其他人员和组织：

（i） 金融服务管理局登记簿所载任何人员和组织；

（ii） 作为苏格兰志愿组织委员会、志愿组织全国委员会、北爱尔兰志愿行动委员会或者威尔士志愿行动委员会成员的任何志愿组织；

（iii） 苏格兰慈善规制者办公室设立的登记簿或者英格兰和威尔士慈善委员会设立的慈善登记簿上的任何组织；

England and Wales;

(iv) Any public limited company regulated by the London Stock Exchange;

(v) Any community interest company registered as such;

(vi) Any trade union or employers association on the list maintained by the Certification Officer (see www.certoffice.org);

(vii) Any body incorporated by statute which is so established to represent or regulate any trade, business or profession;

(viii) The Medical and Dental Defence Union of Scotland, The Medical and Dental Defence Union, and the Medical Protection Society;

(ix) Any person or body, or Member of a class, recognised for this purpose by the Faculty.

Initial list of bodies recognised under part 2 (i):

1. *All professional bodies in the United Kingdom which have been awarded a Royal Charter*
2. *All Designated Professional Bodies under the Financial Services and Markets Act 2000*
3. *Architects Registration Board of the United Kingdom*
4. *Army Legal Service*
5. *Directorate of Legal Services of the Royal Navy*
6. *Naval Prosecuting Authority*
7. *Directorate of Legal Services of the Royal Air Force*
8. *Association of Average Adjusters*
9. *Association of Taxation Technicians*
10. *Insolvency Practitioners Association*

（iv） 伦敦证券交易所管理的任何股份有限公司；

（v） 注册的任何社区利益公司；

（vi） 文书管理官保管的清单上的工会或者雇员协会（参见 www.certoffice.org）；

（vii） 制定法规定成立的代表或者规制任何行业、商业或者职业的组织；

（viii） 苏格兰医师和牙医辩护联盟、医师和牙医辩护联盟、医师保护协会；

（ix） 诉辩律师协会为本目的承认的任何人员或者组织，或者任何集团的成员。

根据 2（i）承认的组织清单：

1. 英国所有被授予皇家特许状的职业组织

2.《2000 年金融服务和市场法》规定的任何指定的职业组织

3. 英国建筑师注册委员会
4. 陆军法律服务处
5. 皇家海军法律服务处
6. 海军检察机关
7. 皇家空军法律服务处
8. 海损理算人协会
9. 税务技术人员协会
10. 破产执业者协会

11. Institute of Indirect Taxation

12. Institute of Chartered Accountants in Ireland

13. Officers of Arms in Ordinary (The Heralds and Pursuivants of the Lyon Court)

14. Incorporated Society of Valuers and Auctioneers

15. Pensions Management Institute

16. Institute of Trade Mark Attorneys

17. The Chartered Insurance Institute or any Member thereof

6. Further list of bodies subsequently recognised under parts 2 (i) or 4 (ix) *:

1. The Society of Messengers-at-Arms and Sheriff Officers and Members thereof

*It is likely that this list will continue to be updated and you should consult the Faculty's Website for a fully updated list at: www.Advocates.org.uk

Direct Access to Advocates: Standard Terms of Instruction

Revised: 14 May 2007

These Standard Terms of Instruction apply whenever the person instructing is neither qualified to practise as a solicitor in Scotland, nor by law authorised to act as a solicitor to a public department in Scotland. The person or body instructing is here referred to as the instructing person, although they may be instructing on their own behalf.

11. 间接税学会
12. 爱尔兰特许会计师协会
13. 常任纹章官（纹章法院纹章官和纹章官助理）
14. 估价师和拍卖师协会
15. 养老金的管理协会
16. 商标律师协会
17. 特许保险协会或者其任何成员

6. 根据 2（i）或者 4（ix）* 随后承认的组织的进一步清单：

1. 执达员和郡行政司法官协会及其会员

* 这一清单有可能继续更新，就完整的更新清单，你应当参考诉辩律师协会网站：www.Advocates.org.uk

直接近用诉辩律师：标准指示条款

2007 年 5 月 14 日修改

只要进行指示的人员无资格在苏格兰作为事务律师执业，或者没有被法律授权在苏格兰公共部门作为事务律师行事，则本《标准指示条款》适用。在这里，进行指示的人员或者组织，称为进行指示的人员，尽管他们可能是在以自己的名义进行指示。

1. Introduction

1.1 Except as otherwise provided hereafter, Advocates will conduct themselves in accordance with the '*Guide to the Professional Conduct of Advocates*' of the Faculty of Advocates and with the Faculty's Direct Access rules, here together referred to as 'the Guide', and these terms of instruction should be read together with the Guide. If instructions are given by a registered European lawyer, or by a lawyer in a country of the European Union other than Scotland, these terms should also be read with Part 5 of the '*Code of Conduct for Lawyers in the European Union*' issued by the Council of the Bars and Law Societies of the European Union.

1.2 Advocates are holders of a public office, who owe duties to the Court and the public as well as to those who instruct them. They cannot in law, and do not, enter into any contractual relationship with those who instruct them or with their clients, and nothing in these terms should be taken to suggest otherwise.

2. Instructions

2.1 General

2.1.1 Subject to the Guide and the provisions below, an Advocate may accept instructions from any person under the Direct Access rules, without the need for instruction through a Scottish solicitor, in relation to any matter.

2.1.2 Such instructions should be in writing (which includes

1. 导言

1.1 除非下文另有规定，诉辩律师应当遵照诉辩律师协会《诉辩律师职业行为指引》和诉辩律师协会《直接近用规则》（这里统称为“指引”）而行为，并且这些指示的条款应当与指引一起解读。如果指示是由注册欧洲律师或者苏格兰之外的欧洲国家的律师作出的，这些条款还应当与欧盟律师协会理事会发布的《欧盟律师行为守则》第 5 章一起解读。

1.2 诉辩律师是公职人员，对法院、公众和指示他们的人员负有职责。在法律上，他们不能、也没有与对他们进行指示的人员或者其委托人形成任何合同关系，这些条款不应当被视为有其他含义。

2. 指示

2.1 一般规定

2.2.1 在遵守指引任何下列规定的情况下，诉辩律师可以从《直接近用规则》规定的任何人员那里就任何事项接受指示，而不需要通过苏格兰事务律师接受指示。

2.1.2 这样的指示应当采取书面形式（包括电子邮件）。它们可以

e-mail) . They may be sent directly to Counsel, or to his or her clerk. If formal acknowledgement is required, the instructions should be sent to the Advocate's clerk with a request for such acknowledgement. As an Advocate cannot be responsible for the general conduct of any matter (see paragraph 2.3 below) , the instructions should specify the particular services which are required from the Advocate. It is important to specify these services as accurately as possible. An Advocate would not normally be expected to provide services beyond those specified in any particular instructions.

2.1.3 It is the responsibility of the Advocate to satisfy himself or herself that any instruction received may properly be accepted in accordance with rule 4 of the Direct Access rules. Whether or not that is the case, an Advocate may decline to accept instructions under these arrangements.

2.1.4 An Advocate is entitled at any stage to require, as a condition of continuing to act in the matter, that a person qualified to practise as a solicitor in Scotland shall take over the instruction of the work concerned or that the services of such a solicitor shall otherwise be retained to assist in the future conduct of the matter, if he or she considers that this is necessary in the interests of the client or the interests of justice.

2.1.5 As Advocates carry out all their work personally and cannot always predict with certainty their other professional responsibilities, instructions under these arrangements are accepted on the basis that the Advocate may be unavoidably prevented, sometimes at short notice, from attending at any

被直接发送给律师，或者其办事员。如果需要正式回执，该指示应当发送给诉辩律师的办事员并请求取得该回执。由于诉辩律师并不负责任何事务的总体处理（参见以下2.3），指示应当列明需要诉辩律师提供的特定服务。尽可能正确地具体列明这些服务很重要。通常情况下，诉辩律师并不会在任何特定指示具体规定的范围之外提供服务。

2.1.3 诉辩律师有责任自己确信，收到的任何指示是遵照《直接近用规则》第 4 条可以适当接收的指示。不论是否是这样，诉辩律师都可以谢绝根据这些做法接受指示。

2.1.4 诉辩律师有权在任何阶段要求，作为就该事务继续行动的条件，有资格在苏格兰作为事务律师执业的人员应当接管有关工作指示，或者聘请这样的律师的服务，以在事务的未来处理中提供协助，如果他或者她认为这对于委托人利益或者正义利益所必需的话。

2.1.5 由于诉辩律师本人办理他们的所有工作，不是总能确定无疑地确定他们的其他职业责任，根据这些安排接受的指示的基础是，根据指引 8.5 和 8.6 规定的在法院出庭的优先次序，诉辩律师可能不可避免地就接受指示事项，不能——有时很急迫—出席任何听证或者其他与事务有关的活动。

hearing or other engagement in connection with the matter on which he or she is instructed on account of the precedence accorded to instructions for Court appearances, in terms of 8.5 and 8.6 of the Guide. However, an Advocate will not discriminate in this respect between instructions which have been accepted under the Direct Access rules and otherwise.

2.1.6 If an Advocate identifies a clash of commitments which is likely to prevent attendance at any hearing, either the Advocate or the Advocate's clerk will warn the instructing person as soon as possible and will, if desired, suggest the names of other Advocates who are willing and able to take over the instructions. The Advocate will co-operate so far as possible with any other Advocate who takes over. In no circumstances, however, will instructions be passed to any other Advocate without the express agreement of the instructing person.

2.1.7 In any case in which an Advocate accepts instructions from a person in his or her capacity as a director, partner, associate, Member or employee of a company, firm or other body, the obligations of the instructing person under these terms of instruction (and in particular obligations to make payment of fees) shall be the joint and several obligations of him or her and that company, firm or other body.

2.2 Categories of work to which these arrangements apply.

2.2.1 An Advocate may accept instructions under these arrangements in relation to any kind of work except as excluded below. There are, however, circumstances in which it will not practically be possible for this to be done, in particular where

然而，在这方面，诉辩律师将不会就根据《直接近用规则》接受的指示和其他指示进行区别对待。

2.1.6 如果诉辩律师发现了担当之间的冲突，可能不能出席任何听证，诉辩律师或者诉辩律师的办事员将尽可能早地告知进行指示的人员，并在有需要的情况下，就愿意并能够接管指示的其他诉辩律师的姓名提出建议。诉辩律师将尽可能配合任何其他接管的诉辩律师。然而，在任何情况下，未经进行指示的人员的明确协议，都不会将指示转给其他诉辩律师。

2.1.7 在任何情况下，如果诉辩律师接受作为公司、事务所或者其他组织的董事、合伙人、非合伙人、成员或者雇员的人员那里以该身份作出的指示，根据这些指示的条款，进行指示的人员的义务（特别是支付律师费的义务）应当是与该公司、事务所或者其他组织的连带义务。

2.2 这些安排所适用的工作类别。

2.2.1 诉辩律师可能根据这些安排就下列被排除的任何工作而接受指示。然而，在一些情况下这么做实际上是不可行的，特别是在苏格兰法院的工作，在这些法院可能必然会涉及苏格兰事务律师的工作。

the work is in a Scottish Court, where it may be necessary for a Scottish solicitor to be involved.

2.3 Excluded Work

2.3.1 However, an Advocate shall not accept instructions:

(a) To receive or handle clients money; or

(b) To do administrative work normally performed by a solicitor, such as entering into correspondence on the client's behalf (as distinct from assistance in drafting correspondence), or ensuring the attendance of witnesses at a hearing; or

(c) To undertake investigative work normally performed by a solicitor, such as the collection of evidence or the instruction of expert witnesses; or

(d) To take responsibility for the management or general conduct of a client's affairs or litigation; or

(e) Which are inconsistent with guidance given by or on behalf of the Faculty of Advocates.

2.4 Documents

2.4.1 All papers will be returned to the instructing person on the completion of the work instructed.

2.4.2 However, unless agreed otherwise, the Advocate is entitled to keep copies of any documents sent for the Advocate's own professional purposes.

2.4.3 Copyright in any work produced remains with the Advocate who is its author, but the instructing person may publish it to any third party to whom publication was contemplated by the instructions in question.

2.3 被排除的工作

2.3.1 然而，诉辩律师不得接受从事下列活动的指示：

（a） 接受或者处理委托人资金；或者

（b） 从事通常由事务律师处理的行政性工作，例如代表委托人进行通信（有别于帮助起草通信），或者确保证人出席听证；或者

（c） 承担通常由事务律师办理的调查性工作，例如收集证据或者指示专家证人；或者

（d） 承担管理或者总体处理委托人的事务或者诉讼的责任；或者

（e） 与诉辩律师协会发布的或者代表诉辩律师协会发布的指引不一致的工作。

2.4 文件

2.4.1 在完成了所指示的工作后，所有文件应当退还进行指示的人员。

2.4.2 然而，除非另有协议，诉辩律师有权为其自己的职业目的，保留所发出的任何文件的复制件。

2.4.3 形成的任何工作的版权仍然属于作为作者的诉辩律师，但是进行指示的人员可以根据有关指示，向旨在作为公布对象的任何第三方公布它。

2.4.4 All documents and other information sent to an Advocate under the Direct Access rules are received in confidence and are subject to legal professional privilege. They will not accordingly be disclosed to any third party except in terms of a statutory or legal requirement on the Advocate to do so; with the express consent of the instructing person to the disclosure; or in terms of the disciplinary rules of the Faculty of Advocates.

3. Payment of Fees

3.1 It shall be the professional obligation of the instructing person to make payment of the Advocate's fees. That is so whether or not the identity of the client is stated. No agreement to the contrary will be of any effect.

3.2 Upon acceptance of instructions, the Advocate will be entitled to payment of a reasonable fee. What is a reasonable fee depends on the whole circumstances of the particular matter on which the Advocate is instructed. Unless otherwise agreed, an Advocate's fees cover all expenses incurred in relation to the matter instructed, such as travelling expenses. All fees are stated as exclusive of, and are subject to, Value Added Tax at the appropriate rate, if applicable.

3.3 Unless otherwise agreed between the instructing person and the Advocate's clerk, a fee note will normally be submitted at the conclusion of each item of work for which the Advocate is instructed. If, by agreement, payment is made in advance, that

2.4.4 根据《直接近用规则》发给诉辩律师的所有文件和其他信息，都是秘密接收的，受到法律职业特免权的保护。因此，它们不会披露给任何第三方，依照制定法或者法律要求、经进行指示的人员作出明确披露同意、依照诉辩律师协会惩戒规则诉辩律师需要这么做者除外。

3. 支付律师费

3.1 向诉辩律师支付律师费，应当是进行指示的人员的职业义务。无论是否说明了委托人的身份，都是如此。与此相反的任何协议都无任何效力。

3.2 在接受指示后，诉辩律师向有权取得合理的律师费。什么是合理的律师费，取决于诉辩律师接受指示的特定事务的全部情况。除非另有约定，诉辩律师的律师费涵盖受指示的事务所发生的全部耗费，例如差旅费。所有列明的律师费不包括所要缴纳的适当增值税。

3.3 除非进行指示的人员与诉辩律师的办事员另有约定，通常情况下，将在诉辩律师受指示的每项工作结束后提交收费单。如果根据协议预先支付律师费，则该律师费不得超过就有关工作商定的合理律师费的估算额。

must not exceed an agreed estimate of a reasonable fee for the work in question.

3.4 It is often helpful to all concerned to agree the amount of a fee and/or the basis of charging in advance. Discussion about such an agreement must take place with the Advocate's clerk or deputy clerks, because professional rules prohibit discussion or negotiation of fees or associated matters directly with the Advocate. Where such an agreement has been reached, neither the instructing person nor the Advocate is entitled to challenge it later.

3.5 Unless otherwise agreed between the instructing person and the Advocate's clerk, an Advocate's fee shall be paid by the instructing person within twenty-one days of submission of each fee note.

3.6 Subject to paragraph 3.4, the instructing person is entitled to challenge the fee proposed or the basis of the charge. In the event of such a challenge, the instructing person should inform the Advocates clerk concerned (or, in the case of fee notes issued by Faculty Services Limited, Faculty Services Limited) in writing as soon as possible and in any event within twenty-one days of the issue of the fee note; and failing such challenge, the instructing person is presumed to agree that the fee proposed is reasonable and becomes responsible to make payment of it.

3.7 If an instructing person challenges the fee proposed, the matter will normally be resolved by negotiation between them and the Advocate's clerk. If they cannot agree, either the instructing person or the Advocate is entitled to require that the matter be

3.4 预先商定律师费的数额和/或收费根据对所有相关人员都常常是有益的。对这样的协议的讨论必须与诉辩律师的办事员或者助理办事员进行，因为职业规则禁止与诉辩律师直接讨论或者谈判律师费或者相关事项。在已经达成这样的协议的情况下，进行指示的人员和诉辩律师都无权随后对它提出质疑。

3.5 除非进行指示的人员与诉辩律师的办事员另有约定，进行指示的人员应当在提交每个收费单后 21 日内支付诉辩律师的律师费。

3.6 在遵守 3.4 的情况下，进行指示的人员有权质疑拟收取的律师费或者收费根据。在提出该质疑的情况下，进行指示的人员应当尽早以书面形式告知诉辩律师的有关办事员（或者在诉辩律师协会服务有限公司发出收费单的情况下，诉辩律师协会服务有限公司），并且在任何情况下应当在发出收费单 21 日内进行该告知。未能提出该质疑，进行指示的人员被推定同意拟收取的律师费是合理的，并要负责支付该律师费。

3.7 如果进行指示的人员对拟收取的律师费提出质疑，该事项通常由他们与诉辩律师的办事员谈判解决。如果他们不能达成协议，进行指示的人员或者诉辩律师有权要求由双方商定的第三方确定该事项，在该第三方不能确定该事项的情况下，

determined by a mutually agreed third party, whom failing by the Auditor of the Court of Session, who shall then adjudicate as to what is a reasonable fee in the circumstances on an agent and client, client paying, basis.

3.8 In the case of fee notes issued by Faculty Services Limited, all fees should be paid to Faculty Services Limited, and not directly to the Advocate.

3.9 An Advocate may not accept a general retainer from the instructing person.

由高等民事法院审计官确定，他将根据代理人和委托人、委托人支付等情况就什么是合理的律师费作出裁决。

3.8 在收费单是由诉辩律师协会服务有限公司发出的情况下，所有律师费应当付给诉辩律师协会服务有限公司，而不是直接支付给诉辩律师。

3.9 诉辩律师不得接受进行指示人员的一般聘请。

APPENDIX E

Guidance as Regards the Proceeds of Crime and Money Laundering

Members are required to acquaint themselves with the provisions of:

- The Proceeds of Crime Act 2002
- The judgement of the Court of Appeal in the case of Bowman v Fels [2005] EWCA Civ 226; and
- The Money Laundering Regulations 2003
- The Money Laundering Regulations 2007 which came into force on 15 December 2007 and can be viewed at: http://www.hm-treasury.gov.uk./consultations_and_legislation/money_laundering_directive/consult_moneylaundering_2007.cfm

The Faculty Council has adopted the Guidance issued by the Bar Council of England and Wales on Proceeds of Crime and Money Laundering. These can be found at: http://www.barcouncil.org.uk/guidance/

附录 E

关于犯罪所得和洗钱的指引

会员自己需要熟知下列规定：

- 2002 年《犯罪所得法》
- 上诉法院在 Bowman v Fels [2005] EWCA Civ 226 案件中的判决；以及
- 2003 年《反洗钱条例》
- 2007 年 12 月 15 日生效的《2007 年反洗钱条例》，可见于：http://www.hm-treasury.gov.uk./consultations_and_legislation/money_laundering_directive/consult_moneylaundering_2007.cfm

诉辩律师协会委员会已经采纳了英格兰和威尔士诉辩律师公会就犯罪收益和洗钱法发布的指引。该指引可见于：http://www.barcouncil.org.uk/guidance/。

Faculty of Advocates Disciplinary Rules 2015

1. (i) These rules are made by the Faculty having regard to its responsibilities in terms of:

   a. The Legal Profession and Legal Aid (Scotland) Act 2007 (asp 5)

   b. The Legal Services (Scotland) Act 2010 (asp 16) – "the 2010 Act" and may be cited as the Faculty of Advocates Disciplinary Rules 2015.

   (ii) These rules have been subject to the approval of the Lord President in terms of Section 121 (2) (a) of the 2010 Act.

Application of Rules:

2. These rules apply to: –

   a. Conduct complaints remitted to the Faculty by the SLCC on or after 7 September 2015;

   b. Any advocate, practising or non-practising, and notwithstanding that he or she may have been suspended from membership of the Faculty or ceased to be a member of Faculty since the time of the events giving rise to a conduct complaint against the advocate.

诉辩律师协会 2015 年惩戒规则

1. （i）本规则由诉辩律师协会虑及下列法律规定的责任而制定：

   a. 2007 年《法律职业和法律援助（苏格兰）法》（asp 5）

   b. 2010 年《法律服务（苏格兰）法》（asp 16）并可以引为《诉辩律师协会 2015 年惩戒规则》。

   （ii） 本规则已经高等民事法院院长依照 2010 年《法律服务（苏格兰）法》121（2）（a）批准。

本规则的适用：

2. 本规则适用于：
   a. SLCC 在 2015 年 9 月 7 日及以后移交诉辩律师协会的行为投诉；
   b. 任何诉辩律师，无论是执业还是非执业诉辩律师，尽管在导致对其行为投诉的事件发生后，他或者她可能已经被停止诉辩律师协会会员资格或者不再是诉辩律师协会会员。

Interpretation:

3. In these rules the following expressions shall, unless the context otherwise requires, have the following meanings:

- "**Clerk to the Tribunal**" means the Clerk of Faculty or such other counsel as the Dean may appoint.
- "**complaint**" means a conduct complaint remitted to the Faculty by the SLCC.
- "**conduct complaint**" means a complaint of Professional Misconduct and/or Unsatisfactory Professional Conduct.
- "**Complainer**" means the person making the complaint.
- "**Complaints Committee**" means a committee appointed in terms of paragraph 72* of these rules.
- "**Dean**" means the Dean of the Faculty of Advocates.
- "**Disciplinary Tribunal**" means the tribunal appointed in terms of paragraph 74 of these rules.
- "**interim suspension**" means suspension from membership of the Faculty pending determination and final disposal of a complaint.
- "**Member**" means the advocate against whom a complaint is made.
- "**Faculty**" means the Faculty of Advocates.
- "**Faculty office-bearer**" means the Dean of Faculty, the Vice-Dean of Faculty, the Treasurer of Faculty, the Clerk of Faculty, the Keeper of the Library, and the Chairman of Faculty Services Limited.
- "**Inadequate Professional Services**" means professional

解释：

3. 在本规则中，除非情境另有要求，下列表述含义如下：

- “**裁判庭书记官**”是指诉辩律师协会书记官或者会长可能任命的其他律师。
- “**投诉**”是指 SLCC 移交的诉辩律师协会的行为投诉。
- “**行为投诉**”是指就职业不端行为和/或令人不满的职业行为进行的投诉。
- “**投诉人**”是指提出投诉的人。
- “**投诉委员会**”是指根据本规则第 72* 条任命的委员会。
- “**会长**”是指诉辩律师协会会长。
- “**惩戒裁判庭**”是指根据本规则第 74 条任命的裁判庭。
- “**暂停会员资格**”是指在查明和最终处理投诉前，停止诉辩律师协会会员资格。
- “**会员**”是指被投诉的诉辩律师。
- “**诉辩律师协会**”是指本诉辩律师协会。
- “**诉辩律师协会执事人员**”是指诉辩律师协会会长、诉辩律师协会副会长、诉辩律师协会司库、诉辩律师协会书记官、图书馆管理人和诉辩律师协会服务有限公司主席。
- “**不足职业服务**”是指在任何方面没有达到可以合理预期的

services which are in any respect not of the quality which could reasonably be expected of a competent advocate.

- "**Investigating Committee**" means a committee in terms of paragraph 76 of these rules.
- "**Professional misconduct**" means any conduct that is a departure from the standards of competent and responsible advocates and that would be regarded by such advocates as serious and reprehensible.
- "**SLCC**" means the Scottish Legal Complaints Commission, established under and in terms of section 1 of the Legal Profession and Legal Aid (Scotland) Act 2007.
- "**Unsatisfactory Professional Conduct**" means conduct that is not of the standard that could reasonably be expected of a competent and reputable advocate, that does not amount to professional misconduct, and that is not merely Inadequate Professional Services.
- "**Lay Member**" means an individual who (i) is resident in Scotland; (ii) is not a solicitor or advocate practising as such in Scotland; and (iii) does not hold and has not held any judicial office.

General:

4. On behalf of the Faculty, the Dean may, if he or she thinks fit, direct another Faculty office- bearer to handle any complaint or complaints in his or her place. Where the Dean makes such a direction, that Faculty office-bearer may exercise all the powers of

称职的诉辩律师的质量水平的职业服务。

- “**调查委员会**”是指根据本规则 76 成立的委员会。

- “**职业不端行为**”是指悖离称职和负责的诉辩律师的标准，将被这样的诉辩律师视为严重和应予谴责的行为。

- “**SLCC**”是指根据和依照 2007 年《法律职业和法律援助（苏格兰）法》成立的苏格兰法律投诉委员会。

- “**令人不满的职业行为**”是指在任何方面没有达到可以合理预期称职和声誉良好的诉辩律师的标准，没有达到职业不端行为，但是也不仅仅是不足职业服务的行为。

- “**非律师人员**”是指（i）居住在英格兰，（ii）本身并不是在苏格兰执业的事务律师或者诉辩律师，并且（iii）并未担任任何司法职务的自然人。

总则：

4. 会长可以代表诉辩律师协会，在其认为适当的情况下，指令诉辩律师协会其他执事人员代表他或者她处理任何投诉。在会长作出该指令的情况下，该诉辩律师协会执事人员可以就投诉行使会长的全部权力。

the Dean in relation to that complaint or those complaints.

5. Where the Dean is the Complainer or the Member, he or she shall direct another Faculty office-bearer to handle that complaint. Where the Dean makes such a direction, the Faculty office-bearer so directed may exercise all the powers of the Dean in relation to that complaint.
6. The Dean may delegate the administration of a complaint, or complaints generally, to the Dean's Secretariat or to another person or persons who may or may not be a member of Faculty.
7. At an appropriate stage in the administration of a complaint, the Dean shall refer the complaint to the Complaints Committee, for determination and disposal in accordance with these rules.
8. A complaint may be withdrawn by the Complainer, in writing, at any time before it is determined. Where a complaint is withdrawn by the Complainer, and unless the Dean directs otherwise, no further steps shall be taken in respect of the complaint.
9. A Complainer is presumed to have waived any right to confidentiality or privilege in respect of the Member, and the Member is entitled to rely upon and to disclose all or any information and documents that he or she considers to be necessary to answer the complaint.

Interim Suspension:

10. The Dean may, if he or she thinks fit, suspend the Member from membership of the Faculty pending the determination and final disposal of the complaint ("interim suspension") .

5. 在会长是投诉人或者会员的情况下，他或者她应当指令诉辩律师协会其他执事人员处理该投诉。在会长作出了该指令的情况下，接受指令的诉辩律师协会执事人员可以就该投诉行使会长的所有权力。

6. 会长可以将某个投诉或者整个投诉工作的管理，委派会长秘书处或者可能是也可能不是诉辩律师协会会员的其他人员。

7. 在投诉管理的适当阶段，会长应当将投诉移送投诉委员会，以遵照本规则确定和处理。

8. 投诉人可以在投诉查明前的任何时候，以书面形式撤回投诉。在投诉人撤回投诉的情况下，除非会长另有指令，就该投诉不应当采取任何进一步措施。

9. 投诉人被推定为就会员放弃了保密和特免权方面的任何权利，会员有权依据和披露他或者她认为就投诉进行答辩所必需的任何信息和文件。

暂停会员资格：

10. 会长在其认为适当的情况下，在对投诉作出确定和最终处理之前，可以停止会员的诉辩律师协会会员资格（“暂停会员资格”）。

11. Before suspending a Member from membership of the Faculty pending a determination and final disposal of the complaint, the Dean may, in his or her discretion, and in appropriate circumstances invite the Member to make such written or oral representations on the matter of his or her possible interim suspension as he or she thinks fit.

12. Where the Member is suspended without having been given the opportunity to make representations as to his or her possible interim suspension, the Dean shall, as soon as is reasonably practicable, invite the Member to make written or oral representations on the matter of interim suspension and shall thereafter review the interim suspension of the Member.

13. A Member who has been suspended from membership of the Faculty pending determination and final disposal of a complaint may, at intervals of not less than six months, and in writing, apply to the Dean to have the interim suspension reviewed. The Dean shall notify the Member in writing of the result of any such review. Where the interim suspension is not lifted the Dean shall also inform the Member of the reasons for the decision.

14. The Member may appeal his or her interim suspension to the Disciplinary Tribunal within fourteen days of being notified of the result of any review by the Dean. Any such appeal shall be in writing and state the grounds upon which it is sought.

15. The Member, the Complainer, and the SLCC shall be notified of the interim suspension of a Member and of any review or appeal that results in a lifting of that interim suspension.

11. 在对投诉作出确定和最终处理之前，停止会员的诉辩律师协会会员资格时，会长可以依照其自由裁量权，并在适当情况下，敦请会员就对其可能的暂停会员资格提出其认为适当的书面或者口头意见。

12. 在会员被停止诉辩律师协会会员资格，但是没有为其提供就可能的停止会员资格提出意见的机会的情况下，会长应当在合理可行的范围内，尽快敦请会员就暂停会员资格提出口头或者书面意见，并应当随后就对会员的暂停会员资格进行审查。

13. 在对投诉作出确定和最终处理之前，诉辩律师协会会员资格被停止的会员，可以在每隔不少于 6 个月的期间内，以书面形式申请会长审查该暂停会员资格。会长应当以书面形式向会员通知该审查的结果。在没有解除暂停会员资格的情况下，会长也应当就该决定的理由告知会员。

14. 在就会长进行的任何审查的结果得到通知后 14 日内，会员可以就暂停其会员资格上诉于惩戒裁判庭。任何这样的上诉应当采取书面形式，并说明理由。

15. 应当就暂停会员资格和导致解除暂停会员资格的任何审查或者上诉，通知会员、投诉人和 SLCC。

Intimation and Investigation of a Complaint:

16. On receipt of a complaint, the Dean's Secretariat shall, as soon as reasonably practicable, inform the Member in writing as to the nature of the complaint, and shall afford to the Member the opportunity to provide a written response to it.

17. The Dean's Secretariat shall have power to make such further enquiry as may be appropriate with a view to –
    a. identifying the issues to be addressed;
    b. investigating the facts relevant to the complaint;
    c. ascertaining whether or not any of those facts bearing on the complaint are substantially in dispute between the Complainer and the Member; and
    d. obtaining any material identified by the Complainer or the Member that may assist the Complaints Committee in its determination and disposal of the complaint.

Action following Investigation:

18. Once a complaint has been referred to the Complaints Committee in accordance with paragraph 7 of these rules, the Complaints Committee may do one or more of the following:
    a. determine that no further action is appropriate;
    b. make such further enquiries as it considers to be appropriate, including remitting the matter to an Investigating Committee (with or without directions) to investigate and report back to the Complaints Committee;

投诉通知和调查：

16. 在收到投诉后，会长秘书处应当在合理切实可行范围内，尽快以书面形式告知会员有关投诉的性质，并应当为会员提供就此进行书面回应的机会。

17. 会长秘书处应当有权进行进一步适当调查，以：

a. 识别所要解决的争议；
b. 调查与投诉有关的事实；
c. 查明投诉人和会员就这些与投诉有关的事实是否存在重大争议；以及

d. 获取投诉人或者会员指明的可以帮助投诉委员会确定和处理投诉的任何材料。

调查后的行动：

18. 一旦遵照本规则第 7 条将投诉移送投诉委员会，投诉委员会可以采取下列一个或者多个行动：

a. 确定不采取进一步行动是适当的；
b. 进行其认为适当的进一步调查，包括将事务移交调查委员会（有或者无指令）调查并向投诉委员会报告；

c. dismiss the complaint;

d. uphold the complaint in whole or in part as a complaint of Professional Misconduct or of Unsatisfactory Professional Conduct (as in their sole discretion they consider appropriate), and impose, if the Committee thinks fit, one or more of the penalties set out below;

e. sist the complaint for a specified period, subject to review by the Complaints Committee at intervals of no longer than three months.

f. (Where the complaint is one of Professional Misconduct) uphold the complaint in whole or in part and remit it to the Disciplinary Tribunal for the imposition of one or more of the penalties that may be imposed by the Disciplinary Tribunal in accordance with paragraph 63 of these rules; or remit the complaint to the Disciplinary Tribunal for determination and disposal.

Investigation by an Investigating Committee:

19. Where the Complaints Committee remits the matter to an Investigating Committee, the Complainer and the Member shall be notified in writing of

a. the fact that the matter has been remitted to an Investigating Committee;

b. the scope of that remit; and

c. the membership of the Investigating Committee;

and shall be provided with copies of such information in relation to the

c. 驳回投诉；

d. （行使其独有的认为适当的自由裁量权）确认投诉全部或者部分是关于职业不端行为的投诉或者是关于令人不满的职业行为的投诉，并在委员会认为适当的情况下，实施下列一个或者多个处罚；

e. 在具体期间内，在不少于 3 个月间隔的情况下，协助投诉委员会对投诉进行审查。

f. （在投诉是关于职业不端行为的投诉情况下）确认全部或者部分投诉，并将其移交惩戒裁判庭实施其遵照本规则第 63 条可以实施的一个或者多个处罚；或者将投诉移交惩戒裁判庭进行查明和处理。

调查委员会的调查：

19. 在投诉委员会将事务移交调查委员会的情况下，应当以书面形式就下列事项通知投诉人和会员：

a. 该事务已经移交调查委员会之事实；

b. 该移交的范围；以及

c. 调查委员会成员；

并应当提供诉辩律师协会掌握的与投诉有关的信息的复制件。

complaint as in the Faculty's possession.

20. Subject to any directions given by the Complaints Committee, the Investigating Committee shall –

    a. invite the Complainer and the Member to make such written representations in relation to the complaint as they think fit;

    b. make such other investigations as it thinks fit.

21. Without prejudice to the generality of paragraph 20 of these rules, the Investigating Committee may at its discretion interview or take statements from such witnesses (including the Complainer, the Member and any other person) , and ingather such documents or other evidence, as it considers may bear upon the facts of the case.

22. On completion of their investigations the Investigating Committee shall report in writing on such evidence as it has obtained to the Complaints Committee. The Investigating Committee may, if it thinks fit, comment on the credibility and reliability of any such evidence, and shall set out the facts that they find admitted or proved.

23. A copy of the report of the Investigating Committee shall be provided to the Complainer and the Member. The Complainer and the Member shall be given the opportunity to make such written representations in relation to the report of the Investigating Committee as they think fit.

24. Having considered the report by the Investigating Committee and any comment thereon, the Complaints Committee may do any one or more of the things stated in paragraph 18 of these rules, other than remitting the matter to an Investigating Committee in terms of sub- paragraph 18 (b) of these rules.

20. 在遵守投诉委员会作出的任何指示的情况下，调查委员会应当：

a. 敦请投诉人和会员就投诉提出他们认为适当的书面意见；

b. 进行其认为适当的其他调查。

21. 在不损害本规则第 20 条的通用性的情况下，调查委员会可以依照其自由裁量权会见可能与案件事实有关的证人（包括投诉人、会员和任何其他人员）或者取得其陈述，收集它认为可能与案件事实有关的文件或者其他证据。

22. 在完成调查后，调查委员会应当以书面形式就其获得的证据向投诉委员会报告。调查委员会在其认为适当的情况下，可以就这些证据的可信性和可靠性进行评论，并应当列出他们认为可采的或者已经证明的事实。

23. 调查委员会报告的复制件应当提供给投诉人和会员。投诉人和会员应当有机会就调查委员会的报告提出他们认为适当的书面意见。

24. 在考虑了调查委员会的报告和对此进行的任何评论后，投诉委员会可以采取本规则第 18 条规定的一个或者多个行动，依照本规则 18（b）将事务移交调查委员会者除外。

Imposition of Penalties by the Complaints Committee:

25. Where the Complaints Committee upholds a complaint of Unsatisfactory Professional Conduct it may impose upon the Member one or more of the following penalties:
    a. a written direction, with or without conditions;
    b. a verbal admonition;
    c. a formal written reprimand;
    d. a severe written censure;
    e. an order for cancellation or repayment in whole or in part of any fees charged or chargeable by the Member in respect of the work which has given rise to the complaint;
    f. an order for compensation to be paid to the Complainer not exceeding £3,000;
    g. a fine not exceeding £3,000.
26. Where the Complaints Committee upholds a complaint of Professional Misconduct it may impose upon the Member one or more of the following penalties:
    a. a written direction, with or without conditions;
    b. a verbal admonition;
    c. a formal written reprimand;
    d. a severe written censure;
    e. an order for cancellation or repayment in whole or in part of any fees charged or chargeable by the Member in respect of the work which has given rise to the complaint;
    f. an order for compensation to be paid to the Complainer not exceeding £7500;

投诉委员会实施处罚：

25. 在投诉委员会确认了令人不满的职业行为的投诉后，它可以对会员实施下列一个或者多个处罚：

a. 书面指令，有或者无条件；
b. 口头警告；
c. 正式书面申斥；
d. 严厉书面谴责；
e. 命令会员就引起投诉的工作，取消或者退还收取的或者可以收取的全部或者部分律师费；

f. 命令赔偿投诉人不超过 3,000 英镑；

g. 不超过 3,000 英镑的罚款。

26. 在投诉委员会确认了关于职业不端行为的投诉后，它可以对会员实施一个或者多个处罚：

a. 书面指令，有或者无条件；
b. 口头警告；
c. 正式书面申斥；
d. 严厉书面谴责；
e. 命令会员就引起投诉的工作，取消或者退还收取的或者可以收取的全部或者部分律师费；

f. 命令赔偿投诉人不超过 7500 英镑；

g. a fine not exceeding £7,500;

h. suspension from practice, with or without conditions for a specified period not exceeding one year.

27. Before it imposes any penalty, the Complaints Committee shall invite the Member to make such written or oral representations in relation to penalty as he or she thinks fit.

28. In deciding the appropriate penalty, the Complaints Committee may take into account any period of interim suspension that has already been imposed on the Member in relation to the complaint.

Decisions of the Complaints Committee:

29. Any decision of the Complaints Committee may be unanimous or by a majority.

30. Each member of the Complaints Committee shall have an equal vote in the making of any decision of the Complaints Committee. In the case of a tied vote, the Chairman of the Complaints Committee shall have the casting vote.

31. The Complaints Committee's decision to do any of the things stated in paragraph 18 of these rules (other than the things stated in sub-paragraph 18 (b)) and in relation to any penalty imposed upon the Member in terms of paragraphs 25 and 26 of these rules shall be in writing and with reasons.

32. The Complaints Committee's decision shall be intimated to the Complainer, the Member, and the Dean.

g. 不超过 7,500 英镑的罚款；

h. 停止执业不超过 1 年，有或者无条件。

27. 在实施任何处罚前，投诉委员会应当敦请会员就处罚提出其认为适当的书面或者口头意见。

28. 在确定适当的处罚时，投诉委员会可以考虑就该投诉对会员已经实施的暂停会员资格的任何期间。

投诉委员会决定：

29. 投诉委员会的任何决定可以是全体一致意见，也可以是多数意见。

30. 投诉委员会在作出任何决定时，投诉委员会每个成员应当有平等的投票权。在票数均等的情况下，投诉委员会主席应当有决定性投票权。

31. 投诉委员会采取本规则第 18 条规定的行动（18（b）规定的行动除外）和依照本规则第 25 条和第 26 条对会员实施任何处罚的决定，应当采用书面形式，并说明理由。

32. 投诉委员会的决定应当通知投诉人、会员和会长。

Right of Appeal from a Decision of the Complaints Committee:

33. The Complainer may, with leave of the Complaints Committee, appeal to the Disciplinary Tribunal against the dismissal of the complaint.

34. The Member may, with leave of the Complaints Committee, appeal to the Disciplinary Tribunal against the final disposal of the complaint.

35. Any application to the Complaints Committee for leave to appeal to the Disciplinary Tribunal shall be made to the Dean's Secretariat within fourteen days of intimation (being the date following the date of posting) of the dismissal, or final disposal of the complaint as the case may be. The application for leave to appeal shall be in writing and state the grounds on which it is sought.

36. On receipt of an application for leave to appeal, the Dean's Secretariat shall intimate the application to the Complainer or Member as the case may be and that person shall be invited to make such written representations as to why leave should not be granted as he or she thinks fit.

37. Leave to appeal to the Disciplinary Tribunal shall only be granted on cause shown.

38. The decision of the Complaints Committee to grant an application for leave to appeal shall be final.

39. The decision of the Complaints Committee to refuse an application for leave to appeal shall be final, unless, within seven days of the intimation of the decision (being the date following

对投诉委员会决定的上诉权：

33. 经投诉委员会准许，投诉人可以就驳回投诉上诉于惩戒裁判庭。

34. 经投诉委员会准许，会员可以就投诉的最终处理上诉于惩戒裁判庭。

35. 向投诉委员会提出的准许上诉于惩戒裁判庭的申请，应当在接到驳回投诉或者对投诉的最终处理（视情况而定）通知后 14 日内，向会长秘书处提出。准许上诉申请应当采用书面形式，并说明提出申请的根据。

36. 在收到准许上诉申请后，会长秘书处应当就该申请通知投诉人或者会员，视情况而定，并敦请该人就为什么不应当作出准许提出其认为适当的书面意见。

37. 准许向惩戒裁判庭上诉，仅应当在说明理由后批准。

38. 投诉委员会批准准许上诉申请之决定应当是终局性的。

39. 投诉委员会拒绝准许上诉申请之决定应当是终局性的，除非在发出决定通知后 7 日内（从邮寄之日后起算），会员或者投诉人以书面形式通知会长他或者她希望就该拒绝上诉于惩戒

the date of posting), the Member or Complainer intimates in writing to the Dean that he or she wishes to appeal that refusal to the Disciplinary Tribunal and to have the Disciplinary Tribunal consider the matter of leave to appeal by way of review.

40. A review hearing under paragraph 39 of these rules shall be heard by a committee of the Disciplinary Tribunal, comprising one senior and one junior counsel, and two lay persons appointed by the chairman of the Disciplinary Tribunal from the panel of lay persons maintained under sub-paragraph 77 (c) of these rules.

41. The Disciplinary Tribunal shall not allow an appeal against a decision of the Complaints Committee refusing leave to appeal unless it is satisfied that the decision of the Complaints Committee to refuse leave to appeal was not in accordance with the requirements of these rules or that the Complaints Committee proceeded on a basis of fact contrary to the weight of the evidence.

42. Where leave to appeal a decision of the Complaints Committee is granted the procedure to be followed thereafter shall be as set out below.

Remit to the Disciplinary Tribunal:

43. Where the Complaints Committee remits the complaint to the Disciplinary Tribunal (either for the imposition of penalties or for determination and final disposal of the complaint) the Clerk to the Tribunal shall:

裁判庭，由惩戒裁判庭以审查方式考虑准许上诉事项。

40. 根据本规则第 39 条举行的审查听证，应当由惩戒裁判庭的一个委员会听审，该委员会由一名资深律师和一名资浅律师、2 名惩戒裁判庭主席从根据本规则 77（c）设立的非律师人员专责小组中任命的非律师人员组成。

41. 惩戒裁判庭不得允许对投诉委员会拒绝准许上诉的决定提出的上诉，除非它确信投诉委员会拒绝准许上诉的决定没有遵照本规则的要求作出，或者投诉委员会的行动依据的是有悖于证据证明力的事实。

42. 在投诉委员会准许上诉决定被批准后，应当按照下列程序进行后续活动。

移送惩戒裁判庭：

43. 在投诉委员会将投诉移送惩戒裁判庭（无论是为了实施处罚还是为了确定对投诉的终局处理）的情况下，裁判庭书记官应当：

a. inform the Complainer and the Member of the scope of the remit;

b. inform the Complainer and the Member of the membership of the Disciplinary Tribunal; and

c. provide the Complainer and the Member with copies of such information in relation to the complaint as is in the Faculty's possession.

44. The Complainer and/or the Member may, on cause shown and in terms of paragraphs 80 and 81 of these rules, object to any person selected to be a member of the Disciplinary Tribunal.

Remit to the Disciplinary Tribunal for the Imposition of penalties:

45. Where a complaint is remitted to the Disciplinary Tribunal for the imposition of penalties the Dean shall instruct a solicitor to pursue the complaint, and the solicitor shall in turn instruct counsel from a panel of three counsel of at least ten years' standing approved by the Faculty for this purpose. The Dean shall provide the solicitor with such information in relation to the complaint as is in the Faculty's possession. The solicitor and counsel may arrange for such assistance to be engaged in relation to the complaint as they consider appropriate.

46. Subject to the other provisions of these rules, and in particular the terms of paragraphs 60 to 63 of these rules, the procedure to be followed once a complaint has been remitted to the Disciplinary Tribunal for the imposition of penalties, and the

a. 就移送的范围通知投诉人和会员；

b. 就惩戒裁判庭组成人员通知投诉人和会员；以及

c. 向投诉人和会员提供诉辩律师协会所掌握的与投诉有关的信息的复制件。

44. 投诉人和/或会员可以经说明理由，根据本规则第 80 条和第 81 条之规定，对被选为惩戒裁判庭成员的任何人员提出异议。

移交惩戒裁判庭实施处罚：

45. 在投诉移交惩戒裁判庭实施处罚的情况下，会长应当指令一名事务律师就投诉进行起诉，该事务律师相应应当指示诉辩律师协会为本目的批准的由 3 名至少有 10 年资格的诉讼律师组成的专责小组中的一名诉讼律师。会长应当向该事务律师提供诉辩律师协会掌握的与投诉有关的信息。事务律师和诉讼律师可以就投诉安排取得他们认为适当的协助。

46. 在遵守本规则其他规定的情况下，特别是依照本规则第 60 条至第 63 条，在投诉已经移交惩戒裁判庭实施处罚后遵循的程序，和就实施处罚所举行的任何听证的程序，应当由惩戒裁判庭主席自由裁量。

conduct of any hearing on the imposition of penalties shall be at the discretion of the chairman of the Disciplinary Tribunal.

Remit to the Disciplinary Tribunal for Determination and Disposal of the complaint:

47. Where a complaint is remitted to the Disciplinary Tribunal for determination and final disposal the Dean shall instruct a solicitor to pursue the complaint, and the solicitor shall in turn instruct counsel from a panel of six counsel of at least ten years' standing approved by the Faculty for this purpose. The Dean shall have power to nominate one or more members of Faculty to serve on the panel of prosecuting counsel on an *adhoc* basis. The solicitor and counsel may engage such assistance in relation to the investigation and prosecution of the complaint as they consider appropriate.

48. The Dean shall provide the solicitor with such information in relation to the complaint as is in the Faculty's possession.

49. The solicitor shall instruct counsel to draft a formal charge. The formal charge shall set out the specific charges being made against the Member. The formal charge shall be intimated to the Member, and he or she shall be entitled to lodge answers to it within such period as the Disciplinary Tribunal in its discretion considers reasonable. The formal charge may, on cause shown, be amended at any time prior to the determination of the complaint. Where the formal charge is amended the amendment shall be intimated to the Member and he or she shall be entitled

移交惩戒裁判庭来查明和处理投诉：

47. 在投诉移交惩戒裁判庭进行查明并最后处理的情况下，会长应当指令一名事务律师就投诉进行起诉，该事务律师相应应当指示诉辩律师协会为本目的批准的由 6 名至少有 10 年资历的诉讼律师组成的专责小组中的诉讼律师。会长应当有权临时提名一个或者多个诉辩律师协会会员组成检控律师专责小组。事务律师和诉讼律师可以就投诉的调查和检控取得他们认为适当的协助。

48. 会长应当向事务律师提供诉辩律师协会掌握的与投诉有关的信息。

49. 事务律师应当指示诉讼律师起草正式指控。正式指控应当列明对会员提出的具体指控。正式指控应当通知会员。他或者她应当有权在惩戒裁判庭依照其自由裁量权认为合理的期间内提交答辩。经说明理由，可以在决定起诉前的任何时候对正式指控进行修改。在对正式指控进行了修改的情况下，该修正应当通知会员，他或者她应当有权在惩戒裁判庭依照其自由裁量权认为合理的期间内提交修正后的答辩。

to lodge amended answers to it within such period as the Disciplinary Tribunal in its discretion considers reasonable.

50. The Clerk to the Disciplinary Tribunal shall give the Complainer and the Member at least fourteen days' notice in writing of the date, time and place of any hearing before the Disciplinary Tribunal (including any preliminary hearing or hearings) and of the membership of the Disciplinary Tribunal.

51. Subject to the other provisions of these rules, the procedure to be followed once a complaint has been remitted to the Disciplinary Tribunal, and the conduct of any hearing shall be at the discretion of the chairman of the Disciplinary Tribunal.

52. Where a complaint has been remitted to the Disciplinary Tribunal, the chairman of the Disciplinary Tribunal may hold such preliminary hearing or hearings as he or she thinks fit in order to address any procedural or other issues that may arise in advance of the full hearing. For the purposes of any such preliminary hearing, the Chairman may, at his or her discretion, sit alone or with some, or all, of the other members of the Disciplinary Tribunal.

53. In advance of any hearing before the Disciplinary Tribunal at which evidence is to be led or considered, the Complainer and the Member shall, when ordered to do so: –

a. Exchange lists of witnesses;

b. Exchange witness statements; and

c. Lodge productions with the Clerk to the Tribunal.

54. At any hearing before the Disciplinary Tribunal, the case against the Member shall be conducted by counsel referred to

50. 惩戒裁判庭书记官应当就惩戒裁判庭举行的任何听证（包括任何预备听证）的期日、时间和地点、惩戒裁判庭的组成人员，在至少 14 日之前以书面形式通知投诉人和会员。

51. 在遵守本规则其他规定的情况下，在投诉已经移交惩戒裁判庭后遵循的程序，以及就实施处罚所举行的任何听证，应当由惩戒裁判庭主席自由裁量。

52. 在投诉已经移交惩戒裁判庭的情况下，惩戒裁判庭主席可以举行其认为适当的预备听证，以在正式听证之前解决可能发生的任何程序或者其他问题。为任何这种预备听证之目的，出席可以依照其自由裁量权独任或者与戒裁判庭一些或者全部成员一起听审。

53. 在惩戒裁判庭听证之前，如果在该听证中需要导出或者审议证据，经命令，投诉人和会员应当：

a. 交换的证人名单；

b. 交换证人陈述；以及

c. 将证物提交裁判庭书记官。

54. 在惩戒裁判庭任何听证中，对会员的检控应当由本规则第 47 条所称诉讼律师进行。会员可以自行办理其案件，或者由诉

in paragraph 47 of these rules. The Member may conduct his own case or be represented by counsel, a solicitor-advocate, or a solicitor.

55. Any hearing before the Disciplinary Tribunal shall be held in public unless on its own motion, or on the application of the Complainer, the Member, or the Dean the Tribunal considers that it would be appropriate for it to be held in private.

56. At any hearing, witnesses may be required to give evidence on oath or under affirmation.

57. Any incidental question of law arising in the course of any proceedings before the Disciplinary Tribunal shall be decided by the chairman of the Disciplinary Tribunal.

58. The Disciplinary Tribunal shall determine the complaint either by dismissing the charges in the formal charge, or by finding some or all of them proved.

59. The decision of the Disciplinary Tribunal determining the complaint may be unanimous or by a majority.

60. Subject to paragraphs 52 and 57 of these rules, each member of the Disciplinary Tribunal shall have an equal vote. In the case of a tied vote, the chairman of the Disciplinary Tribunal shall have the casting vote.

61. The Disciplinary Tribunal's decision determining the complaint shall be in writing and with reasons.

62. The Disciplinary Tribunal's decision determining the complaint shall be intimated to the Complainer, the Member, and the Dean.

讼律师、事务律师—诉辩律师、事务律师来代理。

55. 惩戒裁判庭的任何听证应当公开进行，除非它依照职权或者根据投诉人、会员或者会长的申请，认为不公开听证是适当的。

56. 在举行任何听证时，可以要求证人在宣誓或者郑重陈述后作证。

57. 在惩戒裁判庭任何程序中发生的任何附带性法律问题，应当由惩戒裁判庭主席决定。

58. 惩戒裁判庭在查明投诉后，应当要么驳回正式指控，要么认定指控中的一些或者全部已经被证明。

59. 惩戒裁判庭查明投诉的决定，可以是全体一致意见，也可以是多数意见。

60. 在遵守本规则第 52 条和第 57 条的情况下，惩戒裁判庭每个成员有平等投票权。在票数均等情况下，惩戒裁判庭主席应当有决定性投票权。

61. 惩戒裁判庭查明投诉的决定应当采用书面形式并说明理由。

62. 惩戒裁判庭查明投诉的决定应当通知投诉人、会员和会长。

Imposition of penalties by Disciplinary Tribunal:

63. Where the complaint has been remitted by the Complaints Committee to the Disciplinary Tribunal: –

a. for the imposition of penalties;

b. or for determination and final disposal, and the Disciplinary Tribunal has upheld the complaint in whole or in part

then, subject to paragraph 65and 66 of these rules, the Disciplinary Tribunal may impose upon the Member, one or more of the following penalties: –

a. A written direction, with or without conditions;

b. A verbal admonition;

c. A formal written reprimand;

d. A severe written censure;

e. An order for cancellation or repayment in whole or in part of any fees charged or chargeable by the Member in respect of the work which has given rise to the complaint;

f. An order for compensation to be paid to the Complainer not exceeding £15,000;

g. A fine not exceeding £15,000;

h. Suspension from practice, with or without conditions for a specified period not exceeding five years;

i. Suspension from membership of Faculty, with or without conditions, for a period not exceeding five years;

j. Expulsion from membership of the Faculty

64. Before it imposes any penalty, the Disciplinary Tribunal shall invite the Member to make such written or oral representations

惩戒裁判庭实施处罚：

63. 在投诉委员会将投诉移交惩戒裁判庭：-

a. 以实施惩罚；

b. 或者为确定和最终处理，且惩戒裁判庭已经全部或者部分支持投诉的情况下，

则在遵守本规则第 65 条和第 66 条的情况下，惩戒裁判庭可以对会员实施下列一个或者多个处罚：

a. 书面指令，有或者无条件；

b. 口头警告；

c. 正式书面申饬；

d. 严厉书面谴责；

e. 就引起投诉的工作，命令会员取消或者退还全部或者部分已经收取的或者可以收取的律师费；

f. 命令向投诉人进行赔偿，不超过 15,000 英镑；

g. 罚款，不超过 15,000 英镑；

h. 停止执业不超过 5 年，有或者无条件；

i. 停止诉辩律师协会会员资格不超过 5 年，有或者无条件；

j. 取消诉辩律师协会会员资格。

64. 在实施任何处罚之前，惩戒裁判庭应当敦请会员就处罚提出其认为适当的书面或者口头意见。

in relation to penalty as he or she thinks fit.

65. In deciding the appropriate penalty to impose, the Disciplinary Tribunal may take into account any period of interim suspension that has already been imposed on the Member in relation to the complaint.

66. Where the Disciplinary Tribunal imposes either of the penalties of suspension from membership of Faculty, or expulsion from membership of Faculty, it shall not be competent for the Disciplinary Tribunal also to impose upon the Member the penalty of a fine.

67. The Disciplinary Tribunal's decision on penalties shall be in writing and with reasons.

68. The Disciplinary Tribunal's decision on penalties shall be intimated to the Complainer, the Member, and the Dean.

The standard of proof and Representation:

69. In the determination of any complaint under these rules the Member shall be given the benefit of any reasonable doubt.

70. Where, in response to an invitation under these rules, the Member chooses to make oral representations, he or she shall be entitled to be accompanied or represented for that purpose by counsel, a solicitor advocate, or a solicitor.

Publication of decisions:

71. Where a complaint is upheld (in whole or in part) by the

65. 在决定实施的适当处罚时，惩戒裁判庭可以考虑就投诉已经对会员实施的暂停会员资格的任何期间。

66. 在惩戒裁判庭实施停止诉辩律师协会会员资格之处罚或者取消诉辩律师协会会员资格之处罚的情况下，惩戒裁判庭不能还对会员处以罚款。

67. 惩戒裁判庭的处罚决定应当采用书面形式并说明理由。

68. 惩戒裁判庭的处罚决定应当通知投诉人、会员和会长。

证明标准和代理：

69. 在根据该规则查明投诉时，会员应当有排除任何合理怀疑之益。

70. 在为回应根据本规则作出的敦请，会员选择提出口头意见的情况下，他或者她应当有权由诉讼律师、事务律师—诉辩律师或者事务律师陪同或者代理。

公布决定：

71. 在投诉委员会或者惩戒裁判庭全部或者部分支持投诉的情况

Complaints Committee or by the Disciplinary Tribunal, details of the determination and of any penalty or penalties imposed, shall be published in a register kept by the Faculty for that purpose and available for inspection.

72. Where a complaint is dismissed by the Complaints Committee or by the Disciplinary Tribunal, details of the determination shall not be published in the register referred to in paragraph 66* unless the Member so requests.

73. The Complaints Committee, or the Disciplinary Tribunal as the case may be, may in its discretion order any additional publicity if it considers that the circumstances of the complaint justify additional publicity.

Petition for Removal:

74. Where a Member is suspended from membership of the Faculty in terms of paragraph 10* above ("interim suspension") , or is suspended or expelled from membership of Faculty, the Dean shall, on behalf of the Faculty, petition the Court of Session to remove the Member from the public office of advocate.

Constitution of Committees and the Disciplinary Tribunal:

75. Complaints Committee: –

a. The Complaints Committee in a particular case shall consist of four persons selected by the Dean's Secretariat as follows:

(i) two persons drawn from the Dean; the Vice-Dean;

下，确定的细节和所实施的任何处罚，应当公布于诉辩律师协会为公布目的设立的登记簿，并可供查阅。

72. 在投诉委员会或者惩戒裁判庭驳回投诉的情况下，该决定的细节不得公布在第 66 条 * 所称登记簿中，除非会员提出该要求。

73. 投诉委员会或者惩戒裁判庭，视情况而定，可以依照其自由裁量权，在它认为投诉情况支持进行其他宣传的情况下，命令进行任何其他宣传。

提请除名：

74. 如果根据前述第 10* 条会员被停止诉辩律师协会会员资格（“暂停会员资格”），或者被停止或者取消诉辩律师协会会员资格，会长应当代表诉辩律师协会，提请高等民事法院将会员从诉辩律师公职中除名。

委员会和惩戒裁判庭的构成：

75. 投诉委员会：

a. 特定案件的投诉委员会应当由会长秘书处选任的下列 4 人组成：

(i) 2 人选自会长、副会长，以及会长提名的诉辩律师

eight other senior members of Faculty nominated by the Dean; and

(ii) two persons drawn from the panel of lay persons nominated by the Scottish Ministers for the purposes of these procedures.

b. The tenure for appointment of lay persons in terms of paragraph a above shall be 5 years; subject to renewal as appropriate.

c. The Dean shall have power to nominate a senior member of Faculty to serve on a Complaints Committee on an *adhoc* basis.

d. The chairman of the Complaints Committee shall be the member of the committee who is most senior as counsel.

76. Investigating Committee: –

a. The Investigating Committee in a particular case shall consist of one senior and two junior counsel (selected by the chairman of the Complaints Committee from a panel of ten senior and twenty junior counsel approved by the Faculty for the purpose) and one lay member from the panel of lay persons nominated by the Scottish Ministers for the purposes of these procedures.

b. The chairman of the Investigating Committee shall be the member of the committee who is most senior as counsel,

c. The Clerk to the Investigating Committee shall be the member of the committee who is most junior as counsel.

d. Where the Complainer or the Member as the case may be, on cause shown, objects within a reasonable time to

协会其他八名资深会员；以及

（ii） 2 人选自苏格兰政府为本程序目的提名的非律师人员专责小组。

b. 根据上述 a 款任命的外行人员的任期应当是 5 年，在适当情况下可以展期。

c. 会长应当有权提名诉辩律师协会资深会员临时任职于投诉委员会。

d. 投诉委员会主席应当是委员会成员中作为律师最资深者。

76. 调查委员会：

a. 特定案件的调查委员会应当由 1 名资深和 2 名资浅律师（由投诉委员会主席从诉辩律师协会为本目的批准的有 10 名资深律师和 20 名资浅律师组成的专责小组中选定）和 1 名非法律人士（从苏格兰政府为本程序目的提名的非律师人员专责小组中选任）组成。

b. 调查委员会主席应当是委员会成员中作为律师最资深者，

c. 调查委员会主席的书记官，应当是委员会成员中作为律师最资浅者。

d. 在投诉人或者会员（视情况而定）根据说明的理由在合理时间内对投诉委员会主席选任的任何人员担任调查委

any person selected by the chairman of the Complaints Committee to be a member of an Investigating Committee, or where any person selected to be a member of an Investigating Committee declines to serve on it, the chairman of the Complaints Committee shall select another member of the panel to serve in place of that person. Any objection shall be made in writing and state the grounds of objection.

e. In the event that one member of an Investigating Committee becomes unable, for whatever reason, to continue to serve on that committee, the other two members of the Investigating Committee may act to complete the investigation into a complaint and to report.

Disciplinary Tribunal:

77. Subject to paragraph (e) below, the Disciplinary Tribunal in a particular case shall consist of a Chairman and five other persons appointed by the Dean as follows: –

   a. The Chairman, who shall be one of a panel of three each of whom shall be a retired member of the Judicial Committee of the House of Lords or Justice of the UK Supreme Court, or a retired Senator of the College of Justice or other appropriate person, and shall be appointed by the Lord President of the Court of Session for a period of three years and, in relation to a complaint remitted to the Disciplinary Tribunal within that period, for such further period as may

员会提出异议，或者被选任为调查委员会成员的人员拒绝担任该职务的情况下，投诉委员会主席应当选择专责小组中其他成员取代该人。任何异议都应当采用书面形式，并说明提出异议的根据。

e. 在调查委员会某个成员不论何种原因不能继续在委员会任职的情况下，调查委员会其他两个成员可以完成对投诉的调查并报告。

惩戒裁判庭：

77. 在遵守下列（e）的情况下，特定案件的惩戒裁判庭应当由下列由会长任命的主席和其他 5 名人员组成：

a. 主席应当是由上议院司法委员会退休成员、英国最高法院大法官、司法院退休参议官或者其他适当人员组成的 3 人专责小组中的一员，并经高等民事法院院长任命，任期 3 年，处理在该期间内移交惩戒裁判庭的投诉，以及根据本规则为实现最终处理所必需的进一步期间内的投诉。

be necessary to achieve a final disposal in terms of these rules.

b. Two counsel (including at least one senior counsel) shall be selected by the Chairman from a panel of ten counsel (including at least six senior counsel) approved by the Faculty for the purpose;

c. Three lay persons shall be selected by the Chairman from the panel of lay persons nominated by the Scottish Ministers for the purposes of these procedures.

78. The Clerk to the Tribunal shall be the Clerk of Faculty or such other counsel as the Dean may appoint.

79. Where, in any particular case, the chairman of the Disciplinary Tribunal considers it appropriate that a solicitor should serve on the Tribunal, he or she shall select one solicitor from a panel of three solicitors of at least 10 years' standing nominated by the President of the Law Society of Scotland for that purpose. Where a solicitor is so appointed he or she shall be appointed in substitution for one of the two counsel referred to in sub-paragraph 77 (b) above.

80. Where the Complainer or the Member as the case may be, on cause shown, objects within a reasonable time to the appointment of any person (other than the chairman) appointed to the Disciplinary Tribunal, or any person (other than the chairman) appointed to the Disciplinary Tribunal declines that appointment, the chairman of the Disciplinary Tribunal shall appoint another person from the same panel to serve in place of that person. Any objection shall be in writing and state the grounds of objection.

b. 2 名律师（其中至少 1 名是资深律师）应当由主席从诉辩律师协会为本目的批准的由 10 名律师（其中至少有 6 名资深律师）组成的专责小组中选任；

c. 3 名非法律人是应当由主席从苏格兰政府为本程序目的提名的非法律人员专责小组中选任。

78. 裁判庭的书记官应当是诉辩律师协会的书记官或者会长任命的其他律师。

79. 在任何特定案件中，在惩戒裁判庭主席认为裁判庭应当有 1 名事务律师的适当情况下，他或者她应当从苏格兰事务律师协会会长为本目的提名的由至少 10 年资历的 3 名事务律师组成的专责小组中选择一名事务律师。在任命了该事务律师的情况下，他或者她应当取代上述 77（b）所称的律师中的 1 个或者 2 个。

80. 在投诉人或者会员（视情况而定）根据说明的理由在合理时间内对任命给惩戒裁判庭的任何人员的任命（主席除外）提出异议，或者被任命给惩戒裁判庭的任何人员（主席除外）谢绝该任命的情况下，惩戒裁判庭主席应当从同一专责小组中认定其他人员来取代该人。任何异议都应当采用书面形式，并说明提出异议的根据。

81. Where the Complainer or the Member as the case may be, on cause shown, objects within a reasonable time to the appointment of the chairman appointed to the Disciplinary Tribunal, or the chairman declines his or her appointment, the Lord President of the Court of Session may appoint another chairman from the panel of chairmen in his or her place. Any objection shall be made in writing and state the grounds of objection.

81. 在投诉人或者会员（视情况而定）根据说明的理由在合理时间内对任命给惩戒裁判庭的主席的任命提出异议，或者主席谢绝该任命的情况下，高等民事法院院长可以从主席专责小组中任命另一名主席来取代他或者她。任何异议都应当采用书面形式，并说明提出异议的根据。

REGULATIONS AS TO INTRANTS

FACULTY OF ADVOCATES

July 2009 Edition

入行者条例

诉辩律师协会

2009 年 7 月版

REGULATIONS AS TO INTRANTS

31 July 1996

(As amended March 2004 and December 2006)

FACULTY OF ADVOCATES

入行者条例

1996年7月31日

（2004年3月和2006年12月修正）

诉辩律师协会

CONTENTS

目录

admission to Membership of the Faculty of Candidates for Admission or Intrants in terms of Regulation 6 (4)

H. Aptitude Test

I. Transitional Provisions in Relation to the commencement of pupillage before 31 December 1997

J. Transitional Provisions in Relation to the requirements of Regulations 2 (1) (d) (i) , (ii) and (iii)

师协会提出的异议规则

附录H　能力验证

附录I　关于1997年12月31日前开始的见习的过渡性规定

附录J　关于条例2（1）（d）（i）、（ii）和（iii）要求的过渡性规定

INTRODUCTION

A candidate for admission to the Faculty is known as an "Intrant" .

The Clerk of Faculty is the officer responsible for advising Intrants and prospective Intrants about the procedure and requirements for admission to the Faculty. All enquiries should be addressed to: -

The Clerk of Faculty
Advocates' Library
Parliament House
Edinburgh, EH1 1RF

Procedure for Admission of an Intrant

An Advocate is not only a member of the Faculty of Advocates but also a member of the College of Justice and an officer of the Court. The Procedure for admission of an Intrant is therefore subject in part to the control of the Court, and in part to the control of the Faculty. The stages in procedure are as follows: -

Court	***Faculty***
1. Petition to the Court	
2. Remit to the Faculty (Regulation 1) by the Court	

导言

准入诉辩律师协会候选人称为“入行者”。

诉辩律师协会书记官负责就准入诉辩律师协会的程序和要求，为入行者和潜在入行者提供建议。所有垂询应当寄至：

诉辩律师协会书记官
诉辩律师图书馆
议会大厦
Edinburgh, EH1 1RF

入行者准入程序

诉辩律师不仅是诉辩律师协会的成员，而且也是司法院成员和法院的官员。因此，入行者的准入程序一部分受法院控制，一部分受诉辩律师协会控制。该程序各个阶段如下：

法院	诉辩律师协会
1. 向法院提交申请	
2. 法院将申请转诉辩律师协会（条例 1）	

Court	*Faculty*
3.	Matriculation (Regulation 2)
4.	Examination in Legal Scholarship (Regulation 3)
5.	Professional Training (Regulation 4)
6.	Application for Admission (Regulation 6)
7.	Admission to membership of the Faculty (Regulation 6)
8. Declaration of Allegiance	
9. Admission by the Court to the public office of Advocate	

Presentation of the Petition is a purely formal procedure. The Petition of an Intrant will be presented to the Court through the Clerk of Faculty.

The remit to the Faculty by the Court follows automatically upon presentation of the Petition, and the prospective Intrant may then proceed to Matriculation. Before matriculating an Intrant must produce to the Clerk of Faculty a certificate of good character and provide references from two persons of standing in the community.

Professional Training. The period of training may, but need not, be undertaken before presentation of the Petition. Prospective Intrants are warned that, although the Faculty may be prepared to grant partial exemption from the prescribed period of training, solicitors may be reluctant to accept trainees for a period of less than 21 months. Prospective

法院	诉辩律师协会
3.	注册（条例 2）
4.	法律知识考试（条例 3）
5.	职业培训（条例 4）
6.	申请准入（条例 6）
7.	准入为诉辩律师协会会员（条例 6）
8. 效忠声明	
9. 为法院所准入，担任诉辩律师之公职	

提交申请是一个纯粹的形式性程序。入行者的申请将通过诉辩律师协会书记官提交法院。

在提交申请后**法院自动转诉辩律师协会**，然后潜在入行者可能进入注册程序。在注册之前，入行者必须向诉辩律师协会书记官提交品性良好证明，并提交在社会上有地位的两个人的推荐信。

职业培训。培训期间可以但不是必须在提出申请之前进行。应当提醒潜在入行者的是，虽然诉辩律师协会可能准备就规定的培训期间给予部分免除，事务律师可能不愿意接受时间不足 21 个月的受训者。潜在入行者最好在开始培训前签订培训合同，以便他们如果愿意，可进入法律职业中的事务律师而非诉辩律师队伍。就符合准入诉辩律师协会之资

Intrants are also advised to enter into a training contract before starting their training in order that they may, if they so wish, enter the Solicitors' rather than the Advocates' branch of the profession. It is not essential, for the purpose of qualifying for admission to the Faculty, that this training should be undertaken in any particular part of Scotland; and it is not desirable that this training should be confined to work in connection with litigation.

Fees Payable by Applicants or Intrants

1. A Court Fee of £180 is payable on the Petition.
2. The Fee for Matriculation is £150, but part of this fee may be refunded if the Intrant's name is removed from the Roll before admission. Payment of the Matriculation Fee entitles the Intrant, subject to Regulation 14, to study in the Advocates' Library.

   The Court and Matriculation fees are normally paid together when the Petition is presented through the Faculty.
3. Entry Money of £850 is payable immediately before admission, subject to the transitional provisions of Appendix F. This may, however, be paid by instalments of £250 per annum, totalling £1,000 over a period of 3 years, the first instalment being due on the date of admission to the Faculty. Entry money represents the Intrant's capital contribution to the corporate facilities provided by the Faculty for its members, and should be compared with the capital outlay which other professional men and women have to make before setting up in practice. Annual Rates, graduated according to status and seniority, are levied after admission on all members of Faculty.

格要求的目的而言，这种培训不一定要在苏格兰的任何特定地方进行；并且不宜将这种培训限于与诉讼有关的工作。

申请人或者入行者支付的规费

1. 在申请时应当向法院缴纳规费 180 英镑。
2. 注册规费是 150 英镑，但如果入行者的姓名在准入前被除名，则该费用可能会被部分退还。在遵守条例 14 的情况下，缴纳注册规费后，入行者有权在诉辩律师图书馆学习。

法院和注册规费一般在通过诉辩律师协会提交申请时一起支付。

3. 在遵守附录 F 的过渡性规定的情况下，应当在准入前缴纳 850 英镑入门费。然而，这可以分期付款，在 3 年期间内每年缴纳 250 英镑，合计 1000 英镑，第一笔分期付款应当在准入诉辩律师协会之日缴纳。入门费是入行者就诉辩律师协会为其会员提供的社团设施所进行的捐助，应当与其他职业人员在开始执业前应当缴纳的资本支出相当。年费，根据地位和资历累进，向准入后的诉辩律师协会所有会员收取。

4. A fee of £150 plus VAT is charged for every examination paper which an Intrant sits in the Faculty examinations. The fee is payable on application. Refunds to candidates who cancel will be made at the discretion of the Treasurer.

5. A fee of £25 is payable by any person who: (a) seeks to matriculate as an Intrant under paragraph (1) (d) (ii) of Regulation 2; or (b) not being a matriculated Intrant, wishes to apply for an exemption other than an automatic exemption under Regulations 8, 9 and 10.

All cheques, etc., should be made payable to:- "The Faculty of Advocates" .

4. 入行者参加诉辩律师协会考试，每次缴纳试卷费 150 英镑，并附增值税。该规费在申请时缴纳。是否向取消考试的候选人退费，由司库裁量决定。

5. （a）根据条例 2 之（1）（d）（ii）申请注册为入行者的人员；或者（b）不是注册的入行者，希望根据条例 8、9 和 10 申请自动免除之外的免除的人员，应当缴纳 25 英镑的规费。

所有支票应当付给“诉辩律师协会”。

REGULATIONS AS TO INTRANTS

General Regulations for Admission

1. The Petition

(1) Every candidate for admission must first present a Petition to the Court, on a form provided by the Faculty, for admission to the public office of Advocate. The Court fee of £180 is due on the Petition.

(2) The Court thereafter remits to the Faculty for matriculation of the candidate as an Intrant.

(3) Not later than 28 days before presenting a Petition to the Court in terms of paragraph (1) of this Regulation, the candidate must intimate his intention to do so to the Clerk of Faculty.

(4) Not later than 21 days before the intended date of presentation of a Petition to the Court by a candidate in terms of paragraph (1) of this Regulation, the Clerk of Faculty shall publish the intimation of the candidate's intention to present a Petition by posting a notice at the outer door of Parliament House, stating (a) the name and address of the candidate; (b) the date on which the

入行者条例

准入通则

1. 申请

（1） 每个准入申请者必须首先以诉辩律师协会规定的形式，向法院提交准入为诉辩律师之公职的申请。法院规费为180英镑，在申请时缴纳。

（2） 此后，法院转诉辩律师协会，候选人作为入行者注册。

（3） 在根据本条例第（1）款向法院提交申请28天之前，候选人必须就其意向通知诉辩律师协会书记官。

（4） 候选人根据本条例第（1）款向法院提交申请的预定日期前不迟于21天，诉辩律师协会书记官应当将拟提交申请的候选人的意向通知以在国会大厦外门张贴的方式加以公布，说明（a）候选人的姓名和地址；（b）候选人拟提交其申请的日期；（c）任何反对候选人准入诉辩律师协会的意见，可以以书面向该候选人本人和诉辩律师协会书记官提出。

candidate intends to present his petition; and (c) that any objection to the admission of the candidate to membership of the Faculty may be made by intimation in writing to the candidate personally and to the Clerk of Faculty.

2. Matriculation

(1) Before any person may be matriculated as an Intrant, and subject to the provisions of Regulation 6 (4) , he must: -

(a) produce to the Clerk of Faculty a certificate in the form in Appendix D, subscribed by the applicant and disclosing: -

(i) any prior criminal convictions or outstanding criminal proceedings;

(ii) any complaints of professional misconduct or negligence which have been upheld against him or which are outstanding; and

(iii) whether he has ever been declared bankrupt, or sequestrated or signed a Trust Deed for creditors, and the circumstances thereof.

(b) provide to the Clerk of Faculty the names of two persons of standing in the community (one or both of whom shall, if the Clerk so requires be members or officers of any professional body to which the Intrant formerly belonged) with knowledge of any matters disclosed in terms of subparagraph (a) hereof from whom references may be obtained regarding the fitness of the applicant to hold the public office of Advocate;

2. 注册

（1） 在任何人作为入行者注册之前，在遵守条例6（4）之规定的情况下，他必须：

（a） 向诉辩律师协会书记官提交附录D所规定形式的证明，由申请人签字并披露：

（i） 任何先前的刑事定罪或者未决的刑事程序；

（ii） 对他提起的被维持的或者未决的任何职业不端行为或者过失投诉；以及

（iii） 他是否曾被宣布破产、罚没财产或者与债权人签订托管契据，以及相关情况。

（b） 向诉辩律师协会书记官提供2名在社会上有地位的人员的姓名（如果书记官提出相应要求，则其中1人或者2人应当是入行者以前所属的任何职业组织的成员或者官员），他们应当知道依照（a）所披露的任何事项，可以从他们这里取得关于申请人担任诉辩律师之公职的适当性的推荐信；

(c) pay to the Faculty a Matriculation Fee of £150; and

(d) subject to the transitional provisions of Appendix J

(i) produce to the Clerk of Faculty a Certificate from a Scottish University showing that he holds a Degree with Honours, Second Class (Division 2) or above, in Scottish Law at that University; or

(ii) produce to the Clerk of Faculty a Certificate from a Scottish University showing that he holds a Degree in Scottish Law at that University, together with a Certificate from a University in the United Kingdom showing that he holds a Degree with Honours, Second Class (Division 2) or above, in another subject at that University; or

(iii) produce to the Clerk of Faculty a Certificate from a Scottish University showing that he holds an Ordinary Degree with Distinction in Scottish Law at that University; or

(iv) produce to the Clerk of Faculty a Certificate from the Attorney-General, or Solicitor-General, of England and Wales that he is a member of the English Bar and that he has completed a full period of pupillage there; or

(v) produce to the Clerk of Faculty a Certificate from the Attorney-General for Northern Ireland that he is a member of the Bar of Northern

（c） 向诉辩律师协会缴纳注册规费 150 英镑；以及

（d） 在遵守附录 J 过渡性规定的情况下：

（i） 向诉辩律师协会书记官提交苏格兰大学的文凭，表明他在该大学取得苏格兰法二等（下）或者以上荣誉学位；或者

（ii） 向诉辩律师协会书记官提交苏格兰大学文凭，表明他在该大学获得苏格兰法学位，并提交英国的大学文凭，表明他取得了在该大学其他学科取得二等（下）或者以上荣誉学位；或者

（iii） 向诉辩律师协会书记官提交苏格兰大学文凭，表明他在该大学取得了苏格兰法优秀普通学位；或者

（iv） 向诉辩律师协会书记官提交英格兰和威尔士总检察长或者副检察长的证明，说明他是英格兰和威尔士出庭律师协会会员，他在那里已经完成了整个见习期；或者

（v） 向诉辩律师协会书记官提交北爱尔兰总检察长的证明，说明他是北爱尔兰出庭律师协会成员，他在那里已经完成了整个见习期；

Ireland and that he has completed a full period of pupillage there; or

(vi) in the case of a legal practitioner from another Member State of the European Community produce to the Clerk of Faculty evidence entitling him to authority to practise pursuant to Regulations of the European Communities (Recognition of Professional Qualifications) Regulations 1991.

3. Examination in Legal Scholarship

(1) Except in the case of a legal practitioner from another Member State of the European Community, or in the cases of a member of the Bar of England and Wales, or a member of the Bar of Northern Ireland (who has completed a full period of pupillage in England or Northern Ireland), before an Intrant may be admitted to the Faculty, he must: -

(a) subject to the provisions of Regulation 9, pass the Faculty examinations covering the subjects listed in Appendix A (1);

(b) subject to the provisions of Regulation 10 and the transitional provisions of Appendix E, obtain the Diploma in Legal Practice from a Scottish University; and

(c) prior to the beginning of the period of pupillage, and in accordance with Regulation 3A, pass the Faculty examination listed in Appendix A (3); or, if no pupillage is required, during the twelve months

或者

（vi） 如果是来自有着共同体其他成员国的法律执业者，向诉辩律师协会书记官提交依照 1991 年《欧洲共同体（职业资格承认）条例》他有执业权的证据。

3. 法律知识考试

（1） 除非是来自欧洲共同体其他成员国的法律执业者，或者是英格兰和威尔士出庭律师协会会员或者是北爱尔兰出庭律师协会成员（已经在英格兰和威尔士或者北爱尔兰完成了整个见习期），在入行者准入诉辩律师协会之前，他必须：

（a） 在遵守条例 9 之规定的情况下，通过了涵盖附录 A（1）所列科目的诉辩律师协会考试；

（b） 在遵守条例 10 之规定和附录 E 的过渡性规定的情况下，在苏格兰大学取得法律实务文凭；以及

（c） 在开始见习期之前，遵照条例 3A，通过了附录 A（3）所列的诉辩律师协会考试；或者，如果没有见习要求，在准入诉辩律师协会前的 12 个月内，通过了附录 A（2）所列的诉辩律师协会考试。

before he is admitted to the Faculty, pass the Faculty examination listed in Appendix A (2).

(2) The general standard of legal scholarship required by the Faculty in the subjects listed in Appendix A (1) is that required for the Degree of Bachelor of Laws at a Scottish University.

(3) The Faculty Examinations will be conducted by the Board of Examiners in accordance with the Rules set out in Appendix B.

(4) Prior to giving notice of intention to commence pupillage, an Intrant shall require to pass or be exempted from all the subjects listed in Appendix A (1) other than Evidence.

(5) In exceptional circumstances the Dean of Faculty may permit an Intrant to commence pupillage notwithstanding the fact that the requirements of Regulation 3 (4) have not been satisfied.

3A. The Examination in Appendix A (3) (Evidence, Practice and Procedure)

(1) In this Regulation:

"diet" means a diet of examination specified in paragraph 4 (a) of Appendix B; "Evidence, Practice and Procedure Examination" means the examination listed in Appendix A (3).

(2) The Evidence, Practice and Procedure Examination shall take place once in each calendar year during the February diet.

(3) An Intrant who is not successful in the Evidence, Practice

（2） 诉辩律师协会就附录 A（1）所列科目的法律学识的一般标准要求，即苏格兰大学法律学士学位的要求。

（3） 诉辩律师协会考试由考试委员会遵照附录 B 所列规则进行。

（4） 在就开始见习期之意图进行通知之前，入行者应当要求通过或者免除附录 A（1）所列的除证据之外的所有科目。

（5） 在特殊情况下，诉辩律师协会会长可以允许入行者开始见习期，尽管存在没有达到条例 3（4）的要求之事实。

3A． 附录 A（3）（证据、实务和程序）考试

（1） 在本条例中：

“日期”是指附录 B 之 4（a）具体规定的考试日期；

“证据、实务和程序”是指附录 A（3）所列的考试。

（2） 证据、实务和程序考试应当在每个日历年二月考试日期举行一次。

（3） 在二月考试日期没有通过证据、实务和程序考试的入

and Procedure Examination at the February diet shall be permitted to resit the examination once only.

(4) The resit shall take place during the May diet of the same calendar year.

(5) An Intrant who is successful in the Evidence, Practice and Procedure Examination at the February or May diet of any calendar year shall commence pupillage in the October of that year.

(6) If an Intrant does not:

(a) pass the Evidence, Practice and Procedure Examination in accordance with paragraph (2), (3) or (4) of this Regulation or any exemption granted under Regulation 10A; or

(b) commence pupillage in accordance with the provisions of paragraph (5) of this Regulation or any such exemption;

his name shall, subject to Regulation 18, be removed from the Roll of Intrants.

4. Professional Training

Except in the case of a legal practitioner from another Member State of the European Community, or in the cases of a member of the Bar of England and Wales, or a member of the Bar of Northern Ireland (who has completed a full period of pupillage in England or Northern Ireland), before an Intrant may be admitted to the Faculty: -

(a) he must satisfy the Clerk of Faculty that he has completed, subject to any exemption under Regulation 11, a period of 21 consecutive calendar months' training as, or on the same

行者，应当仅被允许重考一次。

（4）重考应当在同一日历年度五月的考试日期进行。

（5）在任何日历年度二月或者五月考试日期通过证据、实务和程序考试的入行者，应当在该年度十月开始见习期。

（6）如果入行者并没有：

（a）遵照本条条例（2）、（3）或者（4）通过证据、事务和程序考试，或者获得根据条例 10A 批准的任何免除；或者

（b）遵照本条条例（5）或者任何上述免除开始见习期；

在遵守条例 18 的情况下，他的姓名应当从入行者名册中删除。

4. 职业培训

除非是来自欧洲共同体其他成员国的法律执业者，或者是英格兰和威尔士出庭律师协会会员或者是北爱尔兰出庭律师协会成员（已经在英格兰和威尔士或者北爱尔兰完成了整个见习期），入行者在准入诉辩律师协会之前：

（a）他必须使诉辩律师协会书记官确信他作为苏格兰事务律师协会批准的事务律师事务所的受训者，或者以一样的条件，已经完成了——在遵守条例 11 规定的任何免除的

basis as, a trainee in a Solicitor's office approved by the Law Society of Scotland: provided that up to one-third of the period of training may be served in the office of a lawyer carrying on practice in any one of the Member States of the European Community, the office in question to be approved by the Dean; and

(b) he must satisfy the Dean of Faculty that he has duly completed, subject to any exemption under Regulation 11, a period of such training and education as the Faculty may from time to time provide for Intrants following commencement of pupillage, and full-time pupillage to a junior member of Faculty practising before the Court of Session, in accordance with the provisions of Regulation 5.

5. Pupillage

(1) Except as provided for in the transitional provisions in Appendix I: the period of pupillage shall commence on the first Monday in October each year. An Intrant intending to commence pupillage in any year must give notice in writing to the Clerk of Faculty before 30 June of that year.

(2) Subject to Regulation 11, and paragraph (3) of this Regulation, an Intrant may be admitted no earlier than the last Friday before the Court rises in July in the year following commencement of pupillage.

(3) Subject to Regulation 11, an Intrant who has held a full practising certificate as a solicitor in Scotland for a continuous period of not less than 5 years prior to commencing pupillage may be admitted no earlier than the

情况下——连续 21 个日历月的培训期间，但是在欧洲共同体任何其他成员国执业的律师的事务所的培训，最多占培训期间的 1/3，有关事务所得到了出庭律师协会会长的批准；以及

（b） 他必须使诉辩律师协会会长确信，在遵守条例 11 规定的免除的情况下，他已经妥为完成诉辩律师协会届时为入行者在见习开始后提供的培训和教育，并遵照条例 5 之规定在高等民事法院执业的诉辩律师协会资浅会员那里专职见习。

5. 见习期

（1） 除非附录 I 的过渡性规定另有规定：见习期应当从每年 10 月的第一个星期一开始。意图在任何年度开始见习期的入行者，必须在该年度 6 月 30 日之前以书面形式通知诉辩律师协会书记官。

（2） 在遵守条例 11 和本条条例（3）的情况下，在开始见习后，入行者可以在不早于 7 月法院闭庭前的最后一个周五而准入。

（3） 在遵守条例 11 的情况下，入行者如果已经作为苏格兰事务律师持有完整执业证书，在开始见习期之前连续期间不少于五年，在开始见习后，入行者可以在不早于 6 月法院闭庭前的第一个周五而准入。

first Friday in June in the year following commencement of pupillage.

(4) An Intrant not admitted on the Admission Day specified in either paragraph (2) or (3) of this Regulation, may apply to be admitted on one of the other Admission Days specified in Appendix C.

(5) No member of Faculty may accept an Intrant as a pupil for the purposes of Regulation 4 (b) without the prior consent of the Dean of Faculty.

(6) No member of Faculty or Intrant may make or receive any payment in respect of pupillage.

(7) An Intrant who is an enrolled Solicitor in the United Kingdom must have his name removed from the appropriate Roll of Solicitors before the beginning of his pupillage.

(8) No Intrant shall have duly completed his pupillage unless his Devilmaster completes a report in the prescribed form which confirms that the Intrant has displayed sufficient diligence, competence, and trustworthiness during his pupillage to make him suitable to be admitted as a Member of Faculty.

(9) In the event of the Devilmaster refusing to provide such a Report the suitability of an Intrant for admission to the Faculty shall be referred to a Review Committee who shall report to the Dean, in which event the Intrant shall not be deemed to have duly completed a full period of pupillage unless the said Report is in favourable terms.

（4） 如果入行者没有在本条条例（2）或者（3）具体规定的准入日准入，可以申请在附录C具体规定的其他准入日之一准入。

（5） 未经诉辩律师协会会长事先同意，诉辩律师协会任何成员不得为条例4（b）之目的，接受入行者作为见习生。

（6） 诉辩律师协会任何会员或者入行者不得就见习支付或者收取任何费用。

（7） 如果入行者是英国登记的事务律师，在开始其见习期之前，必须已经将其姓名从适当的事务律师名册中除名。

（8） 任何入行者中没有充分完成其进行，除非其见习生导师按照规定形式填写报告，确认入行者在见习期已经展示了充分的勤勉、称职性和可信性，这使得他适合作为诉辩律师协会会员准入。

（9） 如果见习生导师拒绝提供这样的报告，入行者准入诉辩律师协会的适当性应当提交审查委员会，该委员会应当向会长进行报告，在这种情况下入行者不应当被视为妥为完成了整个见习期，除非所称报告对其有利。

(10) In the event of an Intrant having more than one Devilmaster, the word 'Devilmaster' in Regulation 5 (8) and 5 (9) should be read as meaning his principal Devilmaster.

6. Admission to Membership of the Faculty

(1) When an Intrant has satisfied, or has been exempted from, the requirements of Regulations 1 to 4, or alternatively Regulation 12 or 13, he may be admitted to the Faculty.

(2) Application for admission must be made in writing to the Clerk of Faculty not earlier than ten weeks or not later than six weeks before the Admission Day (see Appendix C) and must be either:-

(a) a written confirmation that since the date of the certificate provided in terms of Regulation 2 (1) (a), there has been no change in circumstances affecting the matters thereby certified; or

(b) a further certificate in the like form replacing the original certificate and covering any such change of circumstances.

(3) Not later than seven days before the Admission Day, the Clerk of Faculty will publish the application by posting a notice at the outer door of Parliament House, stating:-

(a) the name and address of the Intrant; and

(b) the day on which, in the absence of objection, the Intrant will be admitted.

(4) Any objection to the admission of a candidate or the admission of an Intrant may be made at any time after he has intimated an intention to present a Petition to the Court

(10) 如果入行者有多个见习生导师，条例5（8）和5（9）中的“见习生导师”应当被解读为其主要见习生导师。

6. 诉辩律师协会会员准入

(1) 如果入行者已经达到——或者已经被免除——条例1至4之要求，或者条例12或者13之要求，他可以被准入诉辩律师协会。

(2) 准入申请必须以书面形式向诉辩律师协会书记官提出，不早于准入日（参见附录C）前10周，或者不晚于准入日前6周，并且必须：

(a) 书面确认依照条例2（1）(a）提供证明后，与所证明的事项有关的情况没有变化；或者

(b) 以同样格式提供进一步证明，取代原先的证明并涵盖发生的任何情况变化。

(3) 不晚于准入日前的7天，诉辩律师协会书记官应当通过在议会大厦外门张贴通告的方式公布申请，该通告应当说明：

(a) 入行者的姓名和住址；以及

(b) 在没有异议的情况下，入行者将被准入的日期。

(4) 在候选人或者入行者依照条例1（1）表明向法院提交申请的意图后的任何时间，可以对候选人准入或者入行者准入提出异议。该异议应当以书面形式通知准入候选人

in terms of Regulation 1 (1) by intimating the objection in writing to the candidate for admission or the Intrant personally and to the Clerk of Faculty. No objection to his admission may be made any later than 4 p.m. on the day prior to that appointed for his admission as specified in the notice mentioned in paragraph (3) of this Regulation.

(a) No objection to admission shall be competent except on the ground that the candidate for admission or the Intrant is unfitted to hold the public office of Advocate.

(b) An objection to the admission of a candidate or the admission of an Intrant shall be dealt with in accordance with the Rules set out in Appendix G.

(c) In the event of an objection being made to the admission of the Intrant, the admission of the Intrant shall be postponed until the objection has been dealt with in accordance with the Rules set out in Appendix G.

(d) In the event of an objection to the admission of an Intrant being upheld, the name of the Intrant shall thereupon be removed from the Roll of Intrants by the Clerk of Faculty.

(e) In the event of an objection to the admission of a candidate for admission being upheld prior to the candidate matriculating, that candidate shall not be permitted to matriculate as an Intrant.

(5) In the absence of a competent and valid objection, and

或者入行者本人和诉辩律师协会书记官。对其准入的异议可以在本条条例（3）所提及的通知中具体规定的准入期日前的下午 4 点后提出。

（a） 任何准入异议都不适当，除非基于准入候选人或者入行者不适合担任诉辩律师之公职。

（b） 对候选人准入或者入行者准入的异议，应当遵照附录 G 所列规则处理。

（c） 如果对入行者的准入有异议，入行者的准入应当推迟，直至遵照附则 G 所列的规则对异议进行了处理。

（d） 如果入行者准入的异议被支持，诉辩律师协会书记官应当随即将入行者的姓名从入行者名册中删除。

（e） 如果对候选人准入的异议在候选人注册前被支持，该候选人不得注册为入行者。

（5） 在没有适当和有效的异议，并且遵守本条条例（6）的情

subject to paragraph (6) of this Regulation, the Intrant shall be admitted a member of Faculty.

(6) Before an Intrant is admitted to the Faculty, subject to the transitional provisions of Appendix F, he must either pay to the Faculty £850 as Entry Money, or he may elect to pay his Entry Money by instalments. An Intrant who elects to pay his Entry Money by instalments must, before applying for admission, deliver to the Treasurer of Faculty, a deed (duly executed) binding the Intrant to pay to the Faculty within 3 years from the date of his admission £1,000 at the rate of not less than £250 per annum, the first instalment being due on the date of admission to the Faculty.

Exemptions

7. General Provisions in relation to Exemptions

(1) No exemptions from the requirements of the Regulations shall be granted except as provided for in Regulations 8, 9, 10, 10A and 11, and the transitional provisions in Appendix E and I.

(2) No application for exemption shall be considered unless it is made in writing to the Clerk of Faculty.

(3) Any application for exemption by a person who is not a matriculated Intrant, and who seeks exemption on any ground which is not mentioned in Regulation 8, 9 or 10 or

况下，入行者应当被准入为诉辩律师协会会员。

（6） 在入行者被准入诉辩律师协会之前，在遵守附录 F 的过渡性规定的情况下，他必须向诉辩律师协会缴纳 850 英镑入门费，或者选择通过分期付款方式支付其入门费。如果入行者选择以分期付款方式支付其入门费，他必须在申请准入之前，向诉辩律师协会司库递交妥为签字的契据，说明入行者将从其准入之日起的 3 年内向诉辩律师协会缴纳 1,000 英镑，每年不少于 250 英镑，第一笔分期付款应当在准入诉辩律师协会之日支付。

免除

7. 关于免除的一般规定

（1） 本条例之要求不得免除，除非条例 8、9、10、10A 和 11，以及附录 E 和 I 的过渡性规定另有规定。

（2） 任何免除申请不得被考虑，除非该申请是以书面形式向诉辩律师协会书记官提出的。

（3） 任何免除申请的提出者，如果不是注册入行者，并申请以条例 8、9 或者 10 或者附录 E 之外的理由作为自动免除的依据，必须附 25 英镑规费。

Appendix E as a ground of automatic exemption, must be accompanied by a fee of £25.

(4) All applications for exemption should be accompanied by detailed certificates from the appropriate University or other examining body, or other documentary evidence in support of the application.

(5) In an application for discretionary exemption, the age and experience of the applicant and the standard attained by him in his examinations, degree or other qualifications shall be taken into account.

8. Exemption from Regulations 2 (1) (d) (i), (ii) and (iii)

(1) The Dean of Faculty may, after consultation with his Council, in exceptional circumstances, exempt an applicant from the requirements of Regulations 2 (1) (d) (i), (ii) and (iii).

(2) In considering any application under this Regulation, regard may be had, in particular, to such objective evidence of the applicant's intellectual ability as the applicant may produce.

9. Exemptions from Regulation 3 (1) (a)

Automatic Exemptions

(1) Subject to the requirement of paragraph (2) of this Regulation, a graduate in Law of a Scottish University, who has passed Degree examinations at LL.B. standard covering subjects listed in Appendix A (1), shall be granted subject-for-subject exemption from examination in the Faculty examinations on production of a Certificate from

（4） 所有免除申请应当附有适当大学或者其他考试组织提供的详细证明，或者其他支持申请的书面证据。

（5） 在自由裁量免除申请中，应当考虑申请人的年龄和经历，以及他在考试、学位或者其他资格上达到的标准。

8. 条例 2（1）（d）（i）、（ii）和（iii）的免除

（1） 诉辩律师协会会长在与其委员会磋商后，在特殊情况下，可以免除对申请人的条例 2（1）（d）（i）、（ii）和（iii）之要求。

（2） 在根据本条条例考虑申请时，可以虑及——特别是——申请人提出的关于其知识能力的客观证据。

9. 条例 3（1）（a）的免除

自动免除

（1） 在遵守本条条例（2）之要求的情况下，已经通过了其标准涵盖附录 A（1）所列科目的法学学士学位考试的苏格兰大学法律毕业生，应当在提交适当的法学院院长或者法律系主任的证明，说明入行者已经通过了相关学位考试，并具体说明所涵盖的科目和相关考试的日期后，应当就对应科目免于诉辩律师协会的考试。

the Dean or Departmental Head of the appropriate Faculty or Department of Law to the effect that the Intrant has passed the relevant degree examinations and specifying the subjects covered and the dates of the relevant examinations.

(2) Automatic exemption shall be granted only where the pass relied upon was obtained within the period of seven years' immediately preceding the date of the application for exemption.

(3) An Intrant who has passed the Faculty examinations in Criminal Law, Private Law and Mercantile Law shall be exempt from the examination in Scottish Legal System.

(4) An Intrant who has passed the Faculty examination in Appendix A (2) (Evidence, Pleading, Practice and Professional Conduct) or in Appendix A (3) (Evidence, Practice and Procedure) shall be exempt from examination in Evidence (Appendix A (1) (7)).

Discretionary Exemptions

(5) If the Board of Examiners are satisfied that the applicant: -

(a) has passed an examination in any of the subjects listed in Appendix A (1) at a standard at least as high as that required by Regulation 3 (2); or

(b) has passed any of the professional examinations of the Law Society of Scotland, provided that he has passed at a standard at least as high as that required by Regulation 3 (2); or

(c) is a graduate in law of a non-Scottish University and has passed degree examinations in subjects which are

（2） 只有在所称的考试是在申请免除之日前 7 年内通过者，才可以取得自动免除。

（3） 入行者如果已经通过诉辩律师协会的刑法、私法和商法考试，应当免于苏格兰法律制度考试。

（4） 入行者如果已经通过诉辩律师协会附录 A（2）（证据、书状、实务和职业行为）的考试或者附录 A（3）（证据、实务和程序）的考试，应当免于证据考试（附录 A（1）（7））。

自由裁量性免除

（5） 如果考试委员会确信申请人：

（a） 已经通过了就附录 A（1）所列科目，通过了其标准至少和条例 3（2）的要求一样高的考试；或者

（b） 已经通过了苏格兰事务律师协会任何职业考试，只要他通过的考试的标准至少和条例 3（2）要求的一样高；或者

（c） 是非苏格兰大学的法学毕业生，已经通过了学位考试，其科目已经为诉辩律师协会考试所涵盖，但是

covered by the Faculty examinations, but for which the Faculty does not require any special knowledge of Scots Law; or

(d) has qualified by examination for entry to a profession and has passed examinations in subjects which are covered by the Faculty examinations, but for which the Faculty does not require any special knowledge of Scots law.

they may exempt that applicant from examination in that subject or group of subjects.

(6) Where an applicant would have qualified for exemption under paragraph (1), but for the requirement of paragraph (2) of this Regulation, the Dean of Faculty may, after consultation with his Council, exempt that applicant from examination in that subject or subjects.

(7) If the Dean of Faculty is satisfied, after consultation with his Council and with the Board of Examiners, that it would be unreasonable to require an applicant to sit an examination in any subject or subjects, including any part of the Aptitude Test referred to in Regulations 12 and 13, he may exempt that Intrant from examination in that subject or subjects.

10. Exemption from Regulation 3 (1) (b)

Automatic Exemptions

(1) A Solicitor who produces a certificate from the Law Society of Scotland to the effect that he has been actively engaged in practice as a Solicitor in Scotland for at least three years

对此诉辩律师协会并没有要求任何关于苏格兰法的特别知识；或者

（d） 已经通过考试取得进入职业的资格，并且已经通过了其科目为诉辩律师协会考试的科目所涵盖的考试，但是对此诉辩律师协会并没有要求任何关于苏格兰法的特别知识。

他们可以免除申请人在该科目或者这些科目上的考试。

（6） 如果申请人符合（1）规定的免除资格，但是不符合（2）的要求，诉辩律师协会会长在与其委员会磋商后，可以免除申请人在该科目或者这些科目上的考试。

（7） 如果诉辩律师协会会长在与其委员会和考试委员会磋商后，决心要求申请者参加任何科目的考试都是不合理的，包括条例 12 和 13 所称的能力测试的任何部分，他可以免除入行者在该科目或者这些科目上的考试。

10. 条例 3（1）（b）的免除

自动免除

（1） 事务律师，如出具苏格兰事务律师协会的证明，证明其在提交申请前，已经在苏格兰作为事务律师积极职业至少 3 年，并且他是准入诉辩律师协会的适当人选，应当

prior to the presentation of his Petition and that he is a fit and proper person to be admitted to the Faculty, shall be exempt from the requirement of Regulation 3 (1) (b).

Discretionary Exemption

(2) The Dean of Faculty may, after consultation with his Council, in exceptional circumstances, exempt an applicant from the requirement of Regulation 3 (1)(b).

(3) The exemption under paragraph (2) of this Regulation shall be granted only where the exceptional circumstances include other relevant professional experience.

Transitional Provisions

(4) The transitional provisions of Appendix E shall apply to a person presenting a Petition prior to 1st January 1984.

10A. Exemption from Regulation 3A

Discretionary Exemption

(1) The Board of Examiners may in exceptional circumstances exempt an applicant from the requirements of Regulation 3A (2), (3), (4) or (5).

(2) An exemption granted under this Regulation may contain conditions in respect of the resitting of the Evidence, Practice and Procedure Examination and the commencement of pupillage.

免于条例 3（1）（b）之要求。

自由裁量性免除

（2） 诉辩律师协会会长在与其委员会磋商后，在特别情况下，可以免除条例 3（1）（b）对申请人的要求。

（3） 本条条例（2）规定的免除，仅在特殊情况——包括其他相关职业经历——下方得批准。

过渡性规定

（4） 附录 E 的过渡性规定应当适用于在 1984 年 1 月 1 日之前提出申请的人员。

10A. 条例 3A 的免除

自由裁量性免除

（1） 在特殊情况下，考试委员会可以免除条例 3A（2）、（3）、（4）或者（5）对申请人的要求。

（2） 根据本条条例批准的免除，可以包含关于重考证据、事务和程序考试，以及开始见习的条件。

11. Exemption from Regulation 4

Discretionary exemption from Regulation 4

(1) Subject to the provision of paragraph (5) of this Regulation, the Dean of Faculty may, after consultation with his Council, exempt an applicant from the requirement of Regulation 4 in whole or in part, conditionally or unconditionally.

Automatic exemptions from Regulation 4 (a) only

(2) An applicant who is an enrolled Solicitor in Scotland shall be granted exemption from the requirements of Regulation 4 (a).

(3) An applicant who holds a degree in law of a Scottish University with First or Second Class Honours shall be granted exemption from nine months of the period of training required by Regulation 4 (a).

Discretionary exemption from Regulation 4 (a) only

(4) The Dean of Faculty may, after consultation with his Council, exempt an applicant from nine months of the period of training required by Regulation 4 (a) where the applicant holds a University Degree (other than an Ordinary Scottish law degree) or other professional qualification.

Exemption from Regulation 4 (b)

(5) Except as provided in paragraph (1) of this Regulation, no exemption from the requirements of Regulation 4 (b) shall be granted to any applicant unless that applicant undertakes: -

(a) that he will not practise as an Advocate in Scotland immediately after admission; and

(b) that he will not subsequently begin to practise as an

11. 条例 4

条例 4 的自由性裁量免除

（1） 在遵守（5）之规定的情况下，诉辩律师协会会长在与其委员会磋商后，可以全部或者部分、有条件或者无条件免除条例 4 对申请人的要求。

仅适用于条例 4（a）的自动免除

（2） 如果申请人是苏格兰登记的事务律师，应当被免于遵守条例 4（a）之要求。

（3） 如果申请人取得了苏格兰大学法学一等或者二等荣誉学位，应当被免于遵守条例 4（a）所要求的 9 个月的培训期。

仅适用于条例 4（a）的自由裁量性免除

（4） 在申请人取得大学学位（苏格兰法普通学位除外）或者其他职业资格的情况下，诉辩律师协会会长在与其委员会磋商后，可以免除申请人遵守条例 4（a）所要求的 9 个月的培训期。

条例 4（b）的免除

（5） 除非本条条例（1）另有规定，对于任何申请人，不得免除条例 4（b）的要求，除非申请人承诺：

（a） 在准入后他不会立即在苏格兰作为诉辩律师执业；以及

（b） 他随后不会在苏格兰作为诉辩律师开始执业，直至他

Advocate in Scotland until he has undergone such period of pupillage, training and education as the Dean of Faculty for the time being may require him to undergo.

12. Legal Practitioners from other Member States of the European Community

(1) Subject to the provisions of Regulation 9 (7), a legal practitioner from another Member State of the European Community shall be required to pass the Aptitude Test described in Appendix H.

(2) The Aptitude Test shall be conducted by the Board of Examiners in accordance with the Rules set out in Appendix B.

13. English and Northern Ireland Barristers

(1) Subject to the provisions of Regulation 9 (7), a member of the Bar of England and Wales, or a member of the Bar of Northern Ireland, who has completed a full period of pupillage in England or Northern Ireland, shall be required to pass the Aptitude Test described in Appendix H.

(2) The Aptitude Test shall be conducted by the Board of Examiners in accordance with the Rules set out in Appendix B.

Rights and Restrictions

14. Conduct

(1) Every Intrant shall be subject, in matters affecting his conduct as an Intrant, to the discipline of the Dean of

已经完成诉辩律师协会会长要求其完成的见习、培训和教育。

12. 来自欧洲共同体其他会员国的法律执业者

（1） 在遵守条例 9（7）之规定的情况下，来自欧洲共同体其他会员国的法律执业者应当被要求通过附录 H 规定的能力验证。

（2） 能力验证应当由考试委员会遵照附录 B 所列规则进行。

13. 英格兰和威尔士及北爱尔兰出庭律师

（1） 在遵守条例 9（7）之规定的情况下，英格兰和威尔士出庭律师协会成员或者北爱尔兰出庭律师协会成员，如果已经在英格兰或者而北爱尔兰完成了整个见习期，应当被要求通过附录 H 规定的能力验证。

（2） 能力验证应当由考试委员会遵照附录 B 所列规则进行。

权利和限制

14. 行为

（1） 每个入行者就关于其作为入行者的行为的事项，受诉辩律师协会会长的惩戒。

Faculty.

(2) If an Intrant conducts himself in such a manner as to render him unfitted to exercise the public office of Advocate, the Dean of Faculty may, subject to the provisions of Regulation 18 (1), after consultation with his Council, the Lord President of the Court of Session and the Lord Justice-Clerk, order that the name of the Intrant be removed from the Roll of Intrants.

15. Use of the Library

Every Intrant shall be entitled, subject to such Regulations as may be made by the Keeper of the Library, to study in the Advocates' Library.

16. Exclusion from Faculty Examinations or Pupillage

A person who is not an Intrant may not: -

(a) sit any of the Faculty Examinations; or

(b) act as a pupil to a practising member of Faculty for the purposes of Regulation 4 (b).

17. Examinations

(1) If the Examiners are satisfied, having regard to the previous performance of an Intrant in the Faculty examinations, that an Intrant should not be permitted to sit any further examinations or that he should only be permitted to do so subject to conditions, the Dean of Faculty may exclude that Intrant absolutely or conditionally from further examination.

(2) Subject to the provisions of Regulation 18, in the event of an Intrant being excluded absolutely from further examination,

（2） 如果入行者的行为方式使其不适合担任诉辩律师之公职，诉辩律师协会会长可以在遵守条例 18（1）之规定的情况下，在与其委员会、高等民事法院院长和副院长磋商后，命令将入行者的姓名从入行者名册中除名。

15. 使用图书馆

每个入行者在遵守图书馆管理者可能制定的条例的情况下，应当有权在诉辩律师图书馆学习。

16. 禁止参加诉辩律师协会考试或者禁止见习

不是入行者的人员，不得：

（a） 参见诉辩律师协会任何考试；或者

（b） 为条例 4（b）之目的担任诉辩律师协会执业会员的见习生。

17. 考试

（1） 如果考试委员会委员确信，虑及入行者在诉辩律师协会考试中的先前表现，不得允许入行者参加任何进一步考试或者他仅应当在遵守有关条件的情况下参见进一步考试，诉辩律师协会会长可以绝对禁止或者有条件禁止入行者参加进一步考试。

（2） 在遵守条例 18 之规定的情况下，如果入行者被绝对禁止参加进一步考试，其姓名应当从入行者名册中除名。

his name shall be removed from the Roll of Intrants.

18. Removal from the Roll of Intrants

(1) The name of an Intrant may not be removed from the Roll of Intrants in terms of Regulation 3A (6), 14 (2) or Regulation 17 (2) until the Intrant has been given written notice of the grounds on which it is proposed to remove his name, and has been given the opportunity of appearing in person, or being represented by a member of Faculty, and making representations thereon, at a meeting of the Dean and his Council, or of the Dean and the Board of Examiners, as the case may be.

(2) If the name of an Intrant is removed from the Roll of Intrants, either at his own request or under Regulation 3A (6) or 17, the Dean of Faculty may order that up to £50 of the Matriculation Fee be refunded to that Intrant. In determining how much, if any, of the Matriculation Fee should be refunded, the Dean may have regard, inter alia, to the conduct of the Intrant, the use which the Intrant has made of the Library and the cost incurred by the Faculty in examining the Intrant.

Interpretation

19. Interpretation of the Regulations

(1) These Regulations shall apply to any person presenting a Petition, to all persons who are Intrants on 31 July 1996 and to any persons matriculating as an Intrant after that date.

18. 从入行者名册中除名

（1） 入行者的姓名不得依照条例 3A（6）、14（2）或者条例 17（2）从入行者名册中除名，直至以书面形式就准备将其除名的理由通知了入行者，并给他提供了在会长与其委员会或者会长与考试委员会（视情况而定）的会议上本人出面或者通过诉辩律师协会的会员代理就此提出意见的机会。

（2） 如果入行者的姓名被从入行者名册中除名，无论是经其自己请求，还是根据条例 3A（6）或者 17，诉辩律师协会会长可以命令将最多 50 英镑的注册规费返还该入行者。在确定应当返还多少注册规费时，会长可以虑及——特别是——入行者的行为、入行者对图书馆的使用情况以及诉辩律师协会在对入行者进行考试时发生的成本。

解释

19. 条例的解释

（1） 本条例应当适用于所有提交申请的人员，在 1996 年 7 月 31 日是入行者的人员，以及在该日期后注册为入行者的所有人员。

(2) Regulation 3 shall apply to all Intrants irrespective of the date of the presentation of their Petition, but subject to the transitional provisions of Appendix E.

(3) In the Regulations references to the masculine gender include the feminine.

(4) In the Regulations the words 'Scottish University' mean any of the following Universities:

The University of Aberdeen, The University of Dundee, The University of Edinburgh, The University of Glasgow, The University of Strathclyde and such other University in Scotland that is from time to time accredited by the Board of Examiners.*

(5) In any question affecting the application or interpretation of the Regulations, the decision of the Dean shall be final.

---

* The following Universities have been accredited by the Faculty of Advocates: Abertay, Robert Gordon, Stirling, Glasgow Caledonian and Napier

（2） 条例 3 应当适用于所有入行者，无论其提出申请日期如何，但是应当遵守附录 E 的过渡性规定。

（3） 本条例所称男性包括女性。

（4） 本条例中的“苏格兰大学”，是指任何下列大学：

Aberdeen 大学、Dundee 大学、Edinburgh 大学、Glasgow 大学、Strathclyde 大学和考试委员会届时认可的苏格兰其他大学。*

（5） 就关于本条例适用和解释的任何问题，会长的决定应当是终局决定。

---

* 下列大学已经为诉辩律师协会认可：Abertay、Robert Gordon、Stirling、Glasgow、Caledonian和Napier。

APPENDICES

APPENDIX A List of Subjects Covered by the Faculty Examinations

Appendix A (1)

1. Roman Law of Property and Obligations
2. Jurisprudence
3. Constitutional and Administrative Law
4. Scottish Criminal Law
5. Scottish Private Law, including:-
   (a) Obligations including Contract and Delict
   (b) Property, Trusts and Succession including Conveyancing, and Landlord and Tenant, and
   (c) Family Law
6. Commercial Law and Business Institutions
7. Evidence
8. International Private Law
9. European Law and Institutions

Appendix A (2)

Evidence, Pleading, Practice and Professional Conduct

附录

附录 A　诉辩律师协会考试涵盖的科目清单

附录 A（1）

1. 关于财产和义务的罗马法
2. 法理学
3. 宪法和行政法
4. 苏格兰刑法
5. 苏格兰私法，包括：
   （a） 义务（包括契约与侵权）
   （b） 财产、信托和继承（包括转让、业主和租户），以及
   （c） 家庭法
6. 商法和商业制度
7. 证据
8. 国际私法
9. 欧洲法律和制度

附录 A（2）

证据、书状、实务和职业行为

Appendix A (3)

Evidence, Practice and Procedure

APPENDIX B Rules for the Conduct of Faculty Examinations

1. The Board of Examiners

(a) The Board shall consist of the Vice-Dean of Faculty and nine other members of Faculty nominated by the Dean of Faculty. Three Examiners (other than the Vice-Dean) shall go out of office annually, but shall be eligible for re-nomination. Four Examiners shall be a quorum.

(b) The Board of Examiners shall have overall responsibility for all matters affecting the education and examination in legal scholarship of Intrants.

(c) The Vice-Dean of Faculty shall be the Chairman of the Board of Examiners, but may appoint one member of the Board to act as Deputy Chairman, and shall appoint one member of the Board to act as Clerk to the Examiners.

(d) The Vice-Dean of Faculty may make such further arrangements as he thinks fit to secure the efficient discharge of the duties of the Board of Examiners.

2. Assessors

(a) The Examiners may invite persons of learning, who are accustomed to conducting examinations, to assist them in the examination of Intrants.

(b) Each Assessor shall be paid a fee, the amount of which shall be fixed by the Vice-Dean of Faculty after consultation with

附录 A（3）

证据、实务和程序

附录 B　诉辩律师协会考试规则

1. 考试委员会

（a）委员会应当由诉辩律师协会副会长和诉辩律师协会会长提名的其他 9 名诉辩律师协会会员组成。每年应当有 3 名委员（不包括副会长）应当卸任，但是应当有资格再获提名。4 名委员构成法定人数。

（b）考试委员会应当全面负责与入行者法律知识的教育和考试有关的所有事务。

（c）诉辩律师协会副会长是考试委员会主席，但是可以任命委员会一名成员担任副主席，并应当任命委员会一名委员担任委员会书记官。

（d）诉辩律师协会副会长可以作出其认为适当的进一步安排，以保证高效履行考试委员会职责。

2. 考官

（a）考试委员会可以邀请有学识、熟悉考试的人员帮助他们对入行者进行考试。

（b）应当向每个考官支付费用，其数额由诉辩律师协会副会长在与诉辩律师协会司库磋商后确定。

the Treasurer of Faculty.

(c) Each assessor shall deliver to the Examiners a written report on the written paper of the Intrant and shall assist in his oral examination, if necessary.

(d) In the event of it being necessary for an Assessor to assist in the oral examination of an Intrant, he shall be treated for all purposes connected with that examination as if he were a member of the Board of Examiners.

3. Conduct of Examinations

(a) The examinations shall be written in the first instance.

(b) Except in the case of the examination in Appendix A (2) the Examiners may require an Intrant to attend for Oral Examination.

(c) The result of any examination shall be decided by an open vote of the Examiners present, and shall be intimated as soon as practicable to the Intrant concerned and to the Clerk of Faculty.

(d) All examinations will be held in the Advocates' Library, unless otherwise authorised by the Vice-Dean of Faculty.

4. Times of Examinations

(a) Examinations shall be held during the first fortnight of February, the first fortnight of May and the first fortnight of October.

(b) The time for any particular examination, written or oral, shall be fixed by the Clerk to the Examiners.

(c) Where an Intrant gives notice that, if successful in an examination, he intends to apply for admission to the

（c） 每个考官应当就入行者的笔答试卷向考试委员会委员提交书面报告，并在必要情况下帮助对入行者进行口试。

（d） 在考官有必要协助对入行者的口试的情况下，在与该考试有关的所有目的上，应当像他是考试委员会的成员一样对待他。

3. 考试

（a） 考试首先应当采用书面形式。

（b） 考试委员会委员可以要求入行者参见口试，附录 A（2）规定的考试除外。

（c） 任何考试的结果应当由在场考试委员会委员公开投票决定，并应当尽可能早地通知有关入行者和诉辩律师协会书记官。

（d） 所有考试应当在诉辩律师图书馆进行，除非诉辩律师协会副会长另有授权。

4. 考试时间

（a） 考试应当分别在 2 月、5 月和 10 月的头两周举行。

（b） 任何特定考试的时间，无论是书面考试还是口试，都应当由考试委员会书记官确定。

（c） 如果入行者通知说，如果他通过了考试，他希望申请在下一个准入日准入诉辩律师协会，其考试日期应当确定，

Faculty at the next Admission Day, the dates of his examination shall be fixed so as to ensure that the Intrant, if successful, will be able to comply with the provisions of Regulation 6.

5. (a) An Intrant who wishes to sit any of the Faculty Examinations must give notice in writing to the Clerk to the Examiners: -
for the February diet - on or before 31 December for the May diet - on or before 31 March
for the October diet - on or before 31 August

(b) An Intrant who wishes to take advantage of the provisions of Rule 4 (c) above must give written notice of his desire to do so when giving notice under Rule 5 (a).

6. A fee of such an amount as is from time to time fixed by the Board of Examiners will be charged for each examination paper.

APPENDIX C Admission Days

1. The last Friday before the Court rises in March
2. The first Friday in June
3. The last Friday before the Court rises in July
4. The first Friday in November
5. The last Friday before the Court rises in December

以便确保入行者在成功通过考试的情况下，将能够遵守条例 6 之规定。

5. （a） 希望参加诉辩律师协会任何考试的入行者，必须以书面形式通知考试委员会书记官：

就 2 月考试日期——在 11 月 31 日及以前

就 3 月考试日期——在 3 月 31 日及以前

就 10 月考试日期——在 8 月 31 日及以前

（b） 如果入行者希望援用上述规则 4（c）之规定，必须在根据规则 5（a）进行通知时，就其意图进行书面通知。

6. 就每次书面考试，收取考试委员会届时确定的规费。

附录 C 准入日

1. 3 月最后一个周五，法院闭庭前
2. 6 月的第一个周五
3. 7 月最后一个周五，法院闭庭前
4. 11 月的第一个周五
5. 12 月最后一个周五，法院闭庭前

APPENDIX D Certificate referred to in Regulation 2 (I) (a) re Criminal Convictions and Proceedings, etc.

To: The Clerk of the Faculty of Advocates.

I,

being desirous of being matriculated as an Intrant and in due course being admitted a member of Faculty, do hereby solemnly, and truly affirm and declare: -

(1) That I have not been convicted of any criminal offence and that there are no criminal proceedings outstanding against me except:-*

(2) That no complaint of professional misconduct or negligence has been upheld against me and that no such complaint is outstanding against me except:-*

(3) That I have at no time been declared bankrupt or sequestrated or entered into any Trust Deed for creditors except:-*

Dated this day of 19

....

(signature)

*Delete "except" where not applicable.

附录D 条例2(I)(a)所称关于刑事定罪和程序等的证明

致：诉辩律师协会书记官。

我，

渴望注册为入行者，并随后准入成为诉辩律师协会会员，在此庄严、真诚地确认和宣告：

（1） 我没有因任何刑事犯罪被定罪，也没有针对我的未决刑事程序，但是下列情况除外：*

（2） 没有判定对我不利的职业不端行为或者过失投诉，也没有针对我的任何这样的未决投诉，但是下列情况除外：*

（3） 我从没有被宣布破产、财产罚没或者与债权人达成任何托管契约，但是下列情况除外：*

年　　月　　日

……………………………………………………………………

（签字）

* 在不适用的情况下，删除“但是下列情况除外”。

APPENDIX E Transitional Provisions in Relation to the Requirement of a Diploma in Legal Practice in Regulation 3 (1) (b)

A person who presents his Petition to become an Intrant prior to 1 January 1984 and who: -

(a) obtained a degree in law of a Scottish University prior to 1 January 1980, or who was entitled to graduate in such a degree prior to that date notwithstanding that he has not so graduated; or

(b) obtained a degree of any University other than a law degree of a Scottish University prior to 1 January 1980, and a degree in law of a Scottish University prior to 1 January 1981, or was entitled to graduate in such a degree in law prior to the latter date notwithstanding that he has not graduated; or

(c) obtained a degree in law, with Honours, of a Scottish University prior to 1 January 1981, or was entitled to graduate in such a degree notwithstanding that he has not so graduated;

shall be exempt from the requirement of Regulation 3 (1) (b) .

APPENDIX F Transitional Provisions in Relation to the Requirement in Regulation 6 (6) in Respect of Entry Money

Before an Intrant is admitted to the Faculty, he must either pay to the Faculty £275 as Entry Money, or he may elect to pay his Entry

附录 E 关于条例 3（1）（b）中的法律事务文凭要求的过渡性规定

在 1984 年 1 月 1 日前提出成为入行者申请的人员，并且：

（a） 在 1980 年 1 月 1 日前获得了苏格兰大学法律学位，或者在该日之前能够毕业并取得该学位，尽管他尚未毕业；或者

（b） 1980 年 1 月 1 日以前获得苏格兰大学法律学位以外的任何大学的学位，以及 1981 年 1 月 1 日之前获得苏格兰大学的法律学位，或者有权在法律上在后一日期之前能够毕业并取得该学位，尽管他尚未毕业；或者

（c） 1980 年 1 月 1 日以前获得苏格兰大学的法律荣誉学位，或者在该日之前能够毕业并取得该学位，尽管他尚未毕业；

应当免于遵守条例 3（1）（b）之要求。

附录 F 关于条例 6（6）关于入门费之要求的过渡性规定

在入行者准入诉辩律师协会之前，他必须向诉辩律师协会缴纳 275 英镑入门费，或者选择就入门费分期付款。选择就入门费分期付款的入

Money by instalments. An Intrant who elects to pay his Entry Money by instalments must, before applying for Admission, deliver to the Treasurer of Faculty, a deed (duly executed) binding the Intrant to pay to the Faculty within 4 years from the date of his admission £300 at the rate of not less than £75 per annum.

APPENDIX G Rules for dealing with objections made to the admission to Membership of the Faculty of Candidates for Admission or Intrants in terms of Regulation 6 (4)

Application of Rules

1. (1) These Rules shall apply where any objection is made in writing to the Clerk of Faculty in accordance with Regulation 6 (4) to the admission of a candidate for admission or to the admission of an Intrant (hereafter referred to as "the applicant") to membership of the Faculty.

(2) The Clerk of Faculty shall place all objections received by him in terms of Paragraph 1 (1) hereof before the Dean, who shall thereafter deal with such objections in accordance with these Rules.

(3) Where, at any time prior to remitting the objection to the Disciplinary Tribunal in terms of Rule 3 (b) , the Dean is of the opinion that the objection is incompetent, vexatious, frivolous, unfounded in fact, or that, having regard to the public interest, no further proceedings are appropriate, he

行者必须在申请准入前，向诉辩律师协会司库递交妥为签字的契据，说明入行者将在从其准入之日开始的4年内向诉辩律师协会缴纳300英镑，每年不少于75英镑。

附录G 处理依照条例6（4）对候选人或者入行者准入诉辩律师协会提出的异议规则

本规则的适用

1.（1）在遵照条例6（4）就候选人或者入行者（以下称为“申请人”）准入为诉辩律师协会会员向诉辩律师协会书记官提出书面异议的情况下，则应当适用本规则。

（2）诉辩律师协会书记官应当将其依照（1）收到的所有异议提交会长，会长应当遵照本规则处理这些异议。

（3）如果在依照规则3（b）将异议转惩戒裁判庭之前的任何时候，会长认为异议是不适当的、无理纠缠、无端的、没有事实根据，或者虑及公共利益，任何进一步的程序都是不适当的，他可以驳回异议。

may dismiss the objection.

Intimation of Objection

2. The Dean shall as soon as may be inform the applicant in writing as to the nature of the objection and shall ascertain from him whether or not the facts to which the objection relates are substantially disputed by him.

Action by the Dean

3. The Dean may:

(a) dismiss the objection in terms of Rule 1 (3) above; or

(b) remit the objection to the Disciplinary Tribunal for determination.

Remit to the Disciplinary Tribunal

4. (1) Where the Dean remits the objection to the Disciplinary Tribunal he shall:

(a) inform the applicant as to the membership of the Tribunal; and

(b) instruct a member of Faculty to pursue the objection.

(2) The member of Faculty referred to in Paragraph (1) (b) above shall be selected by the Dean from a panel of three members of Faculty of at least ten years' standing nominated by the Dean and approved by the Faculty for the purpose.

(3) The member of Faculty referred to in Paragraph (1)(b) above and the applicant may each engage such assistance in relation to the objection as they think appropriate.

(4) The Dean shall provide the member of Faculty referred to

异议通知

2. 会长应当尽早以书面形式告知申请人异议的性质，并应当查明他就与异议有关的事实是否存在重大争议。

会长采取的行动

3. 会长可以：

（a） 依照上述规则 1（3）驳回异议；或者

（b） 将异议转惩戒裁判庭决定。

转惩戒裁判庭

4. （1） 如果会长将异议转惩戒裁判庭，他应当：

（a） 就裁判庭组成人员通知申请人；并且

（b） 指令诉辩律师协会的一名成员来就该异议承担检控职能。

（2） 上述（1）（b）所称诉辩律师协会会员应当由会长从由会长为本目的提名并经诉辩律师协会批准的 3 名至少有 10 年资格的会员组成的专责小组中选任。

（3） 上述（1）（b）所称诉辩律师协会会员和申请人可以分别就异议提供他们认为适当的帮助。

（4） 会长应当向上述（1）（b）所称诉辩律师协会会员提供他

in Paragraph (1)(b) above with such information as is in his possession in relation to the objection.

(5) A formal objection shall be intimated to the applicant setting out the grounds on which it entitled to lodge answers thereto. The formal objection and any answers thereto may on cause shown be amended at any time prior to the determination of the objection.

(6) The parties to the case shall be given due notice of the date, time and place of a hearing before the Tribunal.

(7) In good time before the date of the hearing, the parties to the case, if it is proposed to call witnesses:

(a) shall exchange lists of witnesses and lodge productions with the clerk to the Tribunal; and

(b) may exchange precognitions of witnesses.

(8) At a hearing, the case against the applicant shall be conducted by the member of Faculty referred to in Paragraph (1)(b) above, and the applicant may conduct his own case or have it conducted on his behalf by Counsel or a Solicitor.

(9) The hearing shall be held in public unless:

(a) the applicant requests that it be held in private, or

(b) the Tribunal considers that it would be prejudicial to the interests of justice if the hearing were not in held whole or in part in private.

(10) The procedure at, and conduct of, the hearing shall be at the discretion of the chairman of the Tribunal, but the Tribunal shall act in accordance with the principles of natural justice.

所掌握的与异议有关的信息。

（5） 正式异议应当通知申请人，列明他有权进行将就此答辩的理由。正式异议和对此提出的答辩，在说明理由后，可以在就异议作出决定前的任何时候进行修正。

（6） 就裁判庭听证的日期、时间和地点，应当及时通知案件当事人。

（7） 在听证期日之前的适当时间，案件当事人如果准备传唤证人，则：

（a） 应当交换证人名单，并向裁判庭书记官提交证物；以及

（b） 可以交换对证人的预先询问笔录。

（8） 在听证时，对申请人的检控应当由上述（1）（b）所称诉辩律师协会会员进行，申请人可以自行辩护，或者由其辩护律师或者事务律师进行辩护。

（9） 听证应当公开进行，除非：

（a） 申请人请求不公开进行，或者

（b） 裁判庭认为如果听证公开或者部分公开进行将有损于正义利益。

（10） 听证程序及其进行由裁判庭主席裁量，但是裁判庭应当遵照自然正义原则行事。

(11) Any question of law arising in the course of the hearing shall be decided by the chairman of the Tribunal.

(12) In the determination of the objection by the Tribunal, any question of fact which may arise shall be determined on a balance of probabilities.

(13) Each member of the Tribunal shall have an equal vote in the determination of the objection and any decision of the Tribunal may be unanimous or by a majority.

(14) The Tribunal may determine the objection by dismissing it or by upholding it.

(15) The Tribunal shall give in writing, with reasons, their decision as to the determination of the objection, and their decision shall be notified to the Dean and to the Clerk of Faculty.

(16) The Clerk of Faculty shall, as soon as may be, intimate to the applicant and to the person who made the complaint the decision of the Tribunal as to the determination of the objection.

Faculty to pay expenses

5. All expenses reasonably incurred by the parties in connection with the handling of an objection under these rules shall be paid by the Faculty. Any dispute as to expenses shall be remitted to the Auditor of the Court of Session whose decision shall be final.

Interpretation

6. In these rules, the following expressions shall, unless the context otherwise requires, have the following meanings respectively assigned to them:-

（11） 在听证过程中发生的任何法律问题都应当由裁判庭主席决定。

（12） 裁判庭在就异议作出决定时，任何可能发生的事实问题都应当按照概率权衡来确定。

（13） 在就异议作出决定时，裁判庭每个成员应当有平等的投票权，裁判庭的决定可以是一致的，也可以是多数意见。

（14） 裁判庭在确定异议时，可以驳回或者支持异议。

（15） 裁判庭应当就异议作出书面决定，并说明理由，其决定应当通知会长和诉辩律师协会书记官。

（16） 就裁判庭对异议作出的决定，诉辩律师协会书记官应当尽可能早地通知申请人和提出投诉的人。

诉辩律师协会支付耗费

5. 就当事人根据本规则处理异议所合理发生的全部耗费，由诉辩律师协会支付。关于耗费的所有争端，应当转高等民事法院审计官，其决定是终局决定。

解释

6. 在本规则中，下列措辞的含义分别如下，除非上下文另有所指：

"applicant" means (a) a candidate for admission in accordance with Regulation 1 or (b) an Intrant;

"counsel" means a member of the Faculty of Advocates;

"Dean" means Dean of Faculty;

"Disciplinary Tribunal" shall be the Disciplinary Tribunal constituted in accordance with the Faculty's Disciplinary Rules and shall have the meaning assigned to it in Rule 16 thereof;

"Faculty" means the Faculty of Advocates;

"objection" means an objection intimated in accordance with Regulation 6 (4) .

Commencement

7. These Rules shall come into operation on 1 October 1989.

APPENDIX H APTITUDE TEST

The test shall be conducted in English and shall consist of the following:

1. A written examination paper in Scots Legal System, Constitutional and Administrative law.
2. A written examination paper covering two topics, to be selected by the candidate, from
   (a) Trust and Succession
   (b) Property and Conveyancing
   (c) Bankruptcy and Diligence
3. An oral examination on: -
   (a) Criminal Law, and
   (b) one of either (i) Contract and Quasi Contract or (ii) Delict and Quasi Delict, to be selected by the candidate.

“申请人”是指（a）遵照条例 1 规定的准入候选人，或者（b）入行者；

“辩护律师”是指诉辩律师协会成员；

“会长”是指诉辩律师协会会长；

“惩戒裁判庭”应当是遵照诉辩律师协会惩戒规则成立的惩戒裁判庭，其含义与该规则 16 所称含义相同；

“诉辩律师协会”是指诉辩律师协会；

“异议”是指遵照条例 6（4）提出的异议。

施行

7. 本规则 1989 年 10 月 1 日施行。

附录 H　能力验证

验证应当用英语进行，并包括下列内容：

1. 苏格兰法律制度、宪法和行政法书面考试。
2. 涵盖候选人从下列科目中选择的两个科目的书面考试：

    （a） 信托与继承

    （b） 财产与转让

    （c） 破产与执行

3. 关于下列科目的口头考试：

    （a） 刑法，和

    （b） 候选人从二者选择的科目之一：（i）契约与准契约，或者（ii）侵权与准侵权。

4. The Faculty examination listed in Appendix A (2).

APPENDIX I Transitional Provisions in Relation to the requirements of Regulations 2(1)(d)(i), (ii) and(iii)

(1) An Intrant who wishes to commence pupillage before 31 December 1997 may apply to the Dean of Faculty for exemption from the provisions of Regulation 5 (1) if the Intrant has a training contract with a firm of solicitors the terms of which prevent the Intrant from fulfilling those provisions in a particular year and the Dean may on such terms and conditions as he decides grant such an exemption in exceptional circumstances, provided that the Intrant commences pupillage before 30 October in the same year.

(2) Such an Intrant may be exempted in whole or part from the requirement in Regulation 4 (b) to complete such training and education as the Faculty may from time to time provide for Intrants following commencement of pupillage.

APPENDIX J Transitional Provisions in relation to the Requirements of Regulations 2(1) (d) (i), (ii) and (iii)

(1) For the period of 5 years from 31 July 1996, any person who: -

(i) was in the course of completing a period of training in a Solicitors Office as at 31 July 1996; or

4. 附录 A（2）所列诉辩律师协会考试。

附录 I 关于 1997 年 12 月 31 日前开始的见习的过渡性规定

（1） 入行者如果希望在 1997 年 12 月 31 日前开始见习，可以向诉辩律师协会会长申请免除遵守条例 5（1）之规定，如果入行者已经与事务律师事务所签订培训契约，其条款将使得入行者在特定年度不能履行这些规定的话。在特殊情况下，会长可以根据其决定的条款和条件批准该免除，只要入行者在该年度 10 月 30 日前开始见习。

（2） 这样的入行者可以全部或者部分免除条例 4（b）之要求，以完成诉辩律师协会可能在见习开始后届时为入行者提供的培训和教育。

附录 J 关于条例 2（1）（d）（i）、（ii）和（iii）要求的过渡性规定

（1） 从 1996 年 7 月 31 日起的 5 年内，任何人员：

（i） 截至 1996 年 7 月 31 日，正在事务律师事务所完成培训期；或者

(ii) is a Solicitor who has held a full practising certificate since before 31 July 1996;

shall be subject to the requirements of Regulation 2 (1) (d) (i), (ii) and (iii) as they existed immediately prior to their amendment on 31 July 1996.

(2) Any person who: -

(i) was in the course of studying for a Degree in Scottish Law at a Scottish University during the academic year immediately preceding 31 July 1996; or

(ii) was in the course of studying for a Diploma in Legal Practice at a Scottish University during the academic year immediately preceding 31 July 1996;

shall, for the period of five years from the date on which he obtained a Diploma in Legal Practice, be subject to the requirements of Regulation 2 (1) (d) (i), (ii) and (iii) as they existed immediately prior to their amendment on 31 July 1996.

(ii) 在 1996 年 7 月 31 日之前持有完整执业证书的事务律师；

应当遵守条例 2（1）(d)（i)、(ii) 和（iii）在 1996 年 7 月 31 日修正之前存在的要求。

（2） 任何人员：

(i) 在 1996 年 7 月 31 日前的学年，正在苏格兰大学学习以取得苏格兰法学位；或者

(ii) 在 1996 年 7 月 31 日前的学年，正在苏格兰大学学习，以取得法律实务文凭；

应当自取得法律实务文凭之日起 5 年内，遵守条例 2（1）(d)（i)、(ii) 和（iii）在 1996 年 7 月 31 日修正之前存在的要求。

重要译名对照表

admission　准入

agent　代理人

call　认许

clerk　办事员　书记官　书记人员

client　委托人

College of Justice　司法院

confession　自白

confidentiality　保密

contractual relationship　合同关系　契约关系

counsel　诉讼律师

court dress　法院服装　出庭服装

Court of Session　高等民事法院

Dean　会长

European lawyer　欧洲律师

Faculty of Advocates　诉辩律师协会

have due regard to　充分重视

High Court of Justiciary　高等刑事法院

instruction　指示

integrity　适正　适正性

law agent　诉讼代理人

lawyer　律师

Lord President　苏格兰高等民事法院院长

member　会员　成员

practising certificate　执业证书

precognition　预审笔录　审前笔录

production　证物

registered European lawyer　注册欧洲律师

rise　闭庭

rules of professional conduct　职业行为规则

Senator　参议官

solicitor　事务律师

tribunal　裁判庭

unstateable　不可辩的

图书在版编目（CIP）数据

苏格兰诉辩律师协会诉辩律师职业行为指引与惩戒规则 / 王进喜译 .—北京：中国法制出版社，2017.5
ISBN 978-7-5093-8564-7

Ⅰ. ①苏… Ⅱ. ①王… Ⅲ. ①律师制度—研究—苏格兰 Ⅳ. ① D956.165

中国版本图书馆 CIP 数据核字（2017）第 104635 号

策划编辑 袁笋冰　　责任编辑 赵 燕　　封面设计 李 宁

苏格兰诉辩律师协会诉辩律师职业行为指引与惩戒规则

译者 / 王进喜
经销 / 新华书店
印刷 / 北京京华虎彩印刷有限公司
开本 /710 毫米 ×1000 毫米 16 开　　印张 /26.75 字数 /359 千
版次 /2017 年 6 月第 1 版　　2017 年 6 月第 1 次印刷

中国法制出版社出版
书号 ISBN 978-7-5093-8564-7　　定价：82.00 元

北京西单横二条 2 号　　值班电话：66026508
邮政编码：100031　　传真：66031119
网址：http://www.zgfzs.com　　**编辑部电话：66034242**
市场营销部电话：66033393　　**邮购部电话：66033288**

（如有印装质量问题，请与本社编务印务管理部联系调换。电话：010-66032926）